Crow
Never
Dies

CROW NEVER DIES

*Life on the
Great Hunt*

LARRY FROLICK

The University of Alberta Press

Published by

The University of Alberta Press
Ring House 2
Edmonton, Alberta, Canada T6G 2E1
www.uap.ualberta.ca

LIBRARY AND ARCHIVES CANADA
CATALOGUING IN PUBLICATION

Frolick, Larry, author
    Crow never dies : life on the great hunt /
Larry Frolick.

Includes bibliographical references and index.
Issued in print and electronic formats.
ISBN 978-1-77212-085-1 (paperback).—
ISBN 978-1-77212-146-9 (PDF). —
ISBN 978-1-77212-144-5 (EPUB).—
ISBN 978-1-77212-145-2 (mobi)

    1. Frolick, Larry—Travel—Canada,
Northern. 2. Native peoples—Canada,
Northern—Social life and customs. 3. Hunting—
Canada, Northern. 4. Ecotourism—Canada,
Northern. 5. Canada, Northern—Description
and travel. 6. Canada, Northern—Social life
and customs. I. Title.

FC3956.F76 2016   971.9   C2016-902868-2
                            C2016-902869-0

First edition, first printing, 2016.
First printed and bound in Canada by Houghton
Boston Printers, Saskatoon, Saskatchewan.
Copyediting and proofreading by Kirsten Craven.
Map by Wendy Johnson.
Indexing by Adrian Mather.

The University of Alberta Press is committed to
protecting our natural environment. As part of
our efforts, this book is printed on Enviro Paper:
it contains 100 per cent post-consumer recycled
fibres and is acid- and chlorine-free.

The University of Alberta Press gratefully
acknowledges the support received for its pub-
lishing program from The Canada Council for
the Arts, the Government of Canada and the
Government of Alberta through the Alberta
Media Fund.

Canada Canada Council Conseil des Arts
for the Arts du Canada

 Alberta
Government

For Sigfrid and Adam—adventurers both.

Contents

Foreword

THERE ARE GRADATIONS TO THE NORTH, and it's not enough to just put yourself up there, a few metres beyond 60, with the boreal forest crowding the edges of a couple dry highways, rough and bumpy, sure, but ever there if you need to bail back south.

That's what I did for the year and a half I spent in Hay River, NT, just a little ways up there on the southern shore of Great Slave Lake. I *did* get to rub against the big, bright clichés of northern life: the inky, swirling aurora and stunning afternoon midnights, the ice jams and driftwood, bison on the ground and ravens in the sky. I got that, because it was there to be had.

But mostly I experienced that other northern cliché, that one you don't read about in the guidebooks and booster-minded consumer magazines. This is the version defined by psychosis, and not the kind you might expect: all those well-trod parables about bush madness and sun frenzies. No, this stuff was urban malaise, sewn up tight and jammed into remote, small-town confines. It was drugs and booze and violence and despair, huge quantities of it, laced with the rollicking good times that come part and parcel with that kind of crashing lifeline.

I didn't get it at the time, but this negative north, this black-eyed north, it was the bastard son of the regal north. It's what happens when people stitch themselves into a culture striving toward the ideal, striving and failing, because only a few of its members are actually *able* to live the dream. Only a few of its members are hardy enough, skilled enough, and strong enough. My girlfriend at the time, she was of that ilk, getting her training wheels, sure, but already halfway down the driveway, top speed and gung-ho, and I guess there are just some people with a mind for it. Some people destined not just for the outposts huddled around 60, but for the huge tracts of land that lead to the coast—and why stop there. Why not head out to sea, as well?

I wasn't so gung-ho. I'm a guy who likes the monuments of man close at hand. They give me confidence, and maybe that's pathetic, maybe that's weak, but take a bushman and drop his ass into the blasting intersections of, say, Mexico City, and we'll see if he even makes it to the sidewalk. Fact is, I like pipes and lights, and when I don't, it's usually just a few days before I start to miss them.

And so it's like I said. The north has a gradation. A physical gradation. An experiential gradation. In a huge country like Canada, all beat up by provincial scorn and regional arrogance, I'd never be considered a northerner, no matter how close to the pole I travelled. I just ain't got the stuff.

But Larry Frolick does. And so do the people he writes about in this book. They're living the dream, replete with Arctic char and snorting caribou, with .22s and .30-30s, *bannock* and *mukluk*, the whole deal, every wheeling bird and fragrant flower, every legend and every folktale—and, yes, there are polar bears. But here's the thing of it. Even though you might think you know this story, might recognize it from some part of the so-called Canadian imagination, odds are you really don't. What you know might just be cliché, runny little scoops of national identity, and we've all had enough of that.

Instead, Frolick offers something sweeter. He offers reality. He offers life. And even though he's talking about a bear when he writes these next five words, fact is, they pretty much apply to the whole experience: "The psychic impact is terrific."

Read on.

PAUL CARLUCCI
Ottawa, June 21, 2015

Preface

THE NORTH FORGIVES EVERY SIN BUT STUPIDITY, they say.

I have lived in the Northwest Territories for the past five years, and before that I travelled regularly to the Arctic since 2005 as a journalist. Much of that time was spent in uncertainty, and careful treading. The novel environment—or should I say environments?—demands strict attention to every waking moment, to getting it right.

This account is inevitably encoloured by stupefied wonderment. Did I write truly and well about its people, its skies, the preternatural light? How its living power shows in every human task, in distant sounds? Echoes of wood chopping. Sandhill cranes in clouds. Spruces falling into shadow.

I hope the north and its peoples forgive me for an excess of delight in the freedom of its wild spaces.

Freedom, yes. There's great comfort in knowing the stories I heard from Elders, hunters and truck drivers, craftspeople and artists, maybe old or invented just yesterday. Either way, they are always momentous stories— freshly told, worth hearing again. The north answers questions I didn't know to ask.

I like its repletion. I like the way it fills you up with pure birdsong in summer and casts your eyes over the dazzling crystals of winter. Everyone here is secretly rich.

Introduction

SUMMER in the boreal forest.

The mad activity of a northern spring has subsided into a green-carpeted silence broken only by occasional chirps and warning whistles. The migratory songbirds have settled their disputes over the boundaries of their territories. Their clockwork patterns of shared nest keeping and foraging duties create an intricate counter-rhythm to the fricatives of the wind rasping through spruces. A grove of white birches frames an endless expanse of detail congealed into hazy abstraction by vast distance. If we could but read the dense textures of the forest, we would know everything.

Perhaps it's even possible.

Some First Nations hunters say we have latent senses buried beyond the traditional six or seven, immersive senses that come alive in the dark and unknowingly tap into the connective energy that underlies all living things. These hunters say they are always inside us, these mysterious powers, and, more, that their daily exercise helps procreate the wild richness of the Land in all its variety and perfection. Today, we have too many workaday concerns to mine this particular vein.

The cluster of remote communities in Canada's far northwest include Inuvik, a town of three thousand, situated in traditional Gwich'in territory two hundred kilometres north of the Arctic Circle. Arviat, in the treeless Eastern Arctic, is home to about two thousand residents, mostly Inuit. Hay River, population three thousand, is the base for a thriving commercial fishery with many local Dene crews.

Rote inner noises dominate our actions: What shall we do, think, say? Are we there yet?

The clarity of presence eludes us. It remains mere background, an undeciphered, aural haze, matched in the material realm by clouds of drifting spruce spores and fuzzy poplar seeds, blowing this way and that.

My attention is riveted to the forest's cleaving counterpoints: snapping branches, sudden shifts of intensity marking the play of unseen incidents.

Humans evolved as more clever prey, our genes hard-wired to fear signs and not just the things themselves, the hissing of snakes and the soft padding of nocturnal hunters. As I head down the overgrown trail, I reach an unsteady point of recollected departure. The unknown woods around me are growing chill in their resistant unfamiliarity. There is a growing sign of something deeper at work than conscious will, and it takes over now despite the calm August sunshine and its artful cloud formations.

The body grows edgy, apprehensive. I begin stubbornly picking my way over the dry duff, involuntarily recoiling at the crackling of twigs underfoot. The heavy hiking boots don't help. They are calling attention to themselves. So is my laboured breathing. A bustle of sandflies rises to my face, drawn by the extra carbon dioxide my exertions produce. I look up at the sky again, following a skein of ducks skidding low and fast. Mergansers. Where are they going?

The body records the sum of these signals, like an antenna of flesh and bone. It vibrates at its own frequency and remains what it was fifty thousand years ago: constitutionally unable to discharge its existential unease on this given green earth. In the wild woods we still walk bowed and deferential, pretenders to the throne of the kingdom despite the Bible's claims, and despite the elimination of our ancient bloody overlords from the peak of the food chain.

Most of them, anyhow. There are still grizzly bears about in these low hills. A few. And wolves, even cougars now.

Knives, guns, hymns of fire. So what? In the deep woods, we *humans* are still prey. Vulnerable. It takes some getting used to. Sharpen the senses, avoid surprises. That's the key.

We are not alone in this. Everything here is alive to the possibility of fatal surprise. On the hunt for treetop prey, dragonflies are using the steady wind off the lake to power their deadly swoops, dropping like stones to investigate the forest's dark understorey and raising again to attack the gnats in the upper branches. Far above us, three bald eagles are doing the same thing, roiling with the currents as they tumble over one another in a mock blitzkrieg. They appear to be parenting adults— teaching their near-grown juvenile how to become an effective aerial combatant before she goes off to face the world alone.

I am walking along a rutted logging trail that leads to the lake. Slowly, taking my time. I have already scared up two spruce grouse that scared me, in turn, with their take-off blasts. It rained last night. I am watching for fresh tracks. The dried mud shows a large whitetail deer, or a small caribou, preceded me here. I cannot say which. We are at the boundary of two ecological zones, the northern Taiga Plains proper and its distinctive subregion, the Hay River Lowland, a mixed-woods region that extends into Alberta to the south and acts as a corridor for opportunistic species brought north by global warming. Hence, the novel possibility of cougars.

Now a mess of speckled feathers greets me on the path. Something has torn apart a spruce grouse earlier today: the blood on its severed head is still wet. A hawk or small owl. The raptors straightaway eat their kill on the ground, tearing smartly into the body and gorging on the good stuff before scavenging ravens or eagles spot the easy snack and oust them.

Neighbours big and small must be accommodated in this daily cycle. Perhaps I ousted the ouster. The sense of being watched by everything always is valid. Once I took a series of photos of a distant flying raven and discovered on blowing them up that he was looking steadfastly back at me the whole time. Some ring gulls take a detour to check out the solitary hiker approaching their bay. One by one, they dip in for a quick look and move on.

Well, the gulls are not really interested in me but in what I might be carrying in my backpack. A squad of blue-winged teal have seen me coming just from the reaction of the gulls and violently thrust out of the reeds near shore. I pause and watch them hustle off until they become imperceptible smudges. The blue of the lake is dazzling and pristine. Not a sound except for the murmuring ring gull colony possessed of a rocky crescent—and the three eagles, which continue their taunts at each other from their own denuded islet of granite and driftwood.

I say the blue of *the lake*, but I have overstated the claim. It is only a bay that I see, and a small one at that. The ten-thousand-year-old lake itself spreads over twenty-five thousand square kilometres. It *can* be seen in its entirety, but only from outer space, not from the shores of itself. The name of this lake is Great Slave Lake, and there must be many other hunters and fishermen and hikers on its vast shores today who are also scanning the horizon at this moment, seeing the same thing. A great shimmering silence, manifested in blue and mauve and green and white. Without other people.

The footpath opens to a grassy knoll overlooking a narrow beach of khaki sand and heaped driftwood. The logs are piled three and four deep on the shore, big logs washed up as far as one can see, poplar and birch and aspen logs that have been transported to the lake from the Hay River and its other tributaries in the cyclical floods of early spring. Tens of thousands of monumental timbers, hundreds of thousands, are dumped here, many of them bearing the gnaw marks of beavers. Their huge numbers attest to the immensity of the lake's drainage area to the south and its innumerable marshes and swamps.

The brisk lake air washes over me. I ease my pack onto a hoary log at the water's edge. My fingers trace the gouges at its base. Deep tooth marks. It, too, has been chewed and felled by a single-minded beaver. It is clear from this massive array that the collective impact of these large rodents on their environment is staggering, if indeterminate as to its exact nature. Do these log heaps provide a refuge habitat between water and forest for some specialized creatures? I can see only tiny insects and spiders scampering after them. Perhaps it's different at night.

I should resist this temptation to make logical connections and identify possible consequences. It is mere intellectual distraction, not what I came here for. A nearby clump of alders offers broken shade, full cover. I position myself within the growing shadows of the afternoon and wait. The first task in the bush is to stay quiet and wait, in perfect stillness.

And see what happens.

WINTER

1 : Perfect Stillness

The unending boreal forest of the Mackenzie River, where another dimension awaits, and beyond that...

Overleaf: The sentient forest plays its tricks, gleefully dumping snow on the trapper just as her picture is taken.

THE INDIGENOUS PEOPLES who live in Canada's Northwest were among the last in the New World to encounter European explorers. While there is evidence of Russian and even Chinese trade goods that found their way into the interior of Yukon and Northwest Territories, these archeological relicts, such as manufactured beads and punched-hole coins, simply highlight the existence of wholly regional trade routes that extended inland from the Pacific coast. The Russian and Chinese traders had no need to find a Northwest Passage to Asia—they were already its proprietors, in their hardy trans-Pacific vessels.

The British and French, on the other hand, were obliged to come overland in flimsy canoes from their distant southeast colonies, a series of intermittent forays financed by fur trading corporations headquartered in Lower Canada. What they found was a composite culture, an unwritten history of competing cultural and political influences that Jean-Jacques Rousseau, writing in 1754 in Geneva, was oblivious to when he penned his magnum opus, *Discourse on Inequality*. Civilization had replaced instinct with justice and passion with civilized artifice, he argued, using the little he understood of New World society to support his revolutionary views against the divine right of kings.

The Seven Year's War and the fall of Quebec in 1759 wrought by the supremacy of the British navy soon eliminated the older French Seigniorial system, but not its influences in these northern reaches. The word for "thank you" is *mahsi* in Gwich'in, a Dene language spoken by the ancestors of about 3,500 Aboriginal people centred on the Mackenzie Delta in the Northwest Territories and the Porcupine River in Yukon. This variant of *merci* was taken up (as the local story goes) from Quebecois traders in the absence of an equivalent courtesy term among Aboriginal people; some of the more cheerful traditional fiddle music played by contemporary Gwich'in musicians also discloses a *Habitant* influence, along with its Orkney roots.

Alexander Mackenzie's celebrated expedition in 1789 finally succeeded in reaching the chill Beaufort Sea despite numerous challenges, environmental and human: it began snowing heavily in late July and his crew grew factional. According to his journal, the contentious expedition party of a dozen Whites and Aboriginals carried limited provisions. They were forced to hunt for whatever game they could find to keep heading north and were dependent on trade for most of their provisions. Swans, fish, an owl, and even a lynx are mentioned as routine comestibles. Without the full historical context, it is easy to gloss over these original travel accounts and miss the implications they have for our understanding of pre-Contact societies.

Today, some traditional Gwich'in trappers (generally, Elders over sixty) still eat portions of the lynx—pronouncing it *link* in the local French vernacular—caught in their number 330 steel Conibears. Peter Ross, a veteran Gwich'in trapper in Aklavik, a small community of three hundred on the Peel River, gave the proverbial answer when asked how lynx meat tastes: "Like chicken, but dark meat. You pan-fry the haunch in lard, with salt and pepper."

The idea of eating a cat, wild or not, or any predator for that matter, strikes urbanized Europeans as unseemly if not horrible. But it's all imaginary, this food, isn't it? It's *the idea* we refuse to taste. There is a great deal of theoretical discussion in the sociological literature as to why this might be so. Do different people's food taboos and food preferences reflect internalized historical survival experiences? Did the French learn to relish frog legs as a functional adaptation to the privations of their Hundred Years War? Did the Israelites justifiably fear biological contagion from alien foods like scaleless fish (eels) or four-legged creatures without hooves (pigs) when they enacted the dietary restrictions of Leviticus, circa 500 BC? Or are these restrictive categories the outcome of initially orderly conceptual rules about the workings of the world carried to their logical outcomes, as the structuralist anthropologist Claude Lévi-Strauss argued in *The Savage Mind*?

It has been demonstrated by numerous psychological experiments that what we see before our eyes is not objective reality but projections generated by unconscious and involuntary processes, utter fictions that include what we expect to see, what we are told by others is actually out there, and what our limited sense data creates for its own convenience through the involuntary compulsions of an inner story editor.

It is important to understand, then, when thinking about European Contact and its history to the present, that these same conditioning processes profoundly influence our perceptions of the northern wilderness and the Indigenous people who live here today. Just to cite one example, there were no "virgin" forests at the time of Contact, because these forests were already well *used*. Indigenous people everywhere in the Americas practised various degrees of effective and intervening land management in their own territories, which included controlled tract burning to foster berry production and new plant growth for browsers like whitetail deer and grouse to discourage catastrophic forest fires, and to reduce nearby insect swarms.

The Canadian government in the 1930s banned the traditional tract fires set by the Gwich'in and other tribes in Yukon, partly to maximize Crown revenues from the growing lumber industry and partly because the sophistication of what seemed to be a makeshift and risky practice was beyond its bureaucratic comprehension. These Indians were despoiling the virginity of their own virgin forest!

Nineteenth-century monumental paintings by American landscape artist Thomas Cole (1801–1848), literary descriptions by transcendentalists Ralph Waldo Emerson and David Thoreau, and the black and white landscape photographs of Ansel Adams (1901–1984) perpetuated the iconic role of the unpopulated virgin forest for generations of city folk.

By the same token, the itinerant Englishman Archie Belaney was able to convince three successive generations of devout readers in the twentieth century that he was a half-Apache named Grey Owl, simply because he had absorbed these same popularized Imperial fictions about romantic Indian life that they largely did, and, more, Belaney acted out these standardized preconceptions with the dedication of a successful method actor.

However, Archie Belaney never mentions eating lynx. Instead, he retails Rousseau's infamous Cartesian divide between instinct and justice, claiming, for instance, that beavers are human in their sentiments and, therefore, in all fairness, they ought to be studied, not hunted for bloody pelts. Archie even kneels before a Manitoba swamp like a rustic Narcissus in his custom-fringed buckskin for a celebrated professional photograph. You may have seen this 1930s publicity shot in grade school: the blue-eyed Grey Owl hand feeds his tamed beaver a jelly roll, and, so, successfully inserts at one go his alien Edwardian fondness for pets, sugary treats, and the picturesque into a stark and morally indifferent world order where a single beaver killed in winter might well mean the difference between a family's starvation and survival—that is, for anybody who was not getting monthly royalties from *Country Life* magazine in England.

Inevitably, then, like the original voyageurs, we come to this boreal land heavily freighted with our own cultural cargo. It is necessary to dump it all in order to freely admit our preconceptions and learn what we can about the vanishing world of the Great Hunt. The northern bush was never virgin. Moreover, we have also inherited thick blinders from our youthful immersion in a corpus of work we can call the timeless Brave, a persistent literary genre that begins with James Fenimore Cooper's ahistorical novel, *The Deerslayer* (1841), if not earlier with Daniel Dafoe's *Robinson Crusoe* (1719), and if not earlier still, with the epic of warrior-king Gilgamesh and his sidekick, the wild man Enkidu, circa 2500 BC.

The common ground of these timeless Brave stories is their utter absence of economic, historical, kinship, or political contexts. They take place in a social vacuum, and their purpose is to enact resolutions about the shifting relations of military power versus binding contract that operate at the dynamic core of urbanized society, according to a deep reading of Western mythology by cultural theorist Georges Dumézil.

Today, revisiting tales of Tonto and the Lone Ranger continues to provide grist for our public speculations on the nature of human artifice, and its complement, the power of nature's artifacts—a place where life and death meet and resolve their differences. They offer interesting metaphysical challenges, these stories, but they also woefully obscure the reality of the First Nations people living on the ground. First Nations people might have been brave, but they were never timeless. They had their histories, too, encoded in the land through oral traditions, through place names, rocks, rivers, heights, and even animals.

These cultural filters must be resolved. This book assumes three basic points about the importance of this exercise:

1. *The subsistence relationship between First Nations people and the Land is meaningfully different from that of agricultural and industrial people and is worth understanding on its own for such differences.*
2. *The remnant features of this subsistence technology point to the ways that Europeans' ancestors might also have followed to survive for thousands of years.*

3. *Northern folkways and traditions offer valuable and universal lessons about human potential in our contemporary era, since First Nations, too, have survived the dangerous crises of history to the present day.*

It must be acknowledged that these three propositions are each theoretically contentious. Here are the counterarguments, in reverse order, starting with the third proposition:

1. *History is pure accident, chance, and random drift, which rules out its usefulness as any practical guide to future productive behaviour. Chance rules.*
2. *How human societies lived in the past is only discernable from advanced scientific studies (micro-archeology, genetics, chemical testing) and not from comparative studies of prehistoric orange societies with modern, if marginalized, apple societies. Our past is dirt, literally.*
3. *And, finally, all people are essentially the same the world over and any claim of generic differences is a form of special pleading, if not chauvinistic.*

This intellectual controversy can only be broken by action, by going into the bush with northern people and actually observing what happens out there.

⋮ So here we are: deep winter in the northern boreal forest.

I am walking along the frozen shoreline of the Mackenzie River with Gwich'in trapper Ellen Firth of Fort McPherson. She is checking on her rabbit snares.

We are in the uppermost northwestern corner of Canada, two degrees above the Arctic Circle, 160 kilometres south of the Beaufort Sea, in a spruce tangle thirty kilometres upriver from the frontier town of Inuvik. It is the country's last community to be serviced by a gravel road. An outpost town in an archipelago of icy outposts.

The temperature today is -38°C. It is calm, at last.

Two days ago, a blizzard from Alaska came through the Richardson Mountains and dumped a few token dustings of dry snow as a bluff and distraction before it tore the new roof off the tiny airport terminal, bringing such air traffic as there was to a complete halt. The electrical power went off for hours. It was interesting to see the town illuminated only by the glow of a few snowmobiles. Their headlights bounced over the snowdrifts as they raced each other in the dark of a late January noon.

Local Elders say we must go back to living on the Land; and, more, that the Land wants us back. It is easy to believe that vast animate forces overrun these hopeful, surveyed urban geographies in the Arctic. For two days the north wind howled like a black creature as it prowled the town streets, ripping out street signs and smashing them against sheet-metal walls and plastic vehicles.

Whatever it wanted, whatever it came for, the storm got in the end. The violence suddenly took up and vanished, signing a goodbye note in shattered glass and twisted debris that proved indecipherable. The townspeople were left with a rekindled anxiety about our ability to pass such extreme climatic tests.

But that was then. Today, the new morning in the forest is calm.

The wind out of the northwest is slight but not lifeless. A flat chill breeze sends tiny frost clouds billowing across the frozen lake like crystal smoke, and subsides to a whisper, then a sigh. A grove of tall spruce and birch trees stands like a sentry before the shaggy gates of another world. The difference in the quality of light between the open frozen marsh and the dense coniferous forest is palpable, magnified further by the hikers' heightened senses.

We enter the blue-green entanglement, a redoubt of spruces, and more spruces. The wind shears and fades away like magic. An unseen bird burbles a pretty warning. It is close by, but it is aware that I am looking. A creeper, it stays hidden on its side of a mottled aspen.

Then, nothing. An inner silence descends to meet the outer. Awareness expands and encapsulates every foggy breath. The stillness is electric, haunting yet strangely comforting at the same time.

There is nothing so quiet as the northern bush in winter. Your own existence becomes a precise quantity, measured in laboured efforts. Walking quietly on an overgrown trail is impossible with modern clothing. Dry twigs tap and scrape across the nylon and twill parka like a stroked kettledrum. Gum and canvas boots clump and whine and creak melodramatically over the icy path.

Wearing yielding furs and animal hides might change this experience for the better, but it would also increase the odds of surprising a bear or a wolf around the next bend. Local people always have an axe or rifle within reach, and tell funny stories about the times they did not. Surprised by big beasts with their pants down, literally.

Something to think about, as another sharp turn in the path appears ahead. Everything changes with each step and nothing changes. Detail piles on detail, yet something else remains unseen behind it all. The interior of the forest is breathlessly expectant, so still and secretive that a low cough or misstep is magnified like a gunshot for lack of background distractions. You are it, the only thing moving obliviously through the stillness of the forest. Signs of a recent incident appear in the snow-filled ravine on the right. Someone's dog had slipped off the trail and nearly fallen into the creek before being caught fast by a clump of alders and scrambling back to safety.

The fresh snow is deceptively even. It is easy enough to trip on an unseen root or hollow hidden under its glittery surface. All animals lose their footing, but they have three other legs to sustain them, whereas we humans only have one—and a propensity for idle daydreaming.

Just ahead, some bigger-than-life ravens are kicking up a fuss over something. Now the senses go on full alert. You pause, look around, up and behind, regain your position. It is more than the risk of falling, alone and unheard, in this extreme cold. You realize that the forest, in turn, is both listening closely to your own ragged breathing and becoming increasingly aware of your limitations in the ongoing accretion of your mistakes, blunders, and hesitations, a record that will surely follow your next move no matter how innocent or successfully executed it proves to be.

The north forgives every sin except stupidity, as the local refrain goes, and it is so easy to be stupid in this glacial cold.

After the recent blizzard, the temperature is still dropping, although the early February sun has finally completed its first post-solstice ascent over the long wall of the Richardson Mountains to the west. The rising afternoon light bathes the upper half of the spruce forest in shockingly pink and apricot rays, contradicting the classic black-and-white iconography of the early European explorers.

The array of subtle radiances and incidental half-tones is at play in the forest understorey, too, an incandescence that the snow reflects and diffuses through the lower branches, making camouflage and stillness even more important for the smaller creatures who do not hibernate, who must venture out daily, risking their lives for an anxious nibble or two of dry grass or lichens.

The path around the lake is criss-crossed with the tracks of innumerable hares. But there is no movement on the forest floor, just signs of earlier movement. Somewhere, close by, a dozen snowshoe hares are sitting perfectly still, appearing as white balls of fresh-dropped snow, even bending their heads to hide their black eyes under their forelegs like demure retainers waiting for a noisy royal procession to pass. They will explode into action only when other animals approach them with direct intent, a heart-stopping moment that even keen hunting dogs sometimes fail to anticipate.

Notwithstanding their collective invisibility, there is enough stray prey about to make it worthwhile for a large owl to overwinter by the frozen lake. Right now, the raptor is patiently patrolling the far shore, keeping its course steady at thirty metres as it scours the alder thickets and animal trails below.

The ravens stay close to the opposite shore, tumbling and swooping over the treetops in eccentric circles, like acrobats practising for a big show. Perhaps there is some purpose to their antics, a display of social dominance or territoriality. Only the ravens know for sure, but one thing is certain, these scavengers know more about us than we know about them. They have flown overhead several times, taking different trajectories to build up a more complete picture of the interesting travellers in their midst.

Like us, moose have long legs and a correspondingly high centre of gravity, so it would be useful to observe precisely how they move through this snow, plopping their hooves down squarely one by one and making sure they have secured that footing before lifting the next leg. It is a tiring process for the uninitiated, as it requires different calf muscles and more attention than what we are used to in a paved world. But there is a fallen log in sight and no reason not to sit on it and let the forest disclose what it chooses to reveal.

Here's something. A silent communication emanates from the spruces. They are heavy with snow. A moment's reflection makes it obvious that the accumulation on their branches is no accident. Clearly, these conifer trees were *designed* to hold snow. Why should this be? A blizzard recently raged here for three days and its winds reached eighty kilometres per hour, yet the branches have retained and even increased their load of snow. Perhaps the conifers protect their needles' moisture from drying winds with insulating blankets?

Another twenty minutes of hiking. We reach the crest of the ridge and look west. The sounds of the camp behind us are faint as improbable memory. The wind from the west blows fresh and cold. The Richardson Mountains fill the horizon, a sea of rugged limestone, bearing the green froth of life on their peaks, peak after peak. This is it, the place we have sought out. The bush.

"Look, these tracks are fresh."

Ellen Firth points to the pugmarks in the snow and smiles lightly as hunting people tend to do when signs of a valuable game animal cross their path.

"Lynx. A big one."

Her eyes follow the large cat's trail where it has zigzagged through the spruce forest. The predator was checking on the same rabbit snares that

Ellen has so carefully placed fifty paces apart, about thirty centimetres above the deliberately tamped-down snow alongside the lake path.

⋮ It is early February, I remind myself. The vast delta of the frozen Mackenzie River in Canada's Northwest Territories is one of the world's last great expanses of untrammelled boreal forest. A quiet and still immensity. Each lump of snow falling from the trees sounds like a blissful sigh.

The late morning sun sits low on the horizon, red and bright and powerful, although spring is a long six weeks away. It hurts even without the painful reflections from the pure white snow. The temperature is now about -35°C. There is no wind. The metallic squeals of the crushed snow under our boots are a reminder that ice is water in its metal state. The arctic air is habitually dry and contributes to the inflammatory power of the sun, which bounces about us and smudges the edge of the forest with blue-gray shadows.

Despite the unyielding cold, Ellen wears only a thin black ski jacket and a black watch cap. When she stops moving, she is difficult to make out in the deep black shadows of the deep black spruce, which is probably the idea. She says she owns a .30-30 Winchester, the same vintage rifle that many northern hunters still prefer today for its reliability, although it has been decades since the company last made this particular model. But today all she carries with her into the forest are a skinning knife and a few wire snares.

The local grizzly bears are hibernating and the chances of encountering a polar bear are remote out here in the inland delta. Still, one has to be ready for anything. Large animals can suddenly appear. The forest is permeable to sharp danger as well as to opportunity.

Ellen's eyes move like a speed reader's, darting about, taking it all in—the depth of the snow crust (so remorselessly white, it appears blue to the unsatisfied eye), the openings and barriers in the spruce forest, the powdery sudden reversals of the lynx's momentum, and the fresher overlaid tracks of a rabbit that bravely emerged from its hiding place to feed on willow bark early this morning. It seems that Ellen sees the lynx in four dimensions, recreating in her mind its size, weight, sex, and, most importantly, assessing its life force from the powdery attitudes of its early dawn passage.

The lynx has made its choices, and so has she.

"Must have smelled rabbit blood, maybe. He's goin' to stick around, I think. I'm going to put out a snare for him. Lots of lynx about these days. My husband took out a hundred of them last season from our camp. Good prices this year."

While she talks, Ellen is already planning exactly where to put the lynx snare. She has taken a large straight branch that she will use to lay across the game trail at a 45-degree angle, rising right to left from fifteen centimetres to two metres, as a visual barrier, carefully orchestrating the same incremental changes to the landscape with sticks and twigs that she uses to direct the snowshoe hares to her snares—but at a larger scale.

Under the hoop of the snare, she implants a row of twigs that she carefully breaks so they all appear jagged sharp and well worth leaping over: animals do not like to scratch themselves any more than people do. These pointy sticks are pure bluff, for they are only plunked down a few centimetres into the soft snow, so they could be pushed over easily—but the animals do not know that, of course. It's a visual bluff.

It seems that this simulation, this deceptive modelling, of the trapper's working environment requires not only the illusive powers of the artist over perspective, scale, and narrative but also the acute analysis of the behavioural psychologist. A successful trapper must see the entire set-up strictly from the animal's point of view.

Not content with her set-up, Ellen walks about it, looking at it from different angles, readjusting her twigs and sticks, analyzing its invisible deficiencies. The hoop is sixteen-gauge steel wire; she wants to cajole the animal to put its head into it: the little one-way slider will do the rest.

After she is satisfied with her lynx set-up, we continue our walk to the edge of a frozen lake. I am about to ask her if she has eaten lynx, but a rabbit has been caught in her second-to-last snare. She wordlessly takes it out, places it down on the path, and carefully redoes that set-up, too, replacing the funnel sticks and stepping back to consider the effect. The rabbit snare and the lynx snare get an equal measure of her attention. Or, rather, should we say, the job at hand always gets its full attention?

The rabbit—actually a snowshoe hare (*Lepus americanus*) weighs about two kilograms and can provide a main course for two adults. The hares offer a secure source of animal protein in the upper registers of their ten-year population cycles. On the lower Mackenzie River lived another group of Dene speakers near the Gwich'in. They were dubbed the Hare people by early explorers, because they specialized in taking rabbits. James Itsi, a Gwich'in Elder who grew up in the nearby community of Fort McPherson in the 1950s, recounted how his mother fed him and his eight brothers and sisters with rabbits she caught in the nearby woods while his father was away for months working a distant trapline: "Some days she'd catch ten or fifteen rabbits. You could make blankets out of their fur, too. Not as warm as other animals but easy to work with."

James repeated a point about First Nations children's upbringing that found universal agreement among the Elders of his generation. Children were traditionally taught to speak only when spoken to, and were encouraged from infancy to observe all the workings of adult society from direct, participatory observation—to learn by example.

"Our school was out-of-doors," James said. "You never interrupted an Elder or crossed his or her path, without showing them proper respect. As a young boy you learned how to watch carefully everything your parents did, and always to keep quiet around them as they worked—two important lessons!"

Robert, another Gwich'in Elder, added his own recollection: "You never looked a grown-up straight in the eye, it was considered disrespectful. Even today, the more traditionally raised Gwich'in students are criticized by their White teachers for not looking at them when they talk. They mistake a sign of respect for inattention, or boredom."

I had heard such exemplary accounts prior to my field trip with Ellen, and knew enough not to pepper her with idle questions as she began skinning the rabbit. A whisky jack joined us at the first cut of her knife, eager to steal a scrap of fresh offal from underfoot, a habit the bird species might have adopted with the first arrival of Clovis hunters over ten thousand years ago. Ellen deftly peeled off the hide and cut the joints low to secure the last bit of desirable leg meat. I recalled watching an extended Inuvialuit family back in the fall that had returned home to Inuvik with two caribou they had taken off the Dempster Highway. Grandmothers, aunt and uncle, parents, and two children, eight people in all, worked wordlessly for an hour to butcher the animals on their gravel driveway.

What was striking about that procedure was how the youngest child, a girl of seven or eight, watched intently as she moved freely through the flashing knives and axes and bloody haunches, and how the older people communicated the mutuality of their tasks with subtle gestures and looks. Everyone had a rightful place in the process. Nobody told the child to stand over there, or to go away and play. Her life demonstration was *three-dimensional*; she was encouraged to explore the inner workings of the entire operation, from the shooting of the animals to the final distribution of the bagged meat to an extended circle of friends and kin.

The flatness of Western instruction, the mainstream cultural reliance on images and graphics, on technical manuals, emphasizes the Renaissance invention of ideal perspective, of the privileged vantage point. Easel painting, book printing, marked seating in public forums (including designated desks in schools and factories), and still photography all work to promote the fixed steady eye of European culture. The White teacher who insists that students look her in the eye speaks volumes for this cultural priority.

Out here in the bush, the local emphasis on respectful silence and attentive instruction is easy to understand. The Arctic is an unpredictably hazardous place. You want to hear approaching bears and wolves and rutting moose before they hear you. You need to commit the full range of your critical senses to environmental cues in a multidimensional realm of wild time and space, staying alert to external opportunities and warnings even as you chop wood or skin rabbits.

Yet one cannot help speculating that the deeper, existential reason for adopting a formal, respectful silence in the deep woods has less to do with the practical utility of the attitude and more about maintaining direct communion with its thrilling inner power. Say what you like, the battered and exhausted landscapes adjoining many of our urban city centres are sadly bereft of this animating *ur*-energy. Their trees still grow, the water still flows, but it's a slack and lifeless familiarity. Wounded, if not comatose, drained of its original vitality, such an overtaxed landscape has stopped speaking to us above a whisper.

More. It seems to me, meandering through this winter-charged escarpment is the exhilarating physical sense of escape into connection. Of having finally completed a circuit, of allowing nature to speak freely to the identical nature mirrored deep within us. This inner-outer correspondence is uplifting, liberating, calming, vivifying. Was it sovereign winter itself that taught generations of mankind to silently reflect on the animated powers that direct our fates?

I trekked ahead to take a photo of Ellen walking through the narrow trail.

As I lift my camera, Ellen, a dozen metres away, pauses. A shift in the air—and a huge load of fluffy snow falls on her from the upper branches just as I snap the picture—on her and nowhere else. She smiles, faintly, shakes off the powdery cloak, and continues walking without comment.

I can't help thinking that the Land has played its little joke on us, and wonder if she is thinking the same thing.

⁝ A few weeks later, I go for a ride on the ice road with an Inuvialuit resident, Liz Gordon, who wants to check on the condition of her hunt camp on the banks of the Mackenzie downriver from Inuvik town. Her younger brother Stan likes hunting rabbits after work, and he favours using a .22 calibre short bullet because its small size damages less meat.

Knowing the hunters' preference, the local store cannily charges more for small bullets than the bigger ones, another example of the exploitive nature of our four-hundred-year-old trading post regime. Stan gives me two fresh rabbits, nicely skinned and ready for the pot, along with some ideas on how to cook them "Native-style."

I decide on the slow-baked method, with carrots, potatoes, and onions in a closed casserole dish, along with a dash of red wine. How did they taste? You must have seen this coming—like lynx, of course!

2 : Hunting Is Trapping

Ellen Firth recovering a snowshoe hare from her trapline in the Mackenzie Delta.

THE YOUNG BULL MOOSE stands at the far shore of the river, undecided. It is morning, a bright clear March day on the Mackenzie Delta, upriver from the small Gwich'in community of Tsiigehtchic. The hamlet overlooks where the Arctic Red River joins the Mackenzie River.

The Mackenzie River at this point is about three hundred metres wide, a frozen expanse of ice, two metres thick, sculpted deceptively flat by the prevailing northwesterly winds. In fact, there are numerous ridges, hollows, and big cracks lying just below the snow cover, which has been laid bare by the wind in some places but sits like a glittery sand trap in others, ready to slow down the large animal that chooses to follow the wrong route through it.

The hunter waits on the other shore, downwind from the moose. He has taken up a position in the broken shadows of a thicket of willow scrub. Now he sits on his snowmobile, motionless.

He has a .30-30 Winchester cradled in his arms and knows the effective range of his rifle to within a metre. The possession of a near-antique .30-30 marks him as a member of the older generation of First Nations hunters, for the younger men, trusting more to technology and progress than to tradition and hard-won skill, favour the newer, flat-shooting bores like the .270 Winchester or the .308 Winchester.

The moose must come within two hundred metres for the hunter to take his shot.

Right now, the moose is about 450 metres away. It could decide to stay right where it is and unaccountably drift back into the bush. Moose are like that. Unpredictable individuals, not herd animals like the caribou.

The moose has decided. He is moving out on the ice. It keeps coming, intent on crossing the frozen river. With a last look upstream, the animal begins its traverse, moving at a leisurely trot, its long legs and wide splayed hooves helping to sustain its passage over the crusty terrain. The hunter knows, or intuits, exactly where the moose wants to make for shore; he has seen moose cross this river many times before, in summer and winter, and he knows their preferences as the abundant game trails disclose in their fixed placement and prominence.

This moose is likely heading for the point about 150 metres upstream from the hunter's position. Noel Andre, the Gwich'in hunter, recounts what happened next:

> I was watching him, this moose. Figuring he'd come across up from where I was. Then I seen how he made up his mind and begins to come over, so I wait. This is the best time to hunt moose, in the morning. They are hungry, looking for food. Later, after they eat some, maybe between 1:00 and 3:00, their ears are really sharp, they can hear everything. Later in the afternoon they are ready to bed down and so they stop moving around.
>
> This one, he comes across, he slows down, and he goes in a circle. Like he's looking for something. [Noel points to the deep tracks in the snow, which show how the bull moose changed its direction twice in short order.]

Then he changes his mind again. And he comes forward towards me. I shoot him once, over there, the first time, then he runs a little bit, maybe twenty yards, and I shoot him again and he falls right here. It is going to take me maybe three hours to butcher him.

The bull moose is enormous, four times the mass of a big man, and Noel is happy to cut it up using only a hunting knife with a fifteen centimetre blade, pushing and pulling the carcass into position with the sheer logic of experienced muscle power. He begins by eviscerating the animal, first separating out the edible organs on the snow from the unwanted ones. What is desirable seems to be a cultural choice.

"We don't eat the lungs," Noel says, making a face. "The best part is the stomach and the esophagus. We eat those first."

The huge stomach is filled with munched-up willow browse, and, as he works, Noel explains a culinary difference between the caribou and the moose.

"We grownups don't eat willow ourselves. It's only a treat for kids in the spring. They take the new growth, peel off the bark and lick the juice. But caribou, they eat moss and other good healthy stuff. Sometimes we take the stomach contents of a caribou and rub it over the meat, to give it a special flavour. Or you can make it in a soup. It's good for you."

Another snowmobile shows up. Noel has got himself a needed helper, a man in his twenties, who, in the respectful tradition of Gwich'in youth in the presence of Elders, says nothing as he joins us. He watches the entire procedure carefully, mutely following the older man's gestures and cues to help him roll the massive animal into a new position, and pulling hard at the joints to allow dismemberment with the solitary little knife.

Noel tells us that the moose hide is already spoken for by one of the ladies in town. She has sent her young nephew over in a snowmobile to make her claim. By nightfall, the moose meat will be completely distributed among Noel's family, friends, and the needy in the Tsiigehtchic community. The remains are left as a feast for ravens and whisky jacks, and perhaps for a wandering nocturnal predator, hungry enough to brave the scent of a human's kill site.

In passing, Noel says something highly revealing about the nature of the First Nations hunting tradition: "I knew there was three of them. The young bull, a cow, and a young calf almost as big as this bull. I seen them around for a while. The other two, they're still out there, somewhere upriver."

So the hunter *already knew*, long before this day, that there were three moose nearby on the frozen river. He had studied their habits and tallied the risks. Much and fast calculation went into his half-hour hunt—astute anticipation and rigorous odds making based on empirical data. Noel pre-visualized this moment, and other moments similar to it, by shading them off into different outcomes, just as a computer model simulates a multiple future by using different vectors.

Here the main vector involved putting oneself into the maximal triangulated position so that, when the moose comes to you, it comes close enough that you can bag it with a relatively lightweight deer rifle. You must know its general moose habits and at the same time understand its individual proclivities.

More, you must trade places with your game animal. You must think and move like the animal does, perhaps even see yourself in the waiting distance as the animal sees you or fails to see you—you, the hunter, waiting motionless in the shadow of the scrub willow.

More, you must read the landscape, understand the terrain, determine all the exit possibilities. You must know that this spot of snow and not that spot is the best place to shoot the animal, for the snow is deeper there and the animal will flounder, giving you a chance for a second final shot should the first one fail.

In fact, this kill was not so much *a hunt* as it was a trap—a trap sprung by a man at the centre of an effective killing radius of two hundred metres. A trap that uses the game trails and habits of the prey animal to slowly and inevitably reduce the quarry's flight opportunity as close to zero as possible. Most creatures are faster than humans. Most game animals can outfly, outrun, outsense, and even outhide us. But they cannot escape the parameters of their own behavioural responses, the cues in the environment that influence them to go right or go left, to go faster or slower. Traps are mankind's first great machines, time machines that operate in a land called *later* and return to the present with their gifts of easy-won fresh meat.

Collectively made traps—elaborate fish weirs and rabbit funnels and caribou corrals made of sticks tied together in elaborate structures—once dotted this same delta landscape for thousands of years until a mere century ago. We do not see snares and animal drive fences in the inventories of Paleolithic archeologists because, unlike bone and stone tools, organic items like woven baskets, fibre fish lines, and hide snares disintegrated long ago.

When the Scottish explorer Alexander Mackenzie first came through this river in 1789, he noted the presence of permanent stick fences used in First Nations community drives to direct the flighty ptarmigan game birds toward hunters waiting at the narrow enclosure.

The Gwich'in once routinely constructed similar drive fences for caribou, and stone funnels to direct geese flights. They also set individual snares made of sinew and cured hide for caribou and smaller game. How productive were these devices? It's an easy enough question to answer; all we have to do is ask a professional Gwich'in trapper.

The technology has changed since Alexander Mackenzie's day, with steel wire replacing the sinew cord of the traditional homemade snare, but the principle of the trap remains the same: understand the cues in the environment from the game animal's perspective; amplify those cues; set the snare at the precise width and height that will allow the quarry to place its head and neck comfortably within the noose before it tightens irreversibly with the drag of the shoulders. Of course, the snare itself is a response to the natural environment over millennia; this same natural environment includes consciousness, human consciousness and animal consciousness, and so one cannot help wondering if life—if the trees, the animals, and even the wind—have all co-evolved in response to the totality of the arctic environment of which human consciousness is itself a necessary and formidable part.

Such speculation is condoned, even encouraged, by the local people who indulge in their own conjectures all the time, who are open to unrestricted conjectures about daily occurrences, both natural and social. It is a necessary part of their survival strategy.

Owing to their remoteness in the Northwest Territories and Yukon, the Gwich'in were among the last First Nations to be affected by European Contact. Even with the significant discovery of oil in the region in the 1920s, and all the geological exploration that followed, the bulk of the population—numbering perhaps 3,500 people—remained on the land and engaged in the subsistence (hunting and trapping) economy of their ancestors. However, a major blow was struck to the subsistence economy after the Second World War with the decline in fur prices and the federal policy to move Aboriginal people off the land and into communities.

The Gwich'in of that generation were keenly aware that these changes were permanent and irreversible. Trapper Stephen Frost, the son of a former RCMP officer and his Gwich'in wife, was in his twenties during this momentous cultural shift, and he was able to reflect on these changes from the perspective of a hale and keen-eyed seventy-seven-year-old man, a woodsman who had not forgotten a thing about his rich life experiences.

"You know," Stephen said, "My parents worked hard to raise us kids. We grew up in a log cabin they built themselves on the Porcupine River. We could buy basic things we needed at the post in Old Crow, flour, sugar, tea, matches. Today we can buy ice cream whenever we want, that's great. That's progress. And a hospital! We have a good hospital now; they fixed up my injured leg here this past week! But in the old days? It was a very hard life for our grandparents. You can't imagine today how hard it was, back then."

Memory and speculation go hand in hand. Memory records patterns; speculation seeks their causes. Speculation is fundamental to the relationship the Gwich'in have with their land because the apparent wealth of local natural resources can so easily disappear overnight.

Most readers will have encountered the statistical fact that rabbit populations are highly cyclical in the north, rising and crashing in response to abstract selection pressures. Few, however, will have heard that the moose population, too, mysteriously disappeared from the entire Mackenzie River region for several decades through the 1930s and 1940s, a natural calamity that has yet to be satisfactorily explained. Gwich'in Elder James Itsi, originally from Fort McPherson in the Northwest Territories, moved to the village of Old Crow in Yukon in the 1990s. He considers the fate of the regional moose population as the direct product of human interest in its existence.

The village of Old Crow, James explains, is not next to the wilderness: "It is *in* the wilderness, a place where you can still get the good life." The good life perpetuates all existence. But human effort must be made, or all natural life suffers.

"The good life," he says, "is to go out on the land, build a fire, put a pot on and make some tea. Hopefully you will sit around and create some stories, and remember where you were last year. If you don't go out, you won't remember."

Stories create the Land, create life—not the other way around. Such lived-out stories, according to James Itsi, not only link people to shared experience but also protect the individual from modern disruption, by conferring meaning on private experience.

"If you don't go out on the land in the dark, and trust the land, you can't see. That's when everything goes into one big lump—when people believe in government, and not in their family luck, in family tradition. It's like bingo; you have to try your family luck, or you'll lose it. When there is only light—no TV, nothing, only light—then you see things, other things. Loons howling, and animals running around. They have taken over our place now! No one goes out anymore, people have got away from living. I can see in the dark, when the light comes right down on you from above."

What does James Itsi mean here, by "the light"? Does he mean something literal, or is it a metaphor? Does he mean that the human space of the hunters' traditional territory is being lost through inaction to an unknown wildness? That their ancient sensory world is shrinking? He says he means a real light, inner light, an absolute power that makes it possible for hunters to see the natural world as it really is: "That's where the world went," he nods, "when they only go out for the day. There was only the light before. No TV, nothing. Only the light."

James Itsi was sixty-nine in 2010; he was born in 1941 to Edward and Doris Chitsi of Fort McPherson, NT, one of seventeen children, some of whom, he says, grew up to become band chiefs and professional people. His mother Doris worked as a midwife and also assisted at the Anglican Mission, where she tirelessly "hauled wood every Sunday to make sure the church was warm inside," as he recounts proudly. The area around Fort McPherson was not as well favoured with game resources as Old Crow, and people like his mother had to do everything they could to keep on going in the 1940s and 1950s.

"We didn't have caribou on our land," James recalls. "So the men went away trapping in winter and the mothers and children would get snare wire and trap rabbits for food and money. You could get a dollar for a rabbit and if you were really good at it you could sell your rabbits and put food on the table. One guy came back with fifty rabbits, that was fifty dollars, a lot of money in those days! My mother would notice where the rabbit trails were and she put up her snares, and catch them."

One sees how it is: a white rabbit hops out of the bush. For southern visitors to the Far North, it is a natural wonder with Latin nomenclature (*Lepus americanus*) and possible associations to literary psychedelia. For this older man, the animal brings a rush of familiar memories. Winter: his father a hundred miles away, trapping marten and Arctic fox up in the McKenzie Delta; his mother coming back from the post store with sugar and flour and maybe raisins, hoping to make it to spring, still three months away. Chopping wood for the church in the snowy darkness. A few hours of dim light in January. Stew bubbling in the iron pot on a wood stove.

Rabbits.

⋮ From its high source in the Olgilvie Mountains, deep in Yukon's interior, the Porcupine River runs clear, cold, and true under the ice, continuing past the Aboriginal community of Old Crow and west into Alaska, where it disappears in the immensity of the Yukon River. Fifty kilometres down from the village, at the point where the rocky Bluefish River eagerly tumbles out of heavy bush to join it, the Porcupine broadens into a series of easy rapids traversing aspen flats, seven-metre sand cliffs, and mossy boreal hills.

A log cabin sits high on the north bank, facing the constant seasonal play of water, ice, and light. This is Bluefish Camp, home of Gwich'in trapper Stephen Frost. His nearest neighbour is fifteen kilometres upriver. Stephen is out working in the yard, getting ready for another marten trapping season. He welcomes us with black tea and bannock but does not otherwise pause from his labours as he chops wood—and keeps an eye out for the large wild animals whose habits take them through his yard in all seasons.

For him, the land is not a place of concrete, objectified data, and every reference to the quantifying mechanical approach of "outside experts" leaves him cold and worried:

This year I got a hundred-something muskrats just from the area back of the cabin. When the fur prices went down it was hardly worth trapping, so everybody left Crow Flats. Your equipment starts rusting. People don't go out, and the animals breed up. There are more of them around then when I was a kid. But then they die off, too, when muskrats eat all the bottom vegetation.

He shows off his harvest of flattened pelts, strung by the dozen to a steel hoop. Bloodstained and stiff with smoke, it looks exactly like what it is—raw currency, the original lifeblood of money. This is where we came from, who we are, as Canadian economist Harold Innis pointed out in 1930. But in this age of experts, how are we going to recall this secret truth: that we come from the blood of animals? The fate of the muskrats is tied to human stewardship, and so, of course, is the fate of the migratory caribou and people that depend on them like the Gwich'in.

"Don't know what's happening to the Porcupine caribou herd," Frost says. "Used to be 200,000, now it's down. Yet the wolf numbers are up. The experts collect their moose and muskrat shit, but they don't know anything about the moose," his voice comes from the deepening shadows of the afternoon. "They don't know anything about the Land."

Stephen Frost shakes his head at the prospect of imminent loss. Over a dinner of new potatoes, fried caribou, and cranberry preserve, we asked him what was important—what did he hope to pass on to his children?

"If you are not sure about where you are, you always look at the sun, the mountain, and wind. And you keep your feeling to the wind."

The Arctic twilight transforms his camp into a glowing apparition as the black spruces rally against the final light of the sky, mythic in their timeless self-assertion.

In fact, the local myths are stated in the conjectural and seem to deliberately raise more questions than they answer, providing a game post around which to organize the barrage of unanswerable feints and stratagems that all living things freely commit in their daily meanderings.

The difference is this: this morning we have moved from a world of concrete, answerable things to this world of random maneuvers and mysterious signs, and out of these hundreds and thousands of signs, signs made of twisted branches and discoloured, shedding bark and loping animal tracks and icy drifts and swooping birds, some signs are indeed meant for *us*.

We must watch out for traps, too.

3 : Northern Dogs

A classic Mackenzie Delta husky, powerful and indomitable but declining in popularity as modern sled racing favours lightweight breeds designed for speed.

Always feed your dogs first.

— GWICH'IN saying

IT IS A WONDERFUL THING to enter a dog lot in the Arctic bush. The grateful noise! The frantic joy! The howling exuberance!

Ten dogs or a hundred, it's a large responsibility that the patient musher cannot shirk. Keeping dogs in the north is hard work for their owners. Not only must the team be fed, watered, and trained but it must also be protected from a grievous array of wild animals.

Originally, wolves and bears posed the greatest threat to the domestic dogs of the north, but since global warming began to change the Arctic environment, the cougar, too, has now appeared on the Arctic scene, following white-tailed deer up into Yukon. And it will routinely kill dogs for sport as well as for food.

Elder James Itsi, a resident of the Gwich'in community of Old Crow in Yukon, keeps ten working dogs at his fish camp a few kilometres downstream from the hamlet, on the banks of the Porcupine River. Powerful animals bred for pulling supply sleds in winter, they are capable of reaching twenty-five kilometres an hour and holding to near that speed for the better part of a full day, if the snow conditions are good. And the native intelligence of the breed really shows through when snow conditions are not so good.

"Everybody running dogs tells the same story," says James. "You're going along, a little confused as to directions maybe, right? But thinking you're headed in the right direction. All of a sudden your dogs get real stubborn on you. They stop. You think you're smarter than them. You yell, force 'em to keep going. What happens?—Bang! Down you go. The ice cracks under your weight. They smelt the ice melting from below a long ways off! Now they pull you and the sled out. Looking at you funny. You're soaked in ice water, shivering. You try to keep warm by gathering them tight around you. Next you do what you should have done before: You let them find the way home again."

Although he has all the usual motorized vehicles, the quad bush buggy, the eight-metre boat, and Japanese kicker, James believes in dogs, believes in the superior power of their extended sensory domain. It is not just a question of their intuitive skill in running risky frozen rivers in winter, either. Climate change in the north has made all Aboriginal travellers aware of the increased risks of relying on their machines for survival.

Gwich'in participant Bernie McNeil of Inuvik recounts a recent incident (February 2012) of travelling overland in his snowmobile close to his bush camp, in sight of the Richardson Mountains some fifty kilometres out of Inuvik.

It was last February. Temperature 30 below, maybe 35. And a good cold winter so far. I was alone. Not going too far, just looking to get some firewood to heat up the cabin. I have been over the same patch of bush a hundred times. I am going about 25 kilometres an hour, when wham! I hit water where there shouldn't be any. Sink into a hidden pool, right under the snow, not too deep. But deep enough that it kills my engine

dead and soaks me up to my waist. I have to walk a mile back to my cabin,
my skin cut bloody from my frozen-hard snow pants. After I warm up and
patch up, I have to go back and winch the snowmobile out, inch by inch.
Two days wasted. With dogs, that never would have happened. The
cause?—Permafrost's melting, the groundwater starts seeping through
layers under the snow, looking for a path of least resistance, even in win-
ter. The thick snow cover keeps it insulated to the point where it comes
out at the surface. Now you can't rely on your memory of the land, because
the whole thing changes without warning. You can't smell meltwater like
a dog can, it's just a crapshoot.

One might suppose that summer is different, since you can clearly see standing pools of thawing meltwater, but here again the superior senses of the northern dog would come in handy. Gwich'in Elder Johnny P. Charlie, based in Fort McPherson on the Peel River, tells some visiting photographers he is escorting down the river on June 21, the longest day of the Arctic summer, that today of all days he must keep his craft in the dead centre of the channel and avoid coming too close to the clay till riverbanks on either side.

"We call it *slumping*." Johnny pointed his cigarette at the mottled, raw, six-metre embankments that showed unmistakable signs of recent erosion. "What happens is these riverbanks suddenly collapse and fall on your boat, and then you're done for. Even if they miss you they can make a big splash that'll swamp your boat, drown you in the cold river. So use your big lenses, boys, and we'll stay away from shore 'til it's safe to land."

It is only at this point that I thought I understood why the Inuit sea hunters I had travelled with in the Eastern Arctic often took a dog out with them into the coastal waters of Hudson Bay. The Inuit are long habituated to a polar marine environment that is in constant flux, an environment of dynamic icebergs and tidal currents and sand bars that were not there yesterday.

Perhaps this extreme environment was what had ended the prehistoric occupations of several of the Inuit's sea ice-adapted predecessors over a five-thousand-year time span, although their material cultures did not appear substantially different from that of the historical hunting people encountered by the Vikings around AD 1000. A dog with a hearing range to distances four times greater than a human's, and the expanded ability to hear the high-frequency sounds generated by grinding sea ice, changing underwater currents, and even earthquakes, is a good companion to take along on trips into changeable seas.

The Gwich'in, whose boreal mountain homeland has been relatively stable since the Great Melting at the beginning of the Holocene period ten thousand years ago, have adapted to a less dynamic ecosystem but now face the new challenges of the *drunken forest*, where shifting subsoil twists and topples one-hundred-year-old spruces to create a surreal landscape only Salvador Dali could have imagined.

Some studies even suggest that the ability dogs have to anticipate another kind of danger is based on an altogether different sense than hearing or smelling. Their ability to read human emotions, and to know when their owners are anxious, fearful, or confused, is an adaptive transfer to human mushers of their instinctual preference for a strong and competent pack leader. Dogs demand responsibility and courage from their owners, and it is their ability to respond heartily to effective, bold leadership that marks the final difference between winning teams and also-rans. Musher Mike Baxter puts the driver up as Dog One:

> You have to be mentally prepared, and race day, if you done all your work then you're just going for another sled ride. However it's not really another sled ride, you don't get to see what is going on around you, your whole focus is directly in front of you. If a dog lifts its head then that is a fraction of a second, so you better be there to talk to him, if the dog stops to bite snow on the way then you failed. You failed because your watering program is not up to par. That mistake costs you 2/10 of a second, that's the difference between first and third place. All these things are no different then any other sport. The people at the top will say the same thing:

what's the difference between first and fifth place. It's how close you pay attention to detail.

I remember at one time [our son] Jason had just won the world championship and North American championship and when we got home, someone brought up the fact that it was the dogs that won the race. It is true to a certain degree but you have to remember for example when we were at the world champion there were 35 teams, within ten teams they were two seconds from one another from winning first and second place. So you have to stand back and say all ten of those teams are equal. So what made the difference...and that is the man behind them.

No one who has attended a winter sled race in the north can doubt that the exchange of positive emotions between the human leader and the team contributes to the final result. If they have that confidence, the dogs will trust you till they bleed. And this quality of heart doesn't depend on the conformation of the animal or its physical attributes. A team of hound-based racers has the same competitive spirit as the huskies of older generations.

"A typical run for traditional working dogs is twenty or forty miles," says Dale Andre, a younger Gwich'in dog breeder with about sixty race dogs in his kennel in Aklavik, NT. "But we found that for long distance racing as opposed to pulling loads, you really want a different breed. Not those old-time big guys."

The dogs provide their owners with a regular physical workout in return. A two-year-old, still-growing juvenile will eat about two kilograms of fish a day. This high-protein diet is an important economic factor we will consider in more detail shortly. When they are not being fed buckets of fish and water, hand-delivered to them over rough terrain in distant dog lots, they must be sorted out from tangled traces and chains. This exercise involves lifting the thirty-kilogram animal bodily in midair with one arm, as the tangles are sorted out with the other hand.

"It saves a lot of money on a set of weights," says the champion youth racer Jason Baxter, with a wry smile.

Meanwhile, today in the Yukon hamlet of Old Crow, Kenny Tetlichi, a neighbour of James Itsi, is cooking hundreds of fat dog salmon for his team of twenty animals, which he sometimes rents out to foreign visitors. Asked exactly how many fish he had to put away for his dogs for winter, Kenny grimaces: "More," he says wearily. "Always *more...*"

A biologist with Parks Canada, who has studied the historical fish populations in the Mackenzie Delta, confirms the large numbers of fish needed for traditional Aboriginal dog teams:

The fish populations have never been healthier than today. In the days before the last war when nobody had snowmobiles, you would see dried fish stacked like cordwood running a hundred feet long beside the smoke-houses. A trapper with a team might take ten thousand fish to see them through the winter. Now there are just a few teams in each community, and the dogs are generally a lot smaller, and don't eat as much.

A classic Aboriginal Canadian working breed, the celebrated Mackenzie Delta husky, distinguished by its large chest size, luxurious long coat, and multicoloured head fur, was common in the 1950s in the Gwich'in Settlement Region spanning Yukon and the Northwest Territories. The photo of a splendid team leader resting after his ten-kilometre race at -35°C during the 2012 Muskrat Jamboree in Inuvik, NT, is the closest example to the delta husky I was able to find that was actually put into racing in four years of attending contemporary Aboriginal sled events.

A few White residents owned similar traditional dogs but kept them primarily as pets and guard dogs. Serious racers are obliged to follow the trends set by successful race breeders like Frank Turner of Whitehorse, who selects for quick, event-focused dominators with greyhound, beagle, Labrador, and even water poodle in the ancestral mix.

From his own Old Crow pack, it is obvious that James Itsi prefers the more old-fashioned breed, which he says is a variant regional mix of malamute, husky, Alaskan, and Canadian Eskimo, with some hound. A half-grown, one-year-old pup, tethered to a leash, bounds up to us and is exceedingly difficult to restrain, showing the independence of spirit that marks the breed. Like him, the adult animals of the team all boast the big shoulders, humpy back, and big paws of arrested juvenile wolf development.

The dogs jitterbug anxiously about their rude doghouses like four-legged Elvis's, yet suddenly freeze to watch the coming buckets of fish with intense appraisal rather than pet-like adoration. Are they part-wolf? They sure look like it.

"Every dog has some wolf in him," James shrugs. "It depends on what part you're talking about."

Aboriginal dog breeders know that despite their best efforts, these old ancestral strains will periodically pop up in a litter with atavistic features that are behaviourally neutral, like big paws, and other features like wild shyness that are not so neutral. Problematic.

Dog breeders don't like problem dogs, but they "will work with them," as Gwich'in team racer Dale Andre of Aklavik advises, inviting me to survey his menagerie of gracile canines that bore scant resemblance to James's wolf-derived pack. Even in such a large and constantly cross-bred selected pack as Dale's, the genes for shyness and aggression and stubborn rebellion show up regularly enough to threaten his large financial investment. A winning race dog is easily worth ten thousand dollars, with top dogs fetching over fifty thousand in the unlikely event they would ever be placed on the market.

Today, sled dog racing has become a highly competitive and specialized international sport, and the gold, as First Nations racers told me over and over again, lies in finding the right combination. This strategy has two components: breeding and management. The careful breeding is about individual characteristics that entirely depend on the particular event the racer is aiming at, with the four-hundred-kilometre Hudson Bay Quest race held on March 21 on the ice pack between Churchill, MB, and Arviat, NU, being a far cry from the straightforward, ten-kilometre, six-dog river race at the Muskrat Jamboree in Inuvik, NT. These are different tests, thrilling in their own right and a supreme challenge for the intermeshed teamwork of human driver and big-hearted animals, regardless of the contest's parameters.

And then there is the management involved in assembling and running the right team. The Gwich'in Baxter family of Inuvik dominates the small team category, with son Jason becoming a world champion in 2001 at age twelve in the four-dog team category. His father Mike Baxter summarizes the relationship between careful breeding and effective team management as follows:

> It's no different than horse racers. You're firmly convinced that world champions are due to be born. Nobody breeds a bad horse or a bad dog. There also comes management, an aspect of the sport, which is huge because if your team dogs are all the same age then you are in for a lot of trouble. It means one year you'll need to change everything out. So it's a constant in-and-out sort of thing. If you have a 6-dog team and have a lot of money, you can go to the high-end people and change that dog out.

The cost of running any dog team is high, but the social rewards in terms of public community esteem are high, too. It is a point of pride with northern breeders that the foundation of their team relies in some subtle part on the domestication of the wolf. Mike Baxter acknowledged that in Inuvik there seems to be an ongoing mixture between wolves and dogs.

> There is some truth in the folklore. The reality is breeding to a wolf is no different then breeding to a hound. We found that this is a good thing but only about an eighth of it, and same with the wolf. Because the only thing you're looking for in the wolf is confirmation and stamina. Too much wolf genes will create horrific dogfights, and they're not manageable. The traits of a wolf are never trusting and always on guard. Why we don't breed to them is because he's too big and bulky for the racing we do.

The regional variation of older northern breeds also had its social and competitive component, as Mike explains:

You see a lot of types of dogs, the Mackenzie husky dog, the Depot dogs,
Yellowknife dogs. These are dogs that are synonymous to regions, dogs that
are developed in a region for a specific thing and when these traits show
up. This is one of the things in our yard, we have Mackenzie Delta huskies
and crossed it with hounds. In Alaska there is the Aurora Husky or a
European hound. What you see is that one particular person in a specific
area, wins everything, and then everyone wants to breed to it. One thing
that occurs is you don't stay on top very long, like seven years, you know
because by then everyone else is caught up to you and has your dogs now,
too. There was a guy who came from Europe in a chartered plane and
spanked everyone for five years. Now he's fighting to stay up there because
people pay huge dollars to get the winner breeding done.

That is racing. Elder James Itsi doesn't race his dogs. He uses them to
travel up and down the frozen Porcupine River and up into the vast Crow
Flats perched high above the hamlet. Winter in Old Crow is mountain winter. It begins in late September with the freeze-up of the Porcupine River
and ends in mid-May, although the locals do not consider April, with its
sunny, flyless days and good travelling snow, to be anything less than perfectly grand. It's a time when the bears begin to rouse themselves from
their dens and lumber off in search of food.

As he checks on the team's physical condition, James searches for fresh
predator tracks around his campsite. It seems he is looking for the tracks
of a scout wolf that might return with its pack in full force, after it has
reconnoitered the lay of the camp. "Animals think like we do," he says.
"They investigate, make plans."

It is apparent that two younger dogs have been deliberately unchained
and left free to run around the older animals. The latter are clearly unhappy
about a happy privilege denied them. But there is good reason for this
arrangement, James explains.

"A white guy once stayed alone here at my camp," Itsi recalls, "and he
didn't have a gun or dog for protection. You can see we have bears all over
the river. He told me his big secret: he walked around naked, no clothes

the whole time. The animals left him alone; they attack clothes, not people."

James laughed, flashing white teeth, and dragged another bucket of fish up to the waiting team. The two young pups raced over to him, trying to snatch up all the fish for themselves. I do not understand the reference to clothes in his story. Is he not worried that the wolves will kill the team some night?

"Wolves won't attack dogs on chains—they think it's a trap. But they'll kill a free dog, and eat it all. Leave nothing but the head."

In other words, these two younger dogs are offered up as bait, potential sacrifices to ensure the protection of the more valuable trained dogs. Now I get his allusion: the dog chains are perceived like clothes by these predators. Yet, surprisingly, unchained dogs do have a fighting chance against the most fearsome predator in the northern bush, the great brown bear.

In 2005, Gwich'in entrepreneur and craftsman Allan Benjamin of Old Crow began importing and breeding what was called a bear dog, selling them locally as protection against marauding grizzlies for about $600 each. This feisty little creature includes the spitz, the beagle, and the border collie in its ancestry. These parental lines are deliberately chosen. Spitz-type dogs are original to northern Asia and have thick hair on the pads of their feet that protect them from ice, while the beagle has such a keen sense of smell it is used as a detection dog at border crossings. The border collie is territorial and quick on its feet, so it is well suited to domestic guard duties. There are undoubtedly other breeds in the still-evolving mix, the progeny of which tend to weigh not more than ten kilograms and are eminently companionable.

The little Aboriginal bear dog in its various iterations has now spread to the farthest northern communities. Mary Mikiyungiak, a resident of the Inuit village of Arviat in Nunavut Territory, owns a nimble bear dog and he happily accompanies the family whenever they travel on the land, which in this case includes sea trips far out into Hudson Bay, where it watches for seals and whales with the same dedication as a cocker spaniel might, acting the lookout for grouse and quail.

Mary is inordinately fond of her ochre-yellow bear dog, and she will recount stories of the courage it shows, barking furiously at polar bears and dodging their claws by "running like hell" under the intruder's belly to attack the predator from the rear.

When it is not travelling, Mary's dog is chained by the front door of their seaside house, where it watches the rocky shoreline devoutly for signs of unwelcome visitors. I was visiting one day after her granddaughters had painted a temporary red circle around one of its eyes, which gave it a comic 1930s retro look. Apparently, this breed is far more popular with Aboriginal women; middle-aged men almost universally criticize these small breeds as "useless as tits on a bull," as one Old Crow hunter commented with wry disapproval over a campfire.

Gwich'in trapper Peter Ross, seventy-three, of Aklavik, NT, echoes a common male sentiment, saying that the arrival of the bear dog marks the impoverishment of the noble lineage of true working dogs and is the sad result of the personal vanity of owners concerned with self-image: "They don't *do* anything. They just eat and bark! If you're a busy person with things to do then who's got time for that?"

While it may be that social status accounts for the popularity of the bear dog, the side effects of the growing cash economy on northern communities are also factors in the perceived need for a small dog that is both highly vocal and territorially courageous.

I was able to document many bear dogs loose on the dirt roads of Old Crow, Inuvik, Arviat, and Fort McPherson, and in most cases they were accompanying Aboriginal women who were out shopping at the North Mart or visiting friends, or just going for a "power walk" in their new hiking shoes. Bears are drawn to edible garbage, and there is simply far more of it lying about these days in the smaller communities, especially as people buy convenience foods like hamburgers and fries and carelessly throw out the remains.

I once observed a gargantuan raven in Inuvik deliberately crawl under a wooden porch to retrieve a foil packet of ketchup, which it then methodically slit open with its beak. It ate all the contents in a minute or two without spilling a drop. How it spotted the little silver packet under the snow-covered boards, how it knew the contents were edible, and how it was able to daintily pry open a devious container that obviously frustrates many humans only an ornithologist can answer. The incident shows that Arctic wildlife are readily adapting to this new cash economy as well.

According to the local landfill manager, in the summer of 2011 the town of Inuvik was obliged to remove no less than sixteen grizzly bears from its landfill site, as well as innumerable black bears. Grizzlies are territorial unless a mass food resource such as a salmon run or a washed-up whale overrides their strong instinct for environmental security. Any community with excess food waste takes on the attraction of a salmon run for gathering bears, and the bear dog, which requires only a fraction of the food supply and daily upkeep needed by a sled dog, becomes a newly valuable and cost-efficient social asset in this potentially volatile situation.

Then there is something else at stake about the new social role of the little bear dog that evidently bothers the older Aboriginal hunters. Sled dogs work as a team; bear dogs are solitary beings that protect the nuclear family from all comers, including human visitors. The biggest social change of the post-war cash economy in the north has been the elevation of the aspiring individual over extended kin links and communal responsibility.

It turns out that the old saw about "selling iceboxes to the Eskimos" hides a serious sociological issue: northern Aboriginal people refer to the growing number of privately owned deep freezers in their communities as "stingy-boxes." The private freezer now allows a successful hunter to store all his game, rather than parcel it out to the community at large as needed before the meat spoils.

Such a seemingly minor technological change expands the cost-benefit analysis for every social transaction, and remakes the economic landscape in fundamental, if subtle, ways. It is easy to see the little bear dog as a harbinger of a new social order, where its esteemed qualities of vocal personal responsibility, social deftness, tactical responsiveness, and exclusive loyalty to the immediate family so directly reflect the changing values of the younger Aboriginal generation—and, not least to say, the bubbly, ingratiating charm that distinguishes this new breed from the confident, tractable, and reserved personalities of the traditional sled dogs.

Today, one can effectively map the varieties of northern dog on a scaled grid, starting with the largest, ferocious-looking, blue-eyed sled dogs belonging to the last of the traditional Inuit hunters like Phillip Kigusiutnak of Arviat village, who at eighty still travels by a wooden, handmade sled and is obliged to feed his team several whales a year. Malamute, husky, wolf—winter fur and eyes of blue fire—Phillip's powerful animals are heroic to behold and need an equally heroic musher to run them. Phillip's dog lot is located on the treeless tundra at five kilometres' distance from the village, where winter temperatures often drop to -50°C. The team has taken Phillip to victory four hundred kilometres across the broken sea ice from Arviat to the port of Churchill in Manitoba and back, a windy trip of endurance that takes four days. His advice to those who would enter the annual Hudson Bay Quest competition is simple: "Keep your breath warm."

From that class of animals, we pass on to the still large but increasingly heterogeneous examples like James Itsi's Old Crow dogs, which show German shepherd and collie in their makeup and temperament, along with the more traditional strains. In this category we might include the legendary Mackenzie Delta husky, one of many long-haired types with local variations that a connoisseur is able to distinguish at a glance.

Such connoisseurs abound in the north. Gwich'in dog breeder Diane Baxter and her husband Mike can tell at a glance exactly which of their forty-five dogs has escaped the lot and is now running freely across the scrubby taiga (crossing fresh wolf and lynx tracks while he is still in sight). But that all five or six of their rural neighbours—who each have their own major populations of canines—are able to identify the Baxter dog at three hundred metres' distance is nothing short of a prodigious feat of collective social memory.

This ability seems common to dog owners; it means that local owners are able to identify at least three hundred different dogs glimpsed at a distance, a detailed catalogue memory based on flashes of individual colour and gait. Anthropologists tell us that it was the need for discriminating social intelligence in hunting groups that launched the human brain into all its adaptive cognitive glory, but perhaps the hunting dog also helped multiply that early social intelligence factor in humans.

The unanswered question is how did the domestication of dogs influence the evolution of early human societies? Was there a feedback mechanism at play? We have already mentioned how traditional Gwich'in hunters were obliged to secure a massive supply of dried fish to feed their dogs over the winter. Inuit, and Inuvialuit of the Western Arctic, did the same using sea mammals. A secure daily supply of two kilograms of high-protein fish, with all its omega fats and calcium, would ensure that the sled dogs were up to the task of carrying heavy loads in winter, and that healthy females would carry their pups to term in the spring. Dogs, like humans, respond directly to nutritional supplements. The Baxters, like other breeders, say the adult dog's maximal caloric intake is 1,800 calories a day, which must be doled out in increments, in addition to vitamins and even mineral-enhanced water to make them work-ready.

The creative explosion of Paleolithic material culture associated with the evolution of *Homo sapiens* fifty thousand years ago approximates to the date of the divergence of dogs from the proto-wolf lineage, according to molecular clock studies. Proper dog skulls showing all the morphological features of shortened jaws and smaller brain cases have been found in Central Europe dating to thirty-three thousand years ago.

The same changes occurred in humans as they evolved from their more robust predecessors, perhaps *Homo erectus*. Wolves, unlike dogs, also regurgitate their food to feed pups, and one wonders whether archaic humans like *Homo erectus* did the same. It is also fascinating to consider that this species ancestral to humans died out even though they might have survived as contemporaries of our earliest direct ancestors, and the same is largely true of domestic cattle, horses, and dogs, since their direct, wild, ancestral populations are all extinct. Recent genetic studies suggest another wolf-like creature was ancestral to the domestic dog, not the wolf, even though they can cross-breed.

Did humans domesticate the dog or did the dog domesticate humans?

Research by Pat Shipman of Pennsylvania State University argues that dogs gave modern humans a specialized hunting advantage over contemporary human competitors like the European Neanderthals, as well as other fierce animal predators, and their intense and successful partnership may have accounted for the eventual extinction of such competitors. Other researchers echo these hypotheses, suggesting the key advantage early humans had over their cousins was a more intense level of resource exploitation, based on role specialization where women collected small game and plant resources and men did the heavy lifting with big game and fishing.

The domesticated Paleolithic dog may have been the third and deciding factor, contributing its sensory awareness to the partnership in exchange for both a steady diet of foodstuffs like protein-and-fat-rich fish, game that its own wild ancestors were incapable of securing on their own, and—more to the point—the interesting intellectual and social challenge of living in a relatively complex little society with its constant emotional outpour, its smoking fires, drum music, and action-packed seasonal activities, as well as its delightfully opulent array of novel odours.

The innovative fishing technologies (bone harpoons, ivory hooks) of the mesolithic period circa eleven thousand years ago have been attributed to a sudden change in climate from a dry cold era to a warmer, wetter pattern when productive bogs and marshlands spread across Europe. As I watched James Itsi lug his buckets of purple-mottled dog salmon and silvery coney (a large whitefish species also known as the inconnu, *Stenodus nelma*) up the steep banks of the Porcupine River to feed his hungry team, I wondered whether some of these technical tool advances were generated by the prehistoric dog population's need for high-value nutritional surpluses to be stored over winter.

The long-term behavioural effects of such a surplus protein economy would include enhanced brain function, longer life spans, and concomitantly extended social memory for both men and dogs. Here is proof: a vigorous, sixty-seven-year-old man, lean and limber, is resolutely feeding his dogs, which appear to be just as vigorous, lean, and limber as he is. When they go upriver tomorrow to hunt for moose, it will be their turn to feed him.

4 : The Drunken Forest

The lush boreal forest on the banks of the upper Porcupine River, enriched by generations of spawned-out salmon.

IT IS MID-MARCH and still pure winter in the Mackenzie Delta. At two in the afternoon the unrelenting rays of the glowering sun remain painfully direct, and the limitless horizon they reveal is epically silent except for the mosquito whine of a distant chainsaw.

The hued shadows tumbling out of the forest's edge read like the pencil crayon colour Peacock Blue; we can imagine that this half-metre of finely granulated snow merely reflects the clear sky like the less dry waters of spring. Spring! We are not quite there yet. Another month, perhaps, or six weeks.

On the frozen river itself invisible beings come and go. A light breeze blows powdery snow over the fresh tracks of bodiless moose and lynx and hares, animals that are nowhere to be seen in the dense spruces lining the shores, yet they cannot be far way.

It is qualitatively different from winter in the south. Northern creatures must have evolved pioneering strategies for maneuvering their way through this frantic icy tangle as the continental glaciers diminished. The boreal forest's ink-blot lines of sight, its muffled sounds and kaleidoscopic flashes of broken colour, the grim democracy of its extreme grasp, all these challenge the senses like nowhere else on Earth.

What is the great forest at the margins of its Arctic domain but a heaving mass of doomed legions, a battlefield of scabby spikes clawing out of the mushy ground? It is pretty enough at the extremes of its scale, both in the miniature close-ups of fractal mosses and lichens and at the grand geometries that blue horizons deliver, but ominous and threatening in the midground. Here, surrounding us at close quarters, the northern forest presents us with nature's routine cruelty, a slightly less picturesque subject than the limpid, tea-stained peat bogs to the north or the coolly pristine pine forests two thousand kilometres south.

Up close, the boreal forest does not appear so pristine, either: rather, it looks hard-used. Botanists claim these skinny black delta spruces, emblazoned with ice scars at the shoreline, take a century to reach a diameter of fifteen centimetres and a height of scarcely ten metres. I once took home a sawn-off section of a ten-centimetre spruce trunk to study it under a magnifying glass, and patiently counted out fifty rings, so they cannot be far off in this estimation.

Things here seem to grow ten times slower. Like the Arctic air itself, the wood section was incredibly dry and quickly crumbled to shreds over winter. Still, when they are alive, the black and white spruces are resilient and incorruptibly supple. They dominate this side of the planet; every other living thing must bow to their existence. Fire is their only master.

Local people make long and family-inherited trails through this implacable bush, and keep to them over the decades with a regularity and precision that is astonishing, given the pathways' mysteriously improbable twists and loops. And these are long trails we are talking about, trails that might run four hundred kilometres or more over hill and dale and bog.

One will appreciate that travel here in summer is generally by boat, given the conditions of constant near flooding that Mackenzie Delta residents must contend with after May's ice breakup. I once made the impolitic mistake of calling it "a swamp" aloud, after it struck me one fine May morning that only a fraction of the river's winter meltwaters ever drained to the sea, with the rest of it just sitting around in pools and furrows and channels waiting to freeze up again.

"It's a giant *swamp*!" I said, like Archimedes in his bath (except I had my clothes on).

"Yes," said the Gwich'in lady who overheard my comment. "But it's our *beautiful* swamp."

Winter travel in the depths of the forest interior, whether by dogsled, snowshoes, or skidoo, has the advantage of easy mobility over frozen ground, and the added benefit of minimizing the traveller's exposure to the dangers of wind chill. I do not know if every particular trail is marked on the comprehensive traditional trail map currently being prepared by the Gwich'in Land Use Planning Board in Inuvik. It may well be, but the point is that the twists and turns of these hunters' trails are decidedly fixed and soundly recorded in the collective memory of the users.

According to Sue Mackenzie, the mapping project's planning coordinator, every senior Aboriginal hunter and trapper who participated in it was able to mark with great precision and accuracy the trails he habitually used, based on abstract satellite landform images, although most had never performed this technical exercise before.

What this ongoing project has succeeded in creating, with the input of scores of hunters, is a map of the collective hunting mind in its home territory of roughly fifty thousand square kilometres, excluding the vast water system itself. The project staff has carefully assigned different trail colours for the various tribal affiliations of users (Gwich'in, Inuvialuit, Dene, Metis, etc.), and the resulting, highly ingenious spaghetti-scrawl clearly shows very little overlap, despite the contiguity of major game concentrations and other local resources. Evidently, the trails are designed to maximize access to a plethora of resources while minimizing contact with other human competitors, and, at the same time, they show in their aggregate the intense level of successful, multicommunity resource exploitation carried on over the whole of the Land.

Two of these communities, the Gwich'in and the Inuvialuit, have had a history of small but bloody skirmishes as recounted in their oral traditions, but today there is a great deal of intermarriage in the hamlets they have since settled in, as the twentieth century brought increased government services and the cash economy to the region. Our hosts today are an example of this trend, which in any case may have been the ongoing reality since before Contact, given the common accounts of wife kidnapping.

My companion Liz Gordon is an Inuvialuit who works for the Gwich'in as a lands and resources officer. Today, we are headed to the hunt camp of the Bourkes, a blended Gwich'in and Inuvialuit family. Gwich'in Martin Bourke and his sons are cutting firewood in the forest today, while his Inuvialuit wife April works back in town at her administrative job. The whine of the chainsaw ahead has ceased, and Liz, a friend of April's, immediately says, "Good, we are just in time for tea!"

Liz is correct. As we pull up to the frozen embankment and make our way to the wood-plank cabin, the smoke plumes of a renewed drum stove fire greet us: a comforting sight. Martin invites us inside for a spread of coffee, tea, cookies, and fried meat. The fat of fried food is always welcome when travelling on the land at -30°C, and traditional foods high in fats have always been especially esteemed by both tribal groups, although these foods vary by culture: the regional Inuvialuit naturally show a preference for available sea mammal delicacies like *muktuk* (whale blubber), while the Gwich'in enjoy local country food like moose headcheese, where a moose head is boiled all day in a large pot and the floating bits are then pressed together in a cheesecloth to form a pink meaty porridge. I have tried both items and do not have any preference.

As we enjoy our snack, Martin fetches a fearsome pointy object about the size of a toaster from the high shelf, saying he found it in the woods.

"What do think?" Martin passes it over using both hands. "A buffalo head, right?"

Yes, and more, it looks like a shrunken giant bison head, right down to the lolling eyes and curled hooked horn. The heavy burl of a tree with pointy growths and knots has been shaped by strange forces into the perfect simulacrum of the fierce beast that once roamed these same valleys in the heyday of the glacial refuge called Beringia. Apparently, Martin has painstakingly carved it during long nights at the camp, but turning it over, I realize it's a natural *objet trouvé*, a lucky find.

"Unbelievable. It's perfect."

I glance at Martin and Liz to catch their reactions to this bold display of botanic mimicry. They are a study in contrasts. Martin stares intently at the buffalo head as if he is trying to x-ray its secrets; Liz telegraphs a look I interpret as, *It's way too spooky for me.* And it *is* spooky, for this knotty wooden animal head points to another nature beyond nature, an order of uncontrolled existence outside the picture frame of our notional social categories.

It occurs to me that I, too, have received these astonishing emanations from time to time out of a volatile underworld, and that Aboriginal people may be more aware of these messages than townsfolk because urban life's sturdy civic infrastructure—with its elaborate protocols of language, consumerist distractions, and social competition—works like a brick wall to keep such provocations away from our tender psyches. Of course, Dali and the rest of the *ur*-magicians going back to Hieronymus Bosche summoned such psychic brambles in through the gates of public consciousness, but only after they were screened in the protective mantle of a formal art theory or moral exegesis.

It is one thing to applaud Picasso for having the audacity in 1943 to combine a bicycle seat and a set of handlebars and call his transgressive gallery piece *Bicycle-seat Bull*; it is quite another to spend a good part of one's life in a forest world where everything around you indicates its extreme variableness in animistic possibilities—when a tree branch at dusk suddenly becomes a giant wildcat's forked tongue or a sixteen-footed moose—especially when you are tired or hungry or fretting that you may be lost.

The northern pioneer's term for this febrile and possibly self-destructive mental condition is "gone bushed" or "bush-crazy," and it has its analogues both in Aboriginal culture and in Western theories of aesthetic cognition, but the susceptibility of our minds to borderline environmental suggestion is shown in numerous local accounts of isolate behaviour, like the Old Crow visitor who ends up stripping off all his clothes so the bears won't eat him, as recounted in the previous chapter.

One might even go so far as to say that this general anxiety about falling prey to isolate behaviour may account for a certain male style of stoic detachment common to many northern men. The man who loses two toes to frostbite and leaves the hospital proclaiming it's okay because he "still has eight toes left" claims for himself an attitude of stout disbelief in anything but his own self-assertion, maintaining it in the face of an indecisive and highly creative toothy nature that ultimately refuses to be confined by such semantic niceties.

It is a face the Christian Bible describes as belonging to *another* creation, ruled by the primal force called the beast or leviathan, or, more abstractly, referred to as the wilderness itself in the sense of a place of spiritual abandonment, of great spiritual temptation—a relict abode because the main work of ordered Creation, with its focus on humanity's historical undertaking, goes on elsewhere. In this Judeo-Christian tradition, the wilderness lies forever outside of history.

Similarly, the Biblical beast is the unbounded force that keeps generating novel life forms, threatening humankind's dominion and our need for order expressed in the achievable certainty of the law. It has its analogues in northern First Nations mythic accounts of the rampages of Wolverine (Dene); the battles of the Gwich'in founder-hero Willow Man (K'aiheenjik, meaning "Willow Creek"), who was attacked by his own people because of his dangerous strength and, pursued, eventually jumped to his death; the adventures of another Gwich'in hero Chit ta ho khei (also spelled Ch'ataiiyuukaih or Atachookaii, meaning "Paddled a Different Route"), who had supernatural powers and travelled the land to battle giant animals so they wouldn't predate on humans; the grisly cannibal Wendigo (Cree, Innu); and, as we will see, the techniques of spirit travel by Inuvialuit and Inuit shamans.

The common theme of these Aboriginal traditions is that a dangerous thing *out there* enlarges itself at the expense of the human community and must be constantly overcome. The beast is the archetype of infinite mutability, of unrestrained engorgement. It is still with us. The blob (radioactive post-bomb flesh) and the borg (metastasizing technology) are among its modern-day equivalents. Variations of this terrible thing, including evil shamans, are said to hide or "consume" all the caribou or seals by keeping them in a secret place where only heroes can enter to recover them. The force breaks boundaries, it blocks healthy flows, and brings hunger and destitution to the Land instead of food and plenty: it expresses all the bleak negatives of human reality.

Several Gwich'in Elders in Old Crow told me how the moose mysteriously disappeared from the Mackenzie Valley in the '30s and '40s, an event that occurred some decades before they were born; the account is already well on its way to becoming a tradition. Gwich'in residents in Tsiigehtchic also told of a local shaman who battled a giant beaver, pointing out a large rock on the Arctic Red River where it happened. Beavers, of course, hold back the water with their dams: giants are bad because they take too much of everything.

In the book and film *Into the Wild*, author Jon Krakauer portrays real-life adventurer Christopher McCandless as intent on confronting the abandoned wilderness, alone and barehanded. McCandless does so by rejecting all maps, compasses, and communication with society, stripping down to his bare essentials just like the naked Old Crow visitor in James Itsi's tale, and suffering or welcoming the disintegration of his raw personality, before his physical death by starvation or poisoning (too little or too much). The stirring up of ambivalent commentary of listeners to his fate is a classic function of myth.

The northern bushman's narrative has become a literary genre in North America, meaning that these stories inevitably follow strict if unconscious conventions, such as the protagonist destined to "find himself" in the wilderness. In the aggregate, they might be read less as objective researches into our living relationships with the bush and more as dialectical or critical responses to other works of the same genre, beginning with *Robinson Crusoe.*

An immediate precursor to Krakauer's character is the true-life British Columbia trapper Michael Oros, whose 1970s wilderness diaries were also found in his remote hideout after his death during a RCMP manhunt. Oros's diaries feature long dialogues with his talking dogs and invisible "sneak-arounds," who kept stealing his possessions, that is, pieces of his mind. As with McCandless, Oros's short life in the bush does not bode well for urban escapees intent on discovering who they really are in a confrontation with the unmediated elements. Winter in the Arctic is the richest time for such speculative anxieties; the ultimate question being whether the Land will once again regenerate life, *this time*, or whether its great stream of living forms (caribou, fish, birds, free-flowing water) will stay hidden and inaccessible, trapped by some force. The Gwich'in of the Mackenzie Delta differentiate not four but eight seasons, the usual four plus transitional periods like ice breakup, when birds fly away, good trapping, and freeze-up.

These eight seasons elaborate a relationship with the Land centred on an annual round of subsistence activities. By late March, the fur season is drawing to a close as the animal pelts begin to lose their thick winter luster. But the standing timber has dried out and the snow makes it easy to drag the six-metre logs back to camp for cutting into commercial firewood. Martin Bourke's boys are napping after their tea; they have already cut a few cords today and will sell them for cash back in town.

The current market price (2013) is $400 per cord. They could cut five cords in a day, but the pickup will only carry a cord and a half at one time, during the thirty-kilometre trip back to town on the ice road, and the danger of leaving unsecured wood in piles around camp is that someone may steal them in their absence. There is an energy shortage in town because the natural gas from Inuvik's local well is unexpectedly running out, and, so, the same market forces that have made cutting firewood profitable have also increased the rate of opportunistic pilfering: the family has already lost a full cord stolen from their truck just this week.

Martin places the mesmerizing bison head tree knot back on the shelf, puts on his coat, and leads the way out into the work yard of his family camp. The work yard holds several newish snowmobiles, scattered heaps of cut wood, two coney fish recently caught through the ice, and a large firepit. No dogs. Martin points out the main feature, three elaborate log towers topped by covered viewing platforms for spotting game. "Moose ladders," in the parlance of the north.

"This one's mine, those my two sons built for themselves. We each have our own."

The lookout towers are elaborately constructed; one might even say, overconstructed. About ten metres high, the towers afford the user with a good clear view of the surrounding countryside and allow him to take advantage of the fact that large game animals like moose, having nothing to fear from bald eagles, rarely look up. Besides spotting game, a user might watch for signs of a family member returning from a long trip. In view of the competitive nature of land holding in the region, which is based on custom supported by actual sustained habitation—"use it or lose it"—the third use might explain the fancy design. The towers announce to all passers-by that three men live here. Three vigorous men, who have the physical capacity to heave fifty-kilogram logs into the air.

It is apparent from a fourth and much more prosaic lookout tower at the back of Martin's work yard that these tall projects serve as neighbourhood displays of power. The fourth tower is the classic moose ladder seen in bush camps everywhere in the north: a spruce tree that has been stripped of its branches with eight or ten trimmed crosspieces serving as rungs secured by nails all the way to the top. The climber scrambles up to the crown, hangs tight, swaying with one arm, and with the other he sees what he can see in his binoculars of approaching game, then scrambles quickly down again. A five-minute exercise. Such a bare-bones moose ladder, casually constructed, calls no attention to itself; it looks like just another dead tree to the casual observer, which is why I only noticed it last of the four.

I found its identical match in the Bluefish Camp of Yukon trapper Stephen Frost. At that time, Stephen pointed out a further use, a critical use in the dry heat of a nightless Arctic summer—as a fire lookout.

> *You smell smoke—or you don't. Either way you go up the moose ladder and see what's blowing, ten, twenty miles way. Enough time to get your stuff into your boats if you think it's coming your way fast. A few years ago a big blaze almost took my camp out, real fast too, but the good boys with Fire Service flew in with their loads of river water and dumped them all around, saved my cabin and my trees and garden. Now there's lots of berries growing back there, too! Help yourself!*

The game-spotting tower might be one of the oldest infrastructure projects in human culture; they could have been employed anywhere herd animals like caribou and horses and possibly aurochs (wild cattle) were hunted collectively in cover, because such animals could be efficiently harvested only if the hunters had a good idea of the speed and direction of their migration in sufficient time to prepare collectively for their arrival. As the Magdalenian peoples of 17,000 B P specialized in hunting reindeer and red deer through to a time when the glaciers were retreating from Europe, and the forests were growing back, such a device would have proved especially useful.

In any event, the concept of raised platforms was already well established at this early date because the roof art in the Altamira caves in northern Spain was produced using three-metre scaffolding. Moreover, it appears that some massed herd animals in the cave art of the Upper Paleolithic—while admittedly produced by different artists over a very long time span, as carbon-dating tests of individual animal drawings show—conform in their aggregate to the perspective one would have from *looking down* at an adjacent killing field from a height of ten metres or so.

This collective, millennia-long vision might well have corresponded to a real seasonal event, repeated over hundreds of generations (34,000 BP to 11,000 BP) in which the artist-hunters painted what they had witnessed down in the killing field. Why would Upper Paleolithic hunters try to bring the wild herds into close proximity of their spotting towers? One can think of several practical reasons for this, based on the ancillary ways spotting towers are used by contemporary Arctic hunters.

Firstly, a number of powerful carnivores such as grizzlies, and even the odd wandering polar bear, still visit the boreal hunt camps, as well as wolves, black bears, wolverines, and, recently, mountain lions. Trapper Stephen Frost, for one, is never more than five fast paces from his loaded Winchester carbine, and he leaves extra shells in little piles on logs all about his garden and woodpile. Climbing the lookout tower to get out of harm's way is a prudent tactic, especially when the fresh blood from fur-bearing animals or the carcass of a game animal inevitably attracts unwelcome and unpredictable attention.

As the Upper Paleolithic cave paintings illustrate, the list of large predators that could have been attracted to a mass kill of reindeer in that era includes cave hyenas, cave bears, cave lions, leopards, and giant wolves. A large lookout tower or group of towers would have offered immediate and effective refuge for the entire hunting-and-butchering party (men, women, and older children) and also provide spearmen with an excellent vantage point from which to wreak havoc down on the growling invaders with little risk to themselves. The game tower could also be used, if it were properly adjacent to the kill site, as a safe refuge for the butchered meat itself, because few of these large predators would be able to climb such a structure to steal the cache, particularly when the hunting party was busy transporting the first choice loads of meat by sledge or shoulder pole back to their huts. Or, perhaps, most of the meat was left there in any event, exposed on high for drying or smoking, since it was already made secure enough from scavengers. Such multi-use structures would have obviated the need for wholesale transport and increased efficient harvesting by local groups accordingly.

Contemporary hunters in Old Crow like Elder Esau Schafer favour elevated hunting for moose from a constructed tree blind, as he told me. The technique that worked best in the autumn—when the moose were optimally fat before they went into rut (which spoils the meat)—was to call the bulls directly to him by using the animal's dried shoulder blades to imitate the sound of rivals' antlers rattling against each other, or by tapping the bones against tree bark. The clattering mimics a bull moose announcing his sexual intentions to a cow.

"What you get is the moose rushing in from some direction, mad as hell and looking for a fight," Esau remarked. "You don't want to be surprised on the ground by a twelve-hundred-pound animal with bloodshot eyes and six feet of antlers. Ten, fifteen feet off the ground means you see him coming, long before he thinks to look up."

In the treeless Arctic, the enterprising and creative Inuit and Inuvialuit traditionally tossed their game spotter up in the air with a hide blanket. His job was to hover up there as long as he could like a cartoon character to spot the coming herd. Gaining even a metre of height in this manner confers a productive advantage.

In Arviat, a hamlet in Nunavut Territory in the Eastern Arctic, I once watched as caribou hunters appropriated the little plywood cabins belonging to other hunters (who were not present that day) as lookout towers. These structures, perhaps 2.5 metres high, typically come equipped with a built-in ladder leading to the roof designed expressly for this purpose. I realized then that many cabins I had photographed in my travels through the north were provided with similar homemade ladders, and that game spotting was their principal function.

My Inuit companions that day spent a longish time (half an hour) on the roof of the hut, lying flat or squatting, and remaining quite still so as not to be seen themselves against the horizon by the migrating caribou. They spotted the moving herd immediately on that occasion, whispering that the main body was about fifteen kilometres away, and estimating it would reach the coast near where we were camped by noon the next day.

What they were doing up there the rest of the time was actively plotting the herd's likeliest course, watching to note what the clumps of animals in the lead were doing and even factoring the presence of waiting polar bears into their trigonometry. When I took the binoculars from the Inuit hunters, what I saw was essentially fine-grained wisps of smoke: the caribou. Two or three barely perceptible white dots were the polar bears, hunkered down across the tundra in ambush, waiting for their supper.

I say "two or three" bears because the third white dot was entirely speculative. I looked exactly at the point my Inuit companions directed me to look ("Left of the gray boulder, at seven o'clock," etc.), but at that fine scale of resolution all tangible detail faded away to be replaced by washes of indiscriminate gray.

To claim I actually saw the thing itself, and not just the place where it was alleged to be, was to grant my eyes a certain creative licence I was unwilling to do, for it meant, ultimately, that I was acknowledging the existence of a whole other dimension of reality we might call the *oblique inordinate*. It's there, all right, but very obliquely so, and its evident prominence does not derive from vision exactly but from a kind of contextual layering that works, as far as I can tell, in the negative rather than the positive.

The third polar bear was indeed there. I can vouch for that, because after a few minutes, it began moving toward us and at some point, around twelve kilometres away, it emerged from its dubious existence to full-blown reality (for me) as the tiniest of three white, floating dots.

It was a struggle, a koan for inexperienced eyes, to make this beast appear. I must have missed that day's lecture in Western Painting 101, for I do not recall anything like this concept of the oblique inordinate in European cultural history. Art since the Greeks is pretty much about boundaries. It did not concern itself with the place where the eye stops functioning on its own power until we get to Turner and the abstract guessworks of early modernity. Things either are, or they suggest other things—and they exist edged in bounded space, which gets its own special treatment in Western definitions of reality.

On the other hand, space that becomes things conversely implies *things that become space*; and, in fact, much Aboriginal mythology occupies itself with a discourse on the relations of this mute interchangeability, a devolving realm that is so dependent on the observer's state of mind for its existence that it calls into question whether the invention of quantum physics is really all that recent. For me, that third polar bear existed as a condition of probability even after I saw it (the white dot) moving. I had not seen *it* yet: this-thing-that-I-know-is-a-polar-bear. As for my companions, they undoubtedly read into (or read from) that same phantasmal scene many other more and necessary concrete things—the carnivore's gender, its size, its location, and its intentions.

These realizable postulations are useful things, hard currencies needed by hunters. But what was the bear itself to them? Was it the sum of their practical knowledge of it? Did it exist apart from this gained knowledge? Was it a simulacrum of their previous experience of bears, or did they impute its unique autonomy from its unpredictable behaviour and acknowledge that it became more real in its unconformity to their expectations? (This seems typically the case—like other hunters, Aboriginal hunters often love to say how the animal they bagged was different or unusual in some way.)

In other words, did the polar bear paradoxically exist because it did not exist in their historical-record-keeping minds or evaded them? I have little doubt that such philosophical questions were fair topics for an interesting discussion with my Inuit friends that day, but, as it happened, a solitary lead caribou had made its way unseen to within a few hundred metres of the rear of our cabin, where it was unconcernedly grazing on moss as the hunters focused on the main herd far in the opposite direction. It was interesting to watch the hunters as they quietly slid down the ladder and proceeded to use the cabin as a blind or screen, warily poking their heads around the corner of the wall like First World War trench solders so as not to alarm the caribou, and then felling it with one clean shot to the heart.

Similarly, our hypothetical Paleolithic hunting tower, clothed in bark walls, might have served the function of a shooting blind as well. Of course, we are doing here what my Inuit companions did that day, squeezing every last drop of perceptual value from the hazards of accessible language and simple analogy in an attempt to comprehend a deeper picture of social evolution.

The contemporary northern game tower, and versions of it, delivers a field of inquiry of over three hundred square kilometres on a good day. That is a lot of ground to comb through at the extreme limits of human eyesight.

Meanwhile, walking through the boreal forest, gun in hand, is an entirely different proposition. Here the experience is primarily acoustic: your field of vision is obscured by the writhing masses of black willow and other vegetation that provide cover to animals who use it adeptly. The delta trees are more twisted and irregular than most, since the melting permafrost is constantly shifting and throwing them off-centre: it is not you, it is the forest that is drunk. You can make things out through this twiggy brawl at a hundred paces, at most, but you can hear crackling fodder that tells you it's either a bear, moose, or squirrel by the texture, pitch, and rhythm of the crackling.

Again, it's a position, a contextual rendering like our infinitesimal polar bear. The creature noise could just as easily fade off into the forest as it might suddenly appear, leaving its tracks as a sign of its near trajectory. Animal tracks can be read for rich detail.

But are its signs the animal itself? Or is this specific, corporeal animal, too, merely a sign of something else—meaning that there are different orders of animal existence, and that a game animal might belong to all of them simultaneously? And that none of these orders of existence—tiny white dot or red bloody carcass or the invisible loud crashing through the woods—are more real, or more dominant, than the others. They are all aspects of an invisible thing beyond our final possession. I think this may be what Aboriginal people mean when they refer to such animals as

Caribou and Wolf in the royal singular, these timeless beings that generate all their occurrences but remain unchanged themselves.

This tendency of wild creatures to pop into view from the undifferentiated ground, and fade away again into the background hum of the forest, bolsters the conviction held by many Aboriginal peoples that all animals emanate from another dimension, and that their being does not reside in any particular individual but within the metasystem or tribe.

So it is Caribou, not caribou; it is a distinction to be honoured, even as my friends are perfectly aware that if they were to fly about in an $800-per-hour helicopter, they would see the wild herds below actually existing in space and in time—but from a perspective no different from that of their game towers. The two technologies simply offer alternative strategies of harvesting what is freely given by the great animal being itself. The difference between hunters and shamans seems to be this: hunters wait at the portal from whence the game emerges, whereas shamans enter the portal freely to make their acquaintance with the animal being directly, as we shall see.

What was given? And what was found? I was going to write about the young woodcutters who have been working undocumented this whole time in the forest clearing across the frozen river. Instead, I remain transfixed by the mysterious artifact of the natural bison head, a curiosity that has found me.

The world's hunters and gatherers took what they saw, and perhaps what the forest gave them—beside the raw materials for snowshoes and canoes and atlatls and fish netting and berry baskets and snares and moose ladders was the image of their desire—three-dimensional *suggestions* of things that could be constructed simply from careful admiration of a tutoring environment.

If the forest can produce the replica of an extinct herbivore in fine detail, why would it not be able to offer technical suggestions, too, such as snares and scale models of snowshoes, or even ways home?

What is the hunter's inspiration but an ability to read the forest for its lavish possibilities? And the ability to resist the panic that arises when the unknown suddenly arrives unbidden around the next bend?

5 : Near and Far

Martin Bourke standing by one of his family's three moose lookouts, among the world's oldest forms of architecture, likely invented in the Paleolithic era.

IN THE LAST CHAPTER, we saw how the boreal forest in winter can provoke an ongoing speculative dialogue with its residents over found natural artifacts such as the wooden bison head. I admit that had I stayed the night in that cabin, I would have had to come to terms with the horned visage gleaming in the firelight on an emotional level, rather than merely intellectually. One of the ways First Nations residents of the Mackenzie Delta resolve this anxious late winter retrospection is through furious outdoor action, occasioned by the longer days of March, when they hold their annual public jamborees as vernal equinox festivals.

Such celebrations are probably old practices, as some of the more modern activities like fiddling contests and snowmobile derbies share the bill with fire-making contests, wood-chopping marathons, and human and sled dog races over the ice river. They act as general warm-up exercises for the coming busy season and a chance to see how everyone has made out over the winter. It is noteworthy that the annual jamborees in Inuvik, Tsiigehtchic, Aklavik, and Fort McPherson typically make good use of the famous Fort McPherson white canvas tents, still made in that community and exported all over the world. The tents recall the time within the living memory of the community's oldest residents when their families were seasonally nomadic and travelled between their winter camps and summer camps, as well as making long side trips to their traditional berry grounds, traplines, and fishing areas.

Many residents of a certain age can recall the sweet smell of freshly cut spruce branches used to line the floors of their families' bush tents, and the bubbling tin pots of black tea—these and other features of the old days are recreated in the winter jamborees and remind one and all that the past truly lives on.

Yet this past is also discontinuous, as everyone readily acknowledges, with older children away in southern schools and electronic toys everywhere. How, then, does the fact of discontinuity play out in such small communities that retain a strong sense of identity in their relative isolation and yet must cope with influences and changes that are ultimately global, including global warming itself?

One aspect of hunting and subsistence gathering that is easy to forget, given the strong association of First Nations peoples with fur trapping in this county, is that in the scheme of things, fur trapping and the skills that go with it are comparatively recent innovations.

The Gwich'in, like other Indigenous people in the north, originally used braided hide or sinew snares for animals ranging in size from hares to caribou, with the focus on food production. Deadfalls and elaborate game fences that could run for thousands of metres were also deployed; ducks and geese were called into bow range using grass decoys. Black bears that had just denned up at the beginning of winter were located by a select group of male hunters and speared by the hunt leader in a ritual, if risky, event. All of these activities were communal and local: the whole camp moved to the scene of the activity. Cleaning a few score ducks and geese before they spoil requires sustained group effort.

The introduction of fur trapping as a commercial trade practice in the eighteenth century changed all that. Fur trapping necessitated a working partnership of two men who could count on each other over the long dark months away from their home camps, as they ran a business that required constant checking of their sets over a course of a hundred or more kilometres. If they survived this social change, the more traditional winter activities had to be relegated to other seasons. The origin, or at least the renewed importance, of the late winter jamboree must lie in its celebratory timing at the end of the trapping season, when the glossy winter furs have been consigned to the trading posts and the hard business wrapped up for another year.

The skill and speed with which the First Nations trappers adapted to the introduced European technology, and the dedication with which they carried it out, underlies the field research of Harold Innis in his 1930 history, which considered the economic and cultural impact of the trade on the nation as fundamental to its development as a modern state. Similarly in the twentieth century, First Nations people made very quick adaptations to the local possibilities of river boats constructed from plywood sheets, and developed a standard dinghy called a *triishoh* (a Gwich'in word used in Old Crow), suitable for carrying cargo, with a low draught and a blunt bow that could be used as a step when negotiating the muddy banks of the delta.

The contemporary riverboat commonly lodged on the banks of the Mackenzie River during ice breakup is seven metres long, which is average. According to Elder Johnny P. Charlie, who makes them in Fort McPherson, this type of boat can be completed from scratch by a single expert craftsperson in three or four days. I watched Elder John Andre of Fort McPherson make one about eight metres long and he took his time with it, looking at the job from different angles and planing the burrs just so. Typical paint colours include gray, blue, and green and "whatever is left over from the porch job," as Johnny says. The boats are designed to work with "kickers" (outboard motors) ranging in power from 9.8 HP up to about 50 HP, although they can easily be poled or rowed if necessary.

Hunters who do not have the skill or time to build one will pay $4,000 for a custom *triishoh*, comparable to a store-bought vehicle that will, however, lack the custom features of the commissioned watercraft.

Another example of adept Aboriginal appropriation of European technology is the ice-fishing rig from Aklavik, a small community on the Peel River with a mix of Gwich'in and Inuvialuit residents. This homemade, short fishing pole of stripped poplar features a stout cord three metres long ending in a handmade wire leader, and a planed and polished bright steel lure six centimetres long, armed with a machined barbless hook, and topped by a square of bright red wool to mimic blood. The fisherman uses a jigging motion, causing the lure to wobble and sink like a wounded minnow. The stark brightness is designed to attract coney in the murky low-light waters under the ice.

Aklavik's fishermen, like others in the delta, have perfected the logistics of gill netting fish through two small augured holes in the ice, which must be exactly so many feet apart relative to the size of the net. One local fisherman was able to describe the complex multiple-step process of a team dragging the net through the holes with the frightening precision of a Japanese television manual, and I can only conclude that the jigging seems to be a lot more fun, even if it is less productive.

A more problematic cultural innovation is the moose-hide boat, a cargo vessel with the capacity to take several families and the season's fur catch down the spring torrents to the trading post. A recent recreation of the moose-hide boat (2013) by Sahtu Dene residents of Tulita, under the inspiration of Maurice Mendo, was about ten metres long, with a high prow and propelled by three-metre oars: it held eight people on its maiden voyage on the Keele River. Maurice recounted to local reporters that his grandfather used such a boat to transport furs in the spring from the family's winter camp in the mountains, and this was the first such moose-hide boat to be constructed in twenty-five years, requiring the daily labour of a dozen or so community members.

Again, the difference in their social context seems plain: the *triishoh* can be knocked out in four days by one person; the earlier moose-hide vessel requires concerted effort by a team of dedicated specialists who can split the sinews, soften the hides in water, and patiently shape the frames and keel over many weeks. The artifact—or an artifact of this process— is the renewed complex of social obligations met and extended, and the exercise and transfer of expert skills useful in so many other applications besides boat building.

The moose-hide boat might only be as ancient as the fur trading business, developed maybe three centuries ago in response to the need to transport bales of furs to a fort in the spring. But the social artifact it embodies is extremely ancient. This ultimately is a mnemonic vessel that transports the traditional skill-knowledge of a people from generation to generation. When we spoke in the previous chapter of the possible "over-elaboration" of Martin Bourke's log game towers, we did not mention the possibility that they served as essential teaching exercises; the likelihood is that the Bourke sons' own towers constituted their "final graduation projects."

Similarly, the complex of stones and logs used for game drives by the Gwich'in when Alexander Mackenzie visited the delta in 1789 performed a real subsistence function, and yet it seems they aimed at an aesthetic social target, as well as a food source. The point is that the First Nations' learning institution is arguably one and the same as the group-produced artifact, and this artifact is "open" in the sense that the learning process is open.

These examples, and others I could cite, suggest the innate capacity of hunting and gathering people to make opportunistic choices from highly variable living conditions. A study by anthropologists working with Inuit and Cree hunters in northern Quebec over the period of 1973 to 1980 documented the wide variety of game (thirty-eight different game species for the Inuit) taken over the course of a year. The statistics, on the one hand, showed distinct food preferences (caribou, ringed seal), and, on the other, included "last-resort species" like owls, porcupines, and a bony little scavenger fish called a sculpin, which was openly despised by the Cree hunters of James Bay for its unpalatable ugliness when I travelled there during that same time period.

The interesting point made by the Aboriginal contributors to that study was that they made a formal distinction in their harvesting activities between "near" and "far," with "near" defined as within range of one day's travel, typically forty kilometres. The extra planning and provisioning that must go into an overnight enterprise defines it as "far"—making it an open question whether the same conceptual rule applies generally to other activities such as boat building or campsite selection.

The question of "near and far" takes on special significance if we consider further how the convergence of teaching and practice affects Aboriginal strategies when it comes to extremely novel challenges like global warming.

Now, as I have mentioned, the melting of the Arctic permafrost is accompanied by *slumping* (the sudden collapse of previously frozen hillocks and shorelines) and by *ice eyes*, the appearance of multiple round holes in a frozen lake surface, caused by gases and warm water bubbling up from the lakebed. These untoward incidents have the cumulative effect of turning the familiar into the unfamiliar, the near into the far.

On one hand, we find traditional skill sets that confidently respond to the "near" (i.e., the familiar) with practical solutions so determinedly refined that they constitute an aesthetic of means, as anyone who has ever examined a pair of handmade Aboriginal snowshoes will confirm. This aesthetic sense is rooted in pure utility, as Old Crow artist Lawrence Dean Charlie says, speaking about the origins of his own artwork: "Our art all comes from making practical things we need to survive in the bush; it's how we make our snowshoes, toboggans from moose hide, birch bark canoes."

On the other hand, there is a taciturn, otherworldly, almost monastic attitude shown by people who spend a great deal of time in the quiet but always rustling land, patiently observing the unending variability of its natural phenomena and anticipating its multiple hazards.

This contingent learning never ceases; there are different ranks of problems and mysteries to be solved, beyond the ever-present risks of freezing, drowning, bear attacks, starvation, and the rest. There are social dangers and psychic dangers, invisible inner battles to be waged and won as well. The far can be quite close at hand, is quite close at hand.

I once watched local Old Crow hunter, Elder James Itsi, spend half an hour at his camp studying a flock of pine siskins that appeared to be feeding on the buds of a unique willow tree. Mysteriously, the dozen tiny birds were all hanging upside down, and yet the twigs appeared intact and unmarked on close inspection afterwards. The vivacious birds eventually flew off without revealing their culinary secret. I was unable to offer an explanation of the phenomenon from my Western perspective, and the secret of the little birds that ate nothing in a thousand nips was added to the general stock of mysteries that applied human intelligence has yet to solve.

James Itsi spent a lot of time doing just that, discovering mysteries that lay barely a metre away and that would likely remain mysteries, and this exercise, too, is an attitude of aesthetic appreciation—but one that is best expressed through the ambiguities of painting and storytelling.

Like a dog team, a gun collection, or a meat cache, it appears that every Gwich'in family also has its own store of traditional stories, which constitute a general cache of social knowledge. One series of tales concerns the great Gwich'in mythic hero Willow Man, or K'aiheenjik, a giant who eventually commits suicide by jumping off a cliff because his overwhelming personal power threatens the lifeblood of his own community. K'aiheenjik's self-sacrifice is used to explain the mystery of the red rocks by the sacred Bear Cave Mountain, where this event is said to have happened.

Lawrence Charlie talked about the impact of these old stories on his visual art:

I use black ink with a little red ink for circles in the eyes. There's a man named Willow Man, usually he was a giant, he killed his own people, so he didn't want to do that, so he committed suicide by jumping over the

cliff in Bear Cave Mountain. They believed that red ochre was his blood,
they began painting their tools and weapons with red ochre. I use red now
because that's what they used in the old days, red ochre.

The artist has decorated the plywood walls of his Old Crow cabin with
images of a powerful Gwich'in shaman hunter surrounded by six flapping Crows, possibly using the suggestive curves of the wood grain to
emphasize the subjugation of life to powers that bend and shape our reality. And he says he prefers to use pure black ink for its primal starkness.
The strong contrasts between light and dark are a major feature of his
Gwich'in art, and, as we will see, this style may have been favoured as a
direct response to certain aspects of the local environment, as is so much
of the material culture.

Lawrence recounts how his late grandfather, Charlie Peter Charlie
(1920–2008), a Gwich'in hunter originally from the Tukudh band, was
renowned for running down whole herds of caribou on foot, in snowshoes. Charlie P. firmly advanced the view that there was a historic
migration to the area by their Gwich'in ancestors, who were obliged to
fight other tribes to the south, as well as assorted giant animals, before
they gained control of their present territory.

In 2009, Lawrence discovered his grandfather had left him a sheaf of a
half-dozen mythic accounts, handwritten and typed, much of it on lined
yellow notepaper and translated into serviceable English, set down some
years before his death in 2008. One of these tales, simply entitled "Chit
ta ho khei," in a variant spelling of his name, concerns the primal twin-
hero Atachookaii's hunting adventures. The "Chit ta ho khei" version is six
pages long and begins straight away without any introduction:

This man he fix all the bad animal that animal eating human. The first
thing he started make bow and arrow. He ask for where he could get
spruce gum and person tell him where he could get spruce gum where
spruce gum were always boiling when he got there he push down with his

hand and stop so he take some and then he ask where he could get feather.
Man tell him on top of bluff where eagle nest that eagle also eat man.

The core idea embodied by the tale cycle of Atachookaii is that the unrestrained individual can be more than equal to the whole of his fragile society, so he must limit his aggressive instincts or end destroying the weaker entity of the two. He must accept the obligations of his social role, obligations symbolized by his acceptance of a loaded or costly gift. Gifts create bonds, but usually there is spilled blood involved in the transaction. The Gwich'in hero therefore both opposes and incorporates our darkest tendencies toward antisocial behaviour, which, in these story cycles, are represented by the actions of Wolverine.

The highly useful spruce gum is invariably linked with stories about Wolverine, and a wolverine is, in actuality, a particularly tenacious and solitary predator, one that some hunters say will always brings you bad luck, even if you merely see its tracks.

"It means he is coming straight to your camp to break into it," says James Itsi, flatly.

It is Wolverine's abject solitariness, coupled with its voracious appetite, that brings it to the attention of numerous myths. It deliberately provokes its troubled relations with human society; even the feared grizzly bear is sometimes sociable, and can be seen in family groups fishing for salmon or feasting on a downed moose. Lawrence Charlie notes that spruce gum is medicinal, traditionally used as an antiseptic for cuts, so it offers a cure for the bloody wounds the great hero suffers in discovering its secrets from Wolverine.

This is Lawrence's version of the Atachookaii myth, told from his memory:

Atachookaii traveled up and down the rivers and killed giant animals that were killing people. Lots of people were killed. He killed Wolverine and chased his two young ones and chased them up this tree. He was trying to get them down so he could kill them. They made a deal with him that they

*would share medicine with him in exchange for their life. So he agreed
and they came down and shared with him the spruce gum, pitch...you can
eat it, it's good for your stomach and you can also put it on your cut so it
will suck out the poison from you. You put some on your injury and light a
match on it to melt it down.*

After experiencing the onset of a bad cold, I tried chewing the spruce
gum taken from a tree by James Itsi. I found that it, too, was tenacious.
Sticky, fresh, and menthol clean-tasting at the same time. (I also did not
get the cold that was threatening to become full-blown, either, for the
record.) Spruce gum's cheery stickiness makes it the perfect antidote to
Wolverine's mustelid rankness and rapacious instincts.

Wolverine and spruce gum are categorical opposites: animal/vegetable,
rank/sweet, destructive/healing, solitary-lonely/sticky-collective. The moral
issue negotiated in these hunting tales comes down to man or society, and
the trick for such hunters lies in learning where to stop on the steep trail
to personal enhancement.

Typically, whenever rapid social change adds its novel demands to the
old pot of long-cooking role of manhood, a pressing demand arises: How is
one to find a proper life between obediently following ancestral traditions,
or, trusting to the plain evidence of one's heightened senses against the
seductively lovely grain of the revered past, striking out alone on the rough
and lonely path of selfhood? In other words, the ghost of the father can
haunt the contemporary Gwich'in hunter with especial force and vividness.

There are many elusive mysteries to be encountered in the bush, and
the question is: How much mystery can a human being take before his or
her inner balance is overcome by the dark weight of the unknown?

Hunters' stories belong to the hunter, or his family, inevitably shaping
them in the repeated telling of them and using them in the same manner
as one might use a treasured gun or an axe that has been handed down
as a legacy, as something to treat with respect but also as something that
must confer a living, practical use if it is to help its owners survive in the
new world.

This does not mean there is no controversy or difference of opinion about such matters: Gwich'in hunters can be competitive, independent, proud, private, and disputatious. Bloody revenge and sacrificial generosity remain the twin hallmarks of their oral story cycles, tales that have grown into public counternarratives about human origins and nature. Hunters routinely give half their bagged game to Elders, friends, and kin, in the full knowledge that such public gifts translate into an aura-enhancing status for the benefactor. At the same time, others, less generous townsfolk, while roundly criticized for their stinginess, are paradoxically if grudgingly admired for their adept and steady accumulation of domestic assets, as Lawrence and other informants took pains to point out.

It must be stressed that in this last respect, it seems Gwich'in hunters exhibit profound differences in their cognitive ability from that of White visitors from the south, probably for the reason that for the past four hundred years since Descartes, Europeans have been taught to deny the senses in favour of cartographic reason. Urban sense life is stunted because it has been rigorously devalued in schools and churches. One cannot help but feel that the studied brusqueness of the Gwich'in, in contrast, say, to the typically jovial fellowship of Inuit hunters, stems in part from the uncomfortable arousal of their natural pity at the unnatural ineptitude of White tourists, who have been so protected from everything sharp and bloody by a thick wall of manufactured notions they can barely see straight—or shoot straight, for that matter.

One example will serve to illustrate this sensory gap. Like many who travel in northern Canada, I have heard about the fabled marksmanship of Aboriginal hunters for decades, how they will regularly drop a giant bull moose weighing half a ton with only a small-calibre rifle wrapped in worn-out duct tape, like a .223, whereas Whites must use a "regular" big game gun like a massive .300 Weatherby Magnum, or even a .375 Winchester, with a shell the size of a brass cigarillo, almost 91 mm long (four inches).

However, a few days spent hunting with Gwich'in Elders leads inevitably to the discovery that the truth lies in a complete reversal of this old cliché. It is not that these bush-savvy hunters shoot so well; it is that excitable Whites shoot so poorly. And, to paraphrase Shakespeare, the fault lies not in our fancy, silver-inlaid guns but in ourselves.

An experienced Yukon outfitter confirmed that his wealthy clients routinely miss their shots with shaky disbelief, shots that depend absolutely on the properly composed mental attitude of the hunter—and not much at all on the heady but ultimately inconsequential comparative statistics of bullet trajectory, muzzle velocity, ballistic coefficients, grain weight, and other engineering arcana so beloved by industrial folklore.

The Aboriginal guide will finish off the wounded moose or bear with a single, fatal, and small bullet immediately after the bedeviled tourist bungles it, unless the guest has expressly directed otherwise in his original hunt contract. Naturally, this outfitter does not want his name revealed as the source of this unhappy trade secret, especially when his clients pay as much as $45,000 for the tag to shoot a grizzly bear, plus expenses.

"Good shooting, you got him alright!" the guides might nod to the buck-fevered client, hiding their disturbed reaction under a mask of stoic resolution as they begin to field dress the game. Sometimes the greatest acting consists of a studied silence, and the Gwich'in have developed studied silence to a fine degree.

Disembarking one evening from a fishing scow, I lost my boot in the tight grip of fresh mud at the shoreline along the Porcupine, and I danced around on one foot, haplessly trying to retrieve it from the unyielding muck in a scene that would have struck the Inuit of Hudson Bay as hilariously Chaplinesque. A few Gwich'in men who witnessed the incident suspended all public reaction, although they might have mimicked my one-footed mud dance later that night in the privacy of their cabins.

Divisiveness, doubling, duplicity, and darkness also figure in the Gwich'in cosmos, as much as practical truth and plain talk. The Gwich'in divide themselves into two exogamous clans, Crow and Wolf: Crow must marry Wolf. Lawrence Dean Charlie draws these founding animal figures in his art, using parallel sets of holes, perhaps to signify, for want of a better word, their otherworldly effervescence and utter self-possession. Being wary of humans and highly adroit at camouflage and concealment, few local creatures of the boreal forest allow themselves to be seen by humans for more than a second or two. Even mergansers and other small ducks fly off at three hundred metres from a boat's approach.

Yukon animals are highly indistinct when they are alive: they move like smoke through the ragged and tangled spruce forest, appearing and disappearing at will around the moss-cloaked tree trunks, just as the Porcupine River's grayling trout will spontaneously splash out of fast water and disappear again before the sound reaches your ears. The only proof of its existence is a faint track or a ripple, quickly lost in the immensity of other enigmatic signs and other arbitrary phenomena.

These random apparitions play out against a vast backdrop of monumental stillness. The expansive Mackenzie River in the Northwest Territories only appears to move during spring breakup, and mysteriously even then what moves is not the water itself but the car-sized chunks of ice floating on it.

The Porcupine is a middling-sized silver river that sweeps along as smoothly as a mirror without changing its nature, lazily coursing past a series of lofty, rounded, Yukon mountains—two of which are generally acknowledged to look like giant breasts, even if they are not indeed actual breasts for some invisible cosmic lover to enjoy nightly. The river divides a pair of black jagged lines of unending spruce and willow forest that is redoubled in the perfect water, so that there are always two forests to be traversed, the spiky one of the upper air and its wavering watery twin below. This dark boreal landscape so perfectly echoes the spiky symmetry of the art motifs of local residents that it cannot be mere coincidence. The Land is a concrete embodiment of various dimensions of social truth.

"When we see those two big tits up there, we always know when we are coming home," James Itsi said without a trace of irony as we travelled back to town one evening from a long trip upriver. Earlier, when we were headed upriver, James had commented on the aesthetic differences between Yukon and the Northwest Territories, visible off in the distance (the territorial border lies eighty kilometres east of Old Crow), using another geological-human metaphor:

Those Richardson Mountains are always sunny, with blue skies. The Yukon is always dark and gloomy, cloudy, rainy from Alaska. I always like to be headed into the sunny NWT. It welcomes you with bright arms.

The influence of the boreal landscape on the psyche of its inhabitants is deep and abiding. Lawrence Dean Charlie credits his unique graphic designs to a sudden inspiration that "just pops" into his head, a form of communication from the elemental forces governing nature and perhaps mediated to some degree by inner voices of counsel belonging to his forebears:

Every since I was six-years-old I spent most of my early life in the bush with my grandfather, Charlie Peter Charlie, trapping, fishing, hunting. It's where I got all my morals, my traditional knowledge, all my history from him. He knew all the family lineages, everything. Being in the bush all my life, I knew these animals and use them in my designs. I try to get most of it from stories my grandfather told me. He knew supernatural things that I can't explain.

"The Gwich'in are warriors," Lawrence concludes. "We fought to take this land and now we fight to keep it. We are a tough people."

Typically, given the function of oral accounts, his recollection of his grandfather's version of Gwich'in genealogy differs from published accounts in the professional literature, starting with the Nantsaii, which is usually translated as "First on the Land":

The Nantsaii means the Toolmakers who first learned how to live on the tundra, how to track animals that were here at the time, the habits of the local animals. They did not have stone weapons, but only used horn

implements. These Nantsaii later became the Wolf Clan. The Ravens were
the Chi'ichyaa, who were the second people on the land; they learned
about living on the land, all about the plants. When they were coming
here, back then, babies were being born, that's where they got the name,
it means Babies Being Born. They got their tools from Wolf Clan, and were
considered to be "the Helpers."

Lawrence acknowledges the anomalies and controversies raised by this
account. He says,

When they met up with each other they intermarried and created
Tiinjeeotsii [also known as Teenjiraatsyaa], which means They Are in the
Middle. They don't exist anymore, but this third clan went under the motif
of the Jaeger, the bird. You mostly see jaegers up in Crow Flats closer to
the Coast, not down here. Lots of people disagree with this story; that say
we were always here, that we came from apes that were always here, we
didn't come from anywhere else.

It is tempting to speculate on the significance of various key details in
Lawrence Charlie's account. The parasitic jaeger's coastal diet is made
up mostly of fish stolen from other avian hunters. I wondered if this fact
would have gone unnoticed by those who originally decided to identify
this third, catch-all clan by a morally dubious creature.

The issue of evolution versus traditional history is also uppermost in
the minds of the Gwich'in disposed to larger reflection. In Tsiigehtchic,
a Gwich'in marten trapper in his forties showed me the giant rock at the
shore of the Peel River where a shaman killed a giant beaver "eighty thousand years ago," claiming it for a local history that went back to the very
dawn of the human race.

In other words, many First Nations people are entirely aware of the
propensity of White discourse to associate them with a historyless and
timeless existence—ascribing to them the possession of a purely phenomenal world without internecine wars or hopeless tragedies, fatal mistakes,

or utterly human compromises, a world that is always resolved for the good within the confines of a transcendent folk art, to be fixed forever in carving, in recorded myth, and in epic black-and-white photographs illustrating properly footnoted romantic ethnographies.

Certainly, this view is itself a historical by-product of the nineteenth-century preoccupation with Western aestheticized culture, the world according to Hegel, Wagner, and Walter Pater, not to mention our very own Archie Belaney, whose biography for children, featuring his invented identity as Grey Owl, I was given at age eight or nine. I understood at once, both from the sanctimonious text and its artfully posed black-and-white studio photos, just how pressing was our modern necessity for an original beauty to come forward and reconquer Darwin's miserable legacy of sheer accident and orphaned struggle—especially when its confident acolyte came to the job in fetchingly hand-sewn furs, greeting his lecture audience with the piercing blue eyes of a well-bred city executive.

Like Belaney, the Gwich'in can be good actors, too. They are also a handsome people, moody and intense, handsomely intense in a manner that Shakespeare would have entirely appreciated as fit for the boards of his tragic stage, with dark, expressive faces, bold looks, and full mobile lips that are almost Latinate in their haughty sensuality. They are not selling anything. They *are*.

They are also relatively tall; one hears locals comment knowingly about shorter people in surrounding regions, using a tone of evident pity. The perennial story they recount, of Gwich'in children being kidnapped by the envious Beaver and other rival but lesser Aboriginal peoples, betrays a certain amount of self-conscious appreciation of their own best qualities.

More significantly, though, Shakespeare would have understood their traditional culture far better than urbanites are now able to do. He was closer to the Gwich'in hunters, both in outlook and manner. His dramas of the early 1600s look back to a heroic age when Europeans, too, once walked about with deadly weapons held at the ready whenever they left home. Sword-carrying Europeans, too, were keenly jealous of their reputations and children and extended lineages and territorial privileges and would admit few but the most powerful to speak to them in accents of claimed authority. They, too, once walked deserted beaches and parapets covered with spilled blood and broken bones, past snarling dogs and croaking ravens, a world where death and its ghosts concealed messages from the other world that had to be deciphered on the first step of every journey into the unknown.

These Gwich'in oral traditions may not be our traditional Western past, any more than they are their own past, but something of their past and of our collective human past does live on in them, an immediacy of feeling coupled to an undercurrent of a dread and thrilling ellipsis. If their near is our global far, it is a far that brings us to witness the elemental power behind the ice cracking and the moon rising. This sense of elementalism seems to be driving our own elevation and descent.

Like Lawrence Dean Charlie's immaculately inked crows and wolves, we, too, have all lived with perfect holes cut out of the fabric of our understanding; we, too, once had to stay frightfully and fully awake at all times for fear of falling into the nightly void.

One of my hunting companions, an Elder whose two brothers are both chiefs, was given to waking at three in the morning in his hunt cabin with stifled yells and guttural cries, despite his regal bearing and apparently unruffled composure in the brightness of daylight.

But then what prince of the realm ever sleeps well in Shakespeare?

SPRING

6 : Ice over Water

The Richardson Mountains near Aklavik, NT, in April, when the frozen Peel River buckles and creaks and groans as spring shudders to life underfoot.

Overleaf: *The Mackenzie Delta in May near Inuvik, NT,*
from three hundred metres, the original height of the ice age
glaciers that created these endless bogs and oxbows with
their meltwaters.

APRIL TURNS TO MAY. The season of crashing
water and smashing ice called breakup is now
upon us.

Every afternoon, the people of Inuvik town
go down to the muddy banks of the Mackenzie
River to see how it is proceeding, and not just
out of casual interest, either. The ice moves
downriver like a slow pan in a disaster movie,
an inexhaustible parade of truck-sized chunks
of white, gray, brown, and black ice, and the
onlookers comment: "Oh, there's an ice piece
from Fort McPherson!"—identifying its origin from the distinctive tea stain of a particular
water source. Others are waiting with celebratory anticipation, clutching steel gaffs, tin
buckets, and plastic coolers. They are looking
for a chance to hook a crystalline chunk of can-
dle ice, which they claim makes the best tea
in the world. Pure ice from some pure place
upriver!

Meanwhile, mothers warn their ecstatic children, thrilled by the uproar of the spectacle and its carnival ride delights: "Not too close, my boy! Not too close!"

Two thousand kilometres away down in the Great Slave Lake region, one sees much the same thing, but a few weeks earlier in the season. Some grown-ups are watching the cracking and groaning Hay River with nostalgia for their own youth. "Spring breakup was the best part of growing up here," a resident recalls. "The excitement from all the noise and sudden changes in the river level was like a second Christmas."

It's a wet Christmas. The whole delta region top to bottom is subject to massive flooding, and low-lying Aboriginal communities like Aklavik have experienced flooding as recently as June 2013, while its flood waters in the spring of 2006 required millions of dollars in emergency repair costs.

Ice jamming is the culprit; in 2006, the backed-up water rose more than five metres overnight in Aklavik. Like many communities in the region, Aklavik's municipal boundaries do not include any high ground as a secure base for its building stock, so it routinely gets inundated.

It is the same situation in the towns south of the delta. The Hay River spills into the Great Slave Lake at a point where the surrounding land is barely five metres above the mean shoreline; in 1963, the entire commercial section of the town of Hay River had to be moved two kilometres inland from its original fine prospect on the bay and its white sand beaches after a particularly thick ice jam blocked the river's outflow. At the same time, the mostly First Nations (Dene) residents of low-lying Vale Island preferred to stay where they were, adjacent to the shifting shoreline, choosing the certainty of regular evacuation from their aqueous intimacy—as happened there in 2005, 2007, and 2008—over increased flood protection. Moreover, the erosion caused by the collision of ice and floating logs removes twenty-five centimetres, almost a foot, from the impacted riverbanks each year.

The stubborn residents of Vale Island and Aklavik are not alone. Many Indigenous communities in the north have repeatedly demonstrated a cultural preference for living immediately adjacent to the fluctuating water and have rejected government attempts to relocate them. In the 1960s, the residents of Aklavik (Gwich'in, Metis, and Inuvialuit) were invited to move to a comparatively environmentally stable location less than a two-hour boat ride away where the brand new town of Inuvik was being constructed. The three hundred or so inhabitants who refused en masse cited better access to fishing and hunting resources in Aklavik, which is also only one day's journey to the Richardson Mountains, and, because it lies at an interface between two distinct ecological zones, is so rich in game it supports a robust population of barren ground grizzlies—Aklavik is named after the grizzly.

Water is a peculiar thing in the north. Not much of it falls as rain or snow, which is a good thing in a way, because if more of it fell, the regional flooding problem would be very serious indeed. The Mackenzie Delta Ecoregion, a geographers' concept that includes the area just east of Aklavik, is spotted with lakes and ponds to the extent of 36 per cent of its surface, yet the average annual precipitation is only between two hundred and three hundred millimetres, even less as one moves north.

The boreal forests become dry as toast by midsummer. Scores of natural forest fires, caused by lightning or spontaneous combustion, occur each year and they will eventually reach every section of the entire region within twenty-year cycles. At the same time, most of the surface soil is naturally boggy. Even the hilltops that one might expect to be dry from gravitational runoff are squishy and coldly pooled all summer long. You can see these nondrainage whirligig patterns from the air: the rivers and streams give up and double back, triple back, buckle and writhe, creating clover hitches and reef knots of languid brown water. It has no place to go.

As one might expect, northern people have a rich variety of words to cover the spectrum between wet and *really* wet bushlands. The Gwich'in distinguish creek (*teetshik*) from creek water (*tr'iilii tshu*); and a slough (*eyeendak gwichoo*) from a swamp (*gweelah*); and a marsh (*tloo gwa'al*) from a pond (*te'jiltin*) from open water (*teezri*); while puddles (*tajuudlii*) and rainwater on trees (*dehtshu*) and a mudslide (*gwiinjik*) and groundwater (*nan tshu*) and the water of late spring (*daii chu*) each get their own special words, too.

The most beautiful word ever spoken in any language in my opinion is of Inupiaq Alaskan origin, a term that marks the ultimate convergence of spring light and water and openness and hope and the future—"*qunbuq*," literally "the brightness on the horizon indicating the presence of ice on the ocean."

The two water words that most concern us here are "high water" (*nataniidih*) and "the sound of water running" (*tshuu zhaa*). The sound of water running is thrilling the first time you hear it in early spring: usually its source is a hillside creek that has melted enough in the growing days to run freely, its sweet tinkling echoes against the canyon walls. The Gwich'in word for this delightful creek is *teek'it*. It would be a nice name for a baby girl.

The air is the only thing in the delta you can count on being dry for sure. Everything else is pretty much waterlogged until you get up into the highlands, officially defined as land situated over three hundred metres. The trees of this lower region are stunted and stressed from the ice water. They are gingerly rooted in icy water below, and desiccated by blistering winds, hot and cold, above. The same might have been true of the local people, but, being mobile, they have overcome such watery challenges and learned to thrive on them.

Potamosian (flood-dwelling) societies are actually not uncommon in the world today and were prominent in the past as well, although they are not generally recognized as deserving urban society's unqualified approval, because from the standpoint of industrial efficiency, they appear to be haphazard enterprises lacking reliable infrastructure. Examples include the semi-migratory boat people of southeast Asia, Iraq's marsh Arabs, and the pile-dwelling lake sites of Neolithic Europe from 5000 BC. Rather than being marginal in the sociological sense, potamosian societies have successfully exploited the rich resources and other advantages of these riverine habitats, and, in the case of the First Nations of the Mackenzie Delta, go so far as to link these adaptations to their origins in prehistory.

A children's book, *The Flood* (1996), produced by the Gwich'in Language Teaching and Learning Centre in Fort McPherson, retells a version of the little Muskrat who locates the land for the Gwich'in people's future home. In this account, after Duck fails, Muskrat dives down deep through the floodwaters at the behest of the First Man to secure a mouthful of abysmal soil, which he brings back up to the raft, almost drowning in the attempt. The Man revives Muskrat, and then rolls the bit of earth in his hands until it grows big enough to emerge out of the water. The couple then pole their raft ashore and animals and founder humans exit out into the new earth. Little Muskrat is the hero of another Gwich'in origins story: here again he is more persistent than the other, bigger animals, and, after discovering the great marsh above Crow Mountain in Yukon, Muskrat fakes an injury to fool Beaver into going on ahead, so securing the rich site all to himself.

The hard evidence of enormous floods in the past surrounds the people living in this region and reminds them that the cabin-wrecking floods of 1963, and so on, are but a piffle compared to the catastrophic inundations of 8,500 years ago, which left house-sized boulders sitting atop two-hundred-metre escarpments. Driving along the Dempster Highway by Eagle Plains today, one sees where huge rivers once flowed here and here and there—and also nowhere one might reasonably predict—an observation confirmed by paleo-geological researchers who say that regional drainage patterns in past millennia sometimes ran due eastwards instead of northwards.

Despite their current vast proportions, Great Slave Lake and Great Bear Lake are but remnants of gigantic Lake McConnell, which averaged three hundred metres deep and covered 220,000 square kilometres. What happened that day when the glacial lake, the size of Idaho, drained away during the general Holocene warming is anybody's guess, but the mighty Mackenzie must be a trickle in comparison to that final outpour.

The archeological evidence also shows that humans showed up in certain places in the region sometime before the Holocene warming, and then again soon after it began, but during the final apogee of glaciers that loomed four kilometres high, people would have in all likelihood been

restricted to anomalous ice-free corridors and other exceptionally protected zones. Still, the ancestors of the Indigenous residents of this region
were masters of ice and water for a very long time, and their survival
instincts appear to have been shaped as much by this constant dynamic
climatic flux as by the boreal forest itself.

High water or *nataniidih* has reckoned itself to become a major feature
of the psychological landscape of the region. Take, for example, the illustration used in *The Flood*; it shows First Man and Woman living in a tent
on the raft. It's a simple houseboat, easy to build, easy to repair. Such a
composite vessel would make eminent practical sense where currents are
strong and rivers long. Of course, the motif could simply be a graphic con-
vention adapted from illustrated Bible stories of the ark, but the idea that
human habitation is a floating proposition is seen everywhere in contemporary local practices, including housing. Both in Aklavik (Gwich'in
and Inuvialuit) and on Vale Island (Dene and Metis), one finds Indigenous
houses that are perched on piles and reached by wooden stairways two
and three metres high.

Raised piles protect the permafrost subsoil from melting into mud
due to heat loss from the overtopping structure, of course, but here the
higher-than-necessary elevations also signal a secondary purpose, which
is to raise the living quarters above the spring runoffs or floods. A cultural
value is at work here. White residents of the Hay River area typically elect
to build their dwellings on higher, well-drained lands several kilometres
inland (New Town) and, significantly, seek out permafrost-free patches of
land where they are free to excavate full basements as well. "New Town"
as opposed to "Old Town." This cultural dichotomy can be seen in the territorial capital city of Yellowknife with a heterogeneous population of
twenty thousand, where the underlying granite of the Canadian Shield
makes such excavations extremely expensive. Yet local contractors have
learned that if a new house has a full basement, it will command a premium in the capital's real estate market.

A charming account of life in the 1930s, before the cash economy took
hold in the delta, provides further insight into the long-standing northern

cultural attunement toward *tshuu zhaa*, water running. A Gwich'in couple, Lucy Adams and her husband Jimmy, together with their five-year-old daughter Mary, were travelling by dogsled in the late winter after the trapping season was over, and, as Lucy recounts in the *Gwichin Territorial Park (Campbell Lake) Oral History Project Final Report* in 1994, the dangers of skirting the breaking ice proved ultimately thrilling despite her admitted fears:

That was the first trip I ever make to Sitidgi Lake...with dogteam, we had Mary in the toboggan, she was, you know, just small, maybe four or five. I don't know how many hours it took us. My, a long time!

...It took us a quite a while because the storm came up, and the ice split, ah, and instead of going straight, the dogs follow that edge, and where it's just a little narrow spot, they jump across. And I didn't know all that, me, I was just scared. I was thinking oh we're going to go through the ice any place now. I ask him, "How far now?" "That point, you see that point way over there?" "Oh, okay."

He told me we gotta hit that point, then we get into another, oh for me, it looked like it was took us two days [laughter] I fall asleep in the tobog-gan, when I wake up, still long ways to go! And the worst part of it, we got there in moonlight, you know, we thought we were going to make it back to our tent, we didn't take our tent down, we left it. We camp in open fire. No wood! We look for old Amos' stages [fish racks] and log house, so we could tear it down for wood. We were on this side where it just straight willows. Oh, it was something awful.

...Yeah, it got cold, but he kept the fire going. You know we have eider-downs, but no spruce boughs to put. And he said, "We'll jiggle anyway, maybe we'll get more feed for the dogs." So we did, we just right close to where it's solid enough [on the open creek] to jiggle, and we tried it. We got some big loche!

But we didn't get too many. So he said, "We'll set net when we get up." But I said, "How? We got no boat." "Oh," he said, "I'll show you a way." Till next day we got up, and he said, "You walk across, you go on that side and

*stay across." He fix up the net and he pick up rocks from there. Then he'd
take a long line, and he'd tie a rock on it and he'd throw it across to me.
(Laughter) To think of those days now, it's nice, fun. I wish I could do
that again.*

These incredible travel risks were only possible with dogs in accompani-
ment. Today, the dogsled has been replaced by the snowmobile, but the
sensitivity and skill required to negotiate these shifting conditions continues to be exercised by snowmobilers nonetheless. A typical scene played
out every day during ice breakup in Inuvik is the sport or display or task
(take your pick) of *floe-jumping*. In fact, floe-jumping probably has a local
nickname because it is so prevalent.

The spring snowmobiler, faced with a two-metre gap of melted open
water lying between the packed snow on shore and the still solid river ice
in the middle of the channel, simply revs up his motor and goes for it—
flying through the air and landing with a big *whump* when he hits the pre-
sumably stable ice shelf. From there, spraying gritty snow and meltwater,
he scoots down the ice river, doing the same thing, over and over again,
whenever he is confronted by big thermal cracks or patches of open water.
To be honest, I have to force myself to watch these high-anxiety performances. My attention is drawn to the knot of family members who
inevitably gather at the river's melting edge to wave goodbye to these
daredevils, who likely do not think of themselves in that way but simply
as spring travellers.

The first time I saw floe-jumping, I thought it was some reckless teen-
agers showing off, a local equivalent of drag racing; then I observed two
and even three people hanging on tight to their snowmobiles as they
soared through the air. These were couples and small children heading to
their spring camps. The warming edges of the Mackenzie River are only a
metre or two deep, so a mishap at this point would prove painful but not
fatal. But out in the main channel, where the frigid water ranges from
four to seven metres deep, it is another story.

The frozen river melts from below in spring, so the driver must be attentive to the subtle signs that the ice cover has eroded and is too thin to traverse. At the same time, *rolling bubbles* from the pressure of the currents, and amplified by other vehicles that have passed by earlier in the season, such as supply trucks, may cause discontinuities in the ice structure that are apparent only to experts—whose expertise derives solely from such practical but hair-raising experiences in the field.

In addition to the phenomenon of underwater melt and rolling bubbles, there is also *pressure cracking*, caused firstly by the whole mass of the frozen thing (or very large sections of the river's ice cover) moving incrementally back and forth and from side to side in a tug of war with the water below it (which itself is moving discontinuously at different velocities in different places); and, secondly, by the back pressure from the heaving sections of ice all along the full extent of the river back to its source. This latter effect acts rather like a very long train that cannot stop until every single car in it has stopped, too—which, of course, a frozen river can never do. No, it must keep on moving to the end of its end; its appearance of stillness is only an illusion, even in the dead of winter—a safer illusion than the rest of the year, certainly, but an illusion.

Lastly, there is the incidence of *surface cracking*, caused by the daily heat of direct sunlight, which leaves scary but harmless pools of surface water and shallow cracks that refreeze at night, and which confuse the whole issue further for anybody who does not know how to decipher these cryptic blue hieroglyphs.

The late winter jamborees celebrate a renewed Aboriginal acquaintanceship with the dynamic flux of their postglacial reality. One Saturday morning in mid-April, I drove with a friend to Aklavik for their annual jamboree held on the ice road, and quickly realized it is one thing to drive on the snow-packed ice of deep winter on what looks like a conventional road and quite another to drive atop a sheet of slate blue, wind-scoured, spring ice.

You get out of your vehicle, you stand around, you take clever photos of your heavy insulated boots suspended over cobalt hard water, the whole of it held up by a frail blue fixation, and you wonder if the truck will suddenly sink out of sight with a flatulent groan while you are busy taking pictures of the hoary mountains in the background. A part of your brain constantly recalculates which way you can jump if the surface tension fails.

My friend and I arrived in Aklavik at noon that day, just in time to catch the end of the ten-kilometre dog races, which in the absence of route cameras are more fun for the dogs than for observers. The race consists of dots on the horizon followed by cheers from aficionados in the crowd who have already spotted the apparent winners from the distant turn-around and are eyeing the judges at the prospect of the promised prize money changing hands imminently. The dogs come in ragged and heroic as always, the first teams yelping joyfully and the rest of them in various stages of remorse and despair and hopefulness that their owner did not take his defeat too hard, all of them muzzled in thick frost cakes and some even bleeding steamy red from ice cuts but utterly ignoring their wounds in the general clamour of victory and defeat and *Good run, yo! Better than last time!*

It is hard not to love northern sled dogs, especially with the knowledge that any one of these experienced ice runners, first place or last, knows enough not to take you headfirst into a watery cold grave. They can smell the coming water, they can hear baby cracks before they blister up to the surface, they will tell you with their whining and barking and stubborn resistance not to be a damn fool. You look at these animals and know that without dogs, the first men on this massively glaciated continent would probably not have stood a chance. They would have gone straight back to Central Asia in a huff. Every musher you talk to confirms it: it's the dogs that teach the mushers the hard lessons of ice over water.

Now we have the snowmobile races on the afternoon card. The races in Aklavik begin like all such races with the obligatory half-hour wait while the five judges confer about conferring, and call out to see where the last-minute entry papers are, then look for the last-minute entrants who filed the last-minute entries, then they look for the missing megaphone, then they test it out, then they assure the startled entrants that this was just a test, then they decide to drink the coffee that someone they sent out half an hour ago has finally showed up with, blaming the line-ups that the judges can see for themselves are "way too long"; then, cheered by the hot coffee and two or three rock-hard Eskimo doughnuts, they all decide to pose for some souvenir pictures and hand the phone cameras around one by one to cover all the angles and different group possibilities...

You, the spectator, meanwhile, are stomping your feet from the insistent cold wind and trying to avoid the frenzied seven-year-olds whizzing around in their full-sized snowmobiles, impatiently wondering why snowmobile ice racers of all people cannot seem to get their act together and simply *race*, and so completely missing the point that they are *deliberately* dragging out this whole event because they are all *enjoying themselves* here on the wind-swept ice river in the middle of nowhere, and they are in *no hurry* to go anywhere else or do anything else, as they are *already here* where they *want to be* on a Saturday afternoon in April with the temperature at -30°C and an incandescent fog falling over the mountains and the smell of cut spruce boughs mixed with bulk packs of pork smokies frying on charcoal grills.

The first race begins with roaring and whining and ends, and another one, with equally mysterious rules, begins and ends, and a third; the judges look happy, the spectators look happy, but the racers themselves are all sporting those flamboyant red-and-black helmets that appear to be designed for kabuki actors, so their expressions are frozen in stances of abstract ferocity and they don't talk at all as they step forward like hooded red lizards to collect their envelopes.

My friend and I get back in the four-wheel-drive truck and proceed to venture further along the ice road past Aklavik. There remains three hours of muted daylight to us and the mountains beckon, coyly playing peekaboo behind a veil of inconsistent aerial mist (atr'al). The plowed section of the ice road soon bends in a wide sweep and narrows at the same time. It occurs to us adventurers at the same moment that the road is now impassable by two opposed vehicles. There is no place to turn around and the snowbanks on either side are heavy and impermeable. If another vehicle should come toward us then one of us will have to back up for several kilometres. In spite of this potential problem, it bothers me more that there is not that other vehicle in sight. There is nothing in sight.

Nothing except a skein of wolf tracks chasing deeper moose tracks across our path and an owl that is large and gray, like all the forest animals of winter, and watches us go by from his perch, where he is quite at home in his unidentified being, as we are not.

"Where the hell *are we?*" my friend asks, fortifying his resolution to find the answer with a can of Yukon Gold beer and then another when the first can fails to quell his nagging anxiety. I know what he means. We are ten kilometres west of Aklavik, 68.2203° N, 135.0117° W—yes, thank you, GPS. In plain English we are eight degrees north of the Arctic Circle at an elevation of eight metres above sea level, but that's not *where* we are.

The question is, "*What* the hell are we?" meaning we don't know what this place surrounding us is, in actual substance. Mountains, forest, ice river, snow, sky—familiar words, but what do they mean *here?* Worse, we *know* we don't know anything about this silent landscape that pretends to resemble any number of wilderness images. A mystery, wordless and cold.

It's not the fact that we are on an ice road suspended over black water. It is not the fact that there is not a single wisp of smoke to be seen anywhere, it is not the fact that my friend the driver is getting more inebriated and bolder in his moves to "go with the flow," as he puts it. No. It is

—*buumppp!*

"What was that?"

Flash of panic. Stop the vehicle. Get out and look at the tires.

"Ice roll," the driver says, sipping at his beer held in two fingers like he's at a cocktail party with Lewis and Clarke, who are just over the next mountain securing a moose steak for dinner. "No problem-o."

"Ice roll?" There's a distinct, 1.5-metre undulation to the surface of the wind-blasted ice. "I thought this is called an ice *bubble*."

"Bubble, trouble. Whatever." He drains his beer. "Now what?"

We look ahead to the cheerless prospect of an ever-narrowing path scraped carelessly through drifting snow that might lead us to Fort McPherson. A light frost dusts our faces.

The mountains are in the same place they were half an hour ago.

We have travelled this same river route before but by motorboat through a summer horizon, across waves sparkling at the happy conjunction of thirty-kilometre winds and 50 HP engines, all dedicated to the purposeful green prospect of an endless July afternoon.

And again, flying low in a single-engine Cessna to avoid a hovering dark cloud, beset by crosswinds, bumped and jolted and hanging on tight, hooting and giddy at the prospect of the largest golf course in the world below, we tallied fairways and greens and roughs in uncountable legions, an immense playing field set up just for our recreation and sport.

But now it's winter turning into spring, and the reality of its transformation is not what we expected. We realize the melting of a hard truth: we don't know this heaving land at all.

7 : The Mystery of the Blue Beads

Gwich'in artisan Vincent Cardinal displays his beadwork at the Inuvik Petroleum Show.

IN 1789, the explorer Alexander Mackenzie observed a strong preference for blue beads held by the Aboriginal tribe living along the lower banks of the river that now bears his name. In his *Journal of a Voyage to the Arctic Ocean*, published within *Voyages from Montreal through the Continent of North America to the Frozen and Pacific Oceans in 1789 and 1793 with an Account of the Rise and State of the Fur Trade* in 1903, he wrote:

> About 4 o'clock PM saw Smoke upon the West Shore, traversed & landed. The Natives made a terrible uproar speaking quite loud & running up & down like perfect Madmen. The most of the Women & Children had run off with themselves. I was surprised at their appearing in such a Passion, as the two small Canoes that followed us had been there some time before we landed. (Perceiving the disorder which our appearance occasioned among these people, we waited some time before we

quitted the canoe; and I have no doubt, if we had been without people to introduce us, they would have attempted some violence against us; for when the Indians send away their women and children, it is always with an hostile design.) I made them Presents of some small Articles but they were fonder of the Beads than anything else I gave particularly the Blue Ones. One of them whom I had given a Knife asked me to change it for three Branches of Beads which I did to please him. I bought two shirts for my hunters. Here I learned that they were called Diguthe Dinees *or the* Quarrellers. *Our Conductor like the others wanted to leave us here, he was afraid that we should not come back this way, & besides that the Eskmeaux would perhaps kill us & take their Women from my Men & Indians, & he was afraid of them too. Our Indians told him that we were not afraid & that he need not be.*

The blue trade beads that colour this engrossing account of Mackenzie's first encounter with forty Kutchin people (that is, Gwich'in) present a cultural mystery that holds the key to the inner lives of these former boreal nomads and confirms the challenges of forging a specific group identity within an Arctic subsistence economy. These Gwich'in were part of a distinct tribal nation living between the Hare to the south (another Dene tribal group similar to the Gwich'in) and the much-feared Inuvialuit to the north. It was July 9 and the weather was "sultry," but the tone of Mackenzie's account shifts 180 degrees when they encounter frigid fogs, arriving at the coast a few days later.

Spotting white beluga whales sporting in the icy waves of mid-July, the irrepressible Mackenzie gives chase in a flimsy canoe and almost drowns along with his crew. It is only later, waking on the morning of July 15 to "weather Cold and disagreeable," that he realizes he has reached the Hyperborean Sea, the Arctic Ocean. Confused by the huge quantity of fresh water spilling out into the unsalted sea, and by his Aboriginal guides from the south who refer to it simply as (yet another) "Big Lake," Mackenzie, in his excitement at reaching his final goal, mistakenly labels the next day's entry July 15 as well.

Reading Mackenzie's *Journal of a Voyage to the Arctic Ocean* confirms that, apart from guns, the technical advantages of his superior European Enlightenment traveller's kit were exhausted long before this point, and that it was only Mackenzie's indomitable spirit that keeps the expedition going. The locals' lust for European trade beads and Mackenzie's judicious bartering and gifting of them played no small part in facilitating their daily progress and final success. In truth, Mackenzie bargained his way through to the Northwest Passage.

In addition to securing his crew's safety, Mackenzie uses these manufactured items to buy food (meat, fish, blueberries) from residents along the way, whenever his hired Aboriginal guides failed to catch fish in their nets or bag swans and other game with their bows. Essentially, he and his crew were living off Aboriginal technology, not European, and trade was from the first a two-way street. The bartered Gwich'in shirts mentioned in the above passage might well have been pieces specifically produced by enterprising local women for opportunistic trade with outsiders.

As Mackenzie carefully notes, traditional Gwich'in clothing included caribou hide shirts and leggings, scraped and bleached almost white and fancifully decorated with porcupine quills, mollusk shells (from the Pacific coast), fringes, and tufts of fur—a decorative style that extended to the body in face tattoos and *labrets* (slits in the skin in which small items like feather quills, sticks, and bones were inserted)—but no beads. There were no beads whatsoever to be seen in the actual possession of Aboriginals in 1789 in Mackenzie's hundreds of miles of observant travelling, a point that was commercially extremely significant for a fur trader who was keenly documenting all signs of rival trade and gathering accounts of same, no matter how dubious, from the locals.

Yet, at the same time and for some mysterious reason, blue beads already held a place of honour at Contact's final chapter in North America. And, moreover, the beads continue to do so today, decorating the ceremonial rawhide vests worn at public functions by the male political leaders of the Gwich'in and other northern Dene nations. Where did this preference for clothing beads—and especially blue beads—come from? Was it the case of a market demand created by the suppliers, the European traders?

It also appears from this and other passages in Mackenzie's journal that Aboriginals valued such beads far more than practical items like steel knives. Yet even at this early date, imported knives were still so rare that Mackenzie found some crude flint knives at a recently deserted campsite that same week, and realized from his discovery that he had also reached the final frontier of the continental fur trading network.

Judging from the contemporary beads for sale at the Northern Stores in Inuvik and elsewhere, the blue shade preferred by Aboriginal crafts-people is a bright sky colour similar to American Southwest turquoise. These stores begin stocking fur remnants and beads in the fall for sale to contemporary Aboriginal craftspeople, who do their sewing projects over winter.

The local store in Hay River was still setting up its retail display when I went to look and found that the blue beads were already sold out, along with a complementary uncoloured bead called Pearl White. The Northern Store salesperson confirmed that the local Dene buyers (South Slavey) always buy the blue beads first and habitually complain that the store never stocks enough of them, a consistent market demand that is now hundreds of years old in the region. The pioneering Russians and Chinese traders who set up posts along the Pacific Coast in the early 1700s had no ready access to such items, so one possibility is that turquoise antecedents might have derived from the American Southwest through wholly Indigenous trading routes, long before the French and Spanish signifi-cantly altered these arrangements early in the seventeenth century. They certainly knew the Southwest existed. The Dene people who came to be known as the Apache and Navajo emigrated from the Mackenzie region all the way down to the American Southwest some time after 1100 AD.

Archeological digs initiated by the Gwich'in themselves along the Peel River near Fort McPherson in 2000 found coloured glass beads at most test sites, distinguished by the scientists as Large Beads, Small Beads, Seed Beads, Cylindrical Beads, and Cornaline d'Alleppo Beads, in shades of white, green, and red, with a preponderance of blue beads. Venetian Cornaline d'Alleppo beads were made by winding multicoloured glass around a white core. Produced in Murano, Italy, only from the early 1800s to the 1960s, they were universally known in Canada as Hudson Bay beads and are incontrovertible markers of a post-Contact site.

"Blue" in Gwich'in is *jidii datl'oo*, while "bead" is *naagaii*, and these are wholly Indigenous words—unlike the transliterated imported words for button (*lavadoo*), shawl (*lashel*), and sweater (*lalen yik*), which are all borrowed from French traders (*le bouton, le chale, la laine*, respectively)—again suggesting that this cultural preference was formed pre-Contact. To the extent that turquoise itself, or Native American beads, blue or otherwise, are found to be rare or absent from the pre-Contact sites is not a persuasive argument against this theory, for the reason that it is the *relative rarity* of such an item that confers its value as a status symbol or luxury good in the first instance.

Everybody knows what a Ferrari is; it only takes a few real-world examples in a distant Milanese car show to establish and disseminate what French social philosopher Pierre Bourdieu calls a symbolic good in the strategy of social dominance. In his book, *Distinction: A Social Critique of the Judgement of Taste*, he wrote: "One can never escape from the hierarchy of legitimacies...according to the system of [cultural] objects." I am suggesting here that the canny fur trader Alexander Mackenzie immediately recognized the fact of this "symbolic good" embedded within Gwich'in cultural life, and foresaw the critical importance of (blue) trade beads to the future economic relations between his corporate employers and Indigenous people. His observations proved salient in any event.

The fact that Mackenzie was obliged to buy his men caribou-hide shirts, whether these were decorative trade pieces or not, indicates that their own European-style garments were wearing out soon after their departure from Fort Chipewyan in June. Earlier on the trip, his "Men" (as he calls them) also bought warm muskrat shirts on their own, suggesting a collective response to the highly variable northern weather and the inability of standard European clothing to sustain their comfort and security in the delta even in midsummer. The "sultry" days, as Mackenzie happily refers to them in his journal, were mixed with severe weather—including a July thunderstorm so terrifyingly powerful it blew large stones in the air over their heads like "grains of sand." To call it *unseasonably* bad weather would be a misnomer, because such variability is natural to this interstitial region, where a dry continental climate meets a wet maritime climate over a river channel. The Mackenzie River acts like a bowling alley for the storm gods.

Given the high incidence of frostbite and exposure still suffered by people travelling in the bush today, the problem of appropriate northern clothing remains a critical issue and its full solution continues to elude Arctic residents. By "appropriate," I mean *socially* appropriate, as well as environmentally appropriate, for to ignore the social component of dress is to blind oneself to the social function clothes have as markers of personal status and expert competence that are, if anything, even more important qualities to advertise in the northern bush than in the southern urban environment.

For example, I have often observed how some contemporary Inuit and Inuvialuit women now proudly favour wearing fancy moose-hide or sealskin mukluks and long, calico-and-fur summer parkas (*atigi*) while travelling through airports in the north, and, among other things, these high-status articles signal and reinforce the social connections the women maintain with their Elders and community leaders, which systemic support is itself a form of social capital, as Bourdieu points out.

These customized fashion articles themselves are both labour-intensive in their base construction and trimmed with wild furs that take much effort, luck, and skill to secure, such as ground squirrel, wolverine, ermine, and white rabbit skins. The caribou-hide base layer will be labouriously scraped with a specialized scraper that might itself be also custom-made for the user by a male Elder. These special efforts to produce an authentic standout item are all publicly advertised one way or another in personal web blogs, craft shows, and community feasts, all with no little degree of maker's pride. Further, such a parka will be valued by its producer at $2,500 or more, a sum beyond the means of most middle-class urban residents today, who might count themselves lucky to find a Gor-Tex polyester parka on sale for $400 from a self-described "outfitter" retailer.

Likewise, contemporary Gwich'in women, in addition to wearing large bright kerchiefs, will on special occasions wear an *ineekaii yik* (literally an Inuit parka), being a cotton-lined, caribou-hide, Mother Hubbard parka. This coat typically shows off the excess lining material overhanging the inner caribou hide, which, according to contemporary researchers, is purposefully designed for conspicuous consumption.

There are other ostentatiously modest articles in this same line: mittens, hats, vests, aprons, baby belts, etc., with prices that begin at about three hundred dollars (mittens, Fort McPherson, 2012). I am not convinced that in all cases the homemade, puffy-sleeved, calico "Granny dresses" worn to community dances by some contemporary younger women constitute proof of their domestic thriftiness, either. It seems more of a political statement about holding family values higher than the cash economy, particularly given that the fashion statement here is once again made in the context of a highly public performance before watchful community onlookers, familiar and strangers both, and the real cost of such items, with labour factored in, must be easily five or six times what a similar, mass-produced dress would cost the same buyer online with the click of a button.

To return to the question of the blue bead's mysterious provenance, I am suggesting that its popularity arose from a historically obscure but wholly arbitrary origin—perhaps enough few specimens made their way northwest from colonial United States or Canadian sources in the eighteenth century or earlier, and in sufficient numbers to alert a receptive audience to the fact of their existence, which was enough to trigger its collective selection as a cultural icon. But its selection as a cultural icon does not need to be rational. That is, it need not be linked to any material advantage. On the contrary, its nonutility may well confer it with a social meta-utility.

As Pierre Bourdieu declares, simultaneously echoing Thorstein Veblen's radical views in *The Theory of the Leisure Class* and criticizing Marx's arguments that capital is the ultimate driver of social history, economic capital is used by human actors for social positioning. And it is ultimately expressive of their personal existential constraints; and, more, economic capital is useful only to the extent that it is successful as social capital; and more, deft users do not have to necessarily accumulate this social capital in practice themselves, they merely have to *reference it* in their social interactions. As Bourdieu writes in *Distinction:* "Respondents are only required to express a status-induced familiarity with [the] legitimate...culture."

Why should the obscure origins of a traditional Indigenous cultural icon be a question worth pursuing today? Because the northern bush has defeated so many attempts in the past to husband its resources, and its haphazard human history shows that we need all the help we can get to survive here as individuals and as communities. Evidence of this haphazard history includes the many abandoned settlements and hamlets that litter the northern landscape, both First Nations and White. No one group dominates this harsh landscape, which consistently fractures struggling societies into a mosaic of competitive subcommunities and forces individuals into becoming solitary, heroic risk-takers who run the risk of inner collapse as well, the well-known crisis condition called "bushed."

In the south, we humans are indeed our own worst enemy, luxuriating in wars and meaningless destruction. But in the north the fatal enemy is proud ignorance, the one sin that is unforgiveable.

As a dynamic system, the Arctic continues to pose the greatest of challenges to long-term, sustainable, economic and social relationships within its boundaries; this, because the northern learning curve never ends. It is a tough place to survive, never mind thrive. Nor have we, as a nation still under construction, established, thus far, any sure-footed relationship with the north, notwithstanding various individuals may have been more successful than others at nearing the transitory goal. Even they pay a price for their special knowledge. Nothing comes free in the bush.

Mackenzie himself went back to England after his triumphs and stayed put there. I am mindful of seventy-seven-year-old Gwich'in trapper Stephen Frost's elegiac reflection on the "very hard life" of his grandparents' generation, a sentiment borne out by photographs of the careworn faces of local people circa 1900–1930, especially the women bent double under heavy loads, made old beyond their years. Mackenzie himself not infrequently describes in his journal meeting miserable family groups on his expedition. The list he puts forth includes people obliged to eat rotten meat; facing starvation, or dead of it; victims seriously wounded in recent battles with enemies; a skeletal woman surrounded by keening relatives; and a woman mad with grief for five children she had lost the winter before. These encounters were all in high summer; one can only imagine what horrors he might have encountered travelling in the dead of winter.

Of course, there are also robust First Nations hunters in splendid, culturally unique attire with excellent gear to be found; Mackenzie admires the workmanship of a superb canoe one man has left on a beach, pronouncing it the best he had ever seen. But the risk of fatal danger lies just below the surface of a sultry summer day for everyone, proud or frail. What protection lies between them and starvation, at the best of times? One month's supply of food, or two? Who are the two great antiheroes of the Gwich'in sagas? Their names tell us everything: Without Fire, and Left with Nothing. Heroes—because they survived without fire and somehow made it to spring again without anything. Without Fire is said to have survived by warming himself in the heat of freshly killed rabbit guts.

The high-risk environment of the northern bush has elicited a certain defined spectrum of expressive responses from its residents, the most prominent of which is stark boldness of public gesture and authoritative declamation. The men on the other side of the Richardson Mountains "kill with their eyes," Mackenzie's local informants averred, projecting onto the Yukon horizon a power all might hope to claim in their own daily struggle for social dominance and security. And, yet, as Mackenzie knows full well, these same informants, determined to withhold real information from the nosy explorer, are using these fabulous tales of Yukon ogres as a tactical dodge and a bluff.

Bluff and blind chance are keys to the whole system of northern male agency. The hero Left with Nothing loses all his clothes gambling with an Inuit sharpie, yet his fundamental luck hands him just enough odds to get him home in one piece again.

"I have been *out there*," one contemporary northerner declares of his solo trips deep into the bush. "Right to the edge and beyond!"—and one knows he is not bragging about breaching geological boundaries but psychological ones.

Faced with uncertainty and fatal risk in the field at every turn, the northern hunter cannot afford to show symptoms of weakness or uncertainty himself but must find reasons for his lack of success outside, especially in the breaking of one taboo or another—perhaps he hunted a porcupine the same day he found a beaver in his trap—admitting to untoward technical mistakes rather than personal flaws, for mistakes can be cured by ritual atonement, whereas the weakness and uncertainty that worms its way into one's gut is an unmistakable sign that the whole of his territory may now be encroached on by others with stronger dispositions at will. He must display boldness of manner, as well as boldness of action, to his dying day.

Note that there is nothing inherently or obviously wrong in hunting a porcupine and a beaver in the same day; it is the sheer arbitrariness of the broken rule that fixes one's attention to it as the abstract type of mistake all hunting men commonly make. It's what you do with your chances that counts. The self-declared individual needs to act autonomously, with irrepressible conviction. This image presentation might explain another anecdote in Mackenzie's 1789 account, concerning an armed group led by a man who goes to war to erase the shame of having publicly wept. His weeping was a mistake; the blood of the enemy will be his atonement. What is the line concluding many job ads in the north today? "The possession of a Criminal Record is not necessarily a bar to employment for this position." Character and luck are two different things in the north, and luck is by far desired as the larger.

Similarly, incidents of oratory and rhetoric (or what seem to me to be oratory and rhetoric) pepper the encounters described in Mackenzie's journal. Again and again he is obliged to patiently hear out the English Chief, his main guide, as the man declaims a growing catalogue of griefs and concerns within earshot of his fellows.

Such oratory is part of the local dress code. Everyone is equal except in luck, as it were. Therefore, everyone has the opportunity to address the audience at length, stating a position, or, rather, *restating* a position so as to publicly affirm it—rather than, say, debate an issue to its final resolution with facts and statistics and historical examples, as transpired in the bustling coffee houses of Georgian England of that era, a give-and-take of optimal possibilities explored from the perspectives of the claimed expertise of the technician, merchant, and manufacturer. Mackenzie wore all three hats on his sojourn in the wilds.

The following passage in Mackenzie's journal, dated July 5, 1789, highlights the expressive nature of Slave and Dogrib bands acting in the public forum:

> *During our short stay with those People they amused us with dancing to their own Vocal Music, in neither of which there is no great variety, as least as far as we could perceive. They form a Ring Men and Women promiscuously, the former have a Bone Dagger or piece of Stick between the fingers of the Right Hand which they keep extended above the Head...They jump & put themselves into different Antic Shapes, keeping their Heels, close together. At every pause they make the Men howl in imitation of the Wolf or some other Animal and those that hold out the longest at this strong exercise seem to pass for the best performers; the Women hang their Arms as if without Power of Motion.*

Two hundred years later, contemporary Gwich'in and other Dene nation dancers continue to dance in mixed rings of a dozen or more men and women to fiddle music that has a highly repetitive beat and is limited to just a few chords. The style is probably intended to provide a stable consonance verging on the regimental for the dancers' steady collective heel-to-toe jigging and reels, which can only get more adventurous and personally idiosyncratic as the night wears on. I believe I did hear some of the younger men howl a bit as they swung around the room toward midnight, too, while the amusing Duck Dance, imitating the bobbing of the Arctic oldsquaw duck species that heralds spring in the delta, continues to be an all-ages favourite at such events. These spring (after Lent) and solstice celebratory dances reflect and perhaps encourage the energies of the wild world without. Young and old dance together, chiefs and children, too. The circle dance is necessarily a socially levelling process, democratic, egalitarian, perhaps even what anthropologist Victor Turner calls "liminal," the ground state of all social relations, stripped of excess: this is who we are as human beings in the world.

Making this bright declaration of *who we are* performs a critical function in an environment that threatens to expunge identity at every turn. By all accounts, these northern Dene bands were never larger than a few thousand individuals, and many were much smaller, perhaps five or six hundred people at most, scattered over thousands of square miles. The scattered seasonal resources required scattered seasonal mobility from them, yet they also needed to be assured of their collective interests in the face of unpredictable threats from outside parties, the encroachments of the Cree and the Inuvialuit especially, in this instance. They needed portable institutions and portable symbols to mark their cause of constant vigilance and collective security in the face of ever-present dangers.

I take it as no coincidence that forty Gwich'in managed to muster to meet and engage Mackenzie's party in a display of solidarity on that momentous day in July. Despite the long distances and short warnings, they somehow communicated with each other at the height of their busiest procurement season while fishing and drying meat at their individual camps, and gathered in a showy aggressive attitude for his arrival.

The very arbitrariness of the highly desirable—and virtually nonexistent—blue trade beads signals that arbitrariness can be expressed as a positive virtue, as a way of defining the in-group and asserting a common destiny. Is it too much to say that we can hear the beads talking? We may be small, but we are hard and beautiful, and when we come together, we stand out with polished distinction and reflected celestial power.

Regardless of the historical incidents that may have given rise to this elevated role of the blue bead (and I am suggesting that if they do exist, they are unprovable because its symbolic role is entirely expressive and interpretive, offering an *open* as opposed to a closed script), the bead tradition developed. The Gwich'in succeeded in defining themselves through the elegant aesthetic of choosing such an abstract and portable symbol—which, interestingly enough, no one person or group within the tribe actually produces or controls. Its in-house production would otherwise defeat its purpose as a boundary marker of, and a means to, a self-monitoring destiny based on individual merit, patently recognized by the outside world for hunting, trapping, and negotiating successes, aggregated and elevated to decorate the whole community.

In the likelihood that this speculation seems far-fetched, let me offer some original and more recent third-party research. From the contemporary Gwich'in themselves comes the idea that the trade beads mimic local delta fish eggs, in shape, size, and colour (red, white, orange, yellow, and purple, but not blue), and, more importantly, offer the rich symbol of a generational currency of life. *K'in*, fish eggs, provide an important source of high protein and fat used by Elders and new mothers as a restorative. Then there is the blueberry (*Vaccinium uliginosum*), the single most important plant food harvested in the delta, with the same colour, shape, and size as blue beads, traditionally added to pounded dried meat for flavour and nutritional enhancement. So, *food*, essence of life, pure value, *transformative*.

Next from traditional Gwich'in/Dene story cycles comes the tale of *Naagajj tsal*, Little Beads, an ancient Slavey hero reminiscent of Achilles, as this excerpt from *Gwichya Gwich'in Googwandak* recounts:

Little Beads was the name of the Slavey leader who fought with
Atachuukajj over the woman Lete'tr'aandyaa. ("Moving Back and Forth")
His name describes a special quality of his battle jacket. It was made with
small pebbles ("beads") which, inserted into a hardened mixture of gravel
and spruce gum, were woven into an impenetrable battle jacket. No arrow
spear or dagger could cut through it. Naagajj tsal was accidently killed by
the orphan boy Chitajj...He had a strange kind of arrow, the arrow was
formed just like an ice chisel. Now, Naagajj tsal's coat was made from sand
and gum. Nobody could kill him. But his coat had shoulder straps which
held it together. Now the orphan boy just shot his arrow in the air. It came
down, hit the straps of Naagajj tsal's jacket and cut them. Well, he just
dropped! That's a hard story.

So, *protection*, hard life, careful immunity, *preservative*. Joining these two
opposed forces together, the transformative and the preservative, into
one metonym or word signifier, we arrive at a convergence of the real, the
concrete—with the verbal, the allusive—into the single-point, boundary-
entity, "bead."

From contemporary cognitive research scientists, such as Bo Yao and
his colleagues, we also learn that words and things have been found to
converge *semantically*, meaning, for example, that words denoting bigger
objects or things like "moose" are recognized and processed significantly
faster by their human subjects than those words indicating a smaller
semantic size, like "bead." This holds true "irrespective of the concrete-
ness of the entities," so that big abstract words ("disaster") are recognized
faster than little abstract words ("incident").

If bigger word-things are easier to process than small word-things, like
"bead," then what advantages does thinking about little, hard-to-process
"beads" confer on users? For a possible answer, we can turn to another
line of cognitive research, one that deals with the relationship between
"careful behaviour" and "narrow attention focus." Japanese scientists
Hiroshi Nittono and his colleagues report finding a direct correlation
between people who studied cute/pretty images (*Kawaii* in Japanese) and

their immediate improvement in motor dexterity, all via their increased attention and control over motor actions. This suggests a convergence of aesthetics and engineering at some fundamental level in the way our brains are wired and function when faced with discriminatory/motor tasks.

It may be that simply *thinking* about little things like beads "tunes up" one's motor responses and makes the actor more aware of the incremental changes occurring in his larger environment. And, if the Japanese research is correct, his or her response to new challenges is likely to be more nuanced, and more sensitive to variable outcomes. As we previously pointed out in the matter of distant nonobjects in the Arctic landscape, the ability to scan the environment in a finely grained manner, in a land where the ground under óne's feet constantly shifts ever just so, or the scattering of snowbirds announces something unseen and possibly dangerous, is a paramount undertaking.

We can say this about our lost armoured hero: Naagajj tsal would have been better off to do battle with just one bead in hand, and a highly focused mind, because, if had he done so, he might have noticed Chitajj's ice-chisel arrow flying directly at the one mortal spot he had failed to protect.

This leads us to consider what overall strategies are best adapted for arriving at a more secure life in the Arctic bush. Should we take up sewing and fine crafts on moving to the north as a kind of mental prophylaxis? Lots of people do so, finding satisfaction in the pursuit of technical bush skills like knife making, fine carving, landscape watercolour painting, or jewelry making, skills they often learn from Aboriginal teachers who learned some of their tricks and techniques from pioneer settlers, who learned some of their crafts from old-time *nanaa'jh*, bushmen, who...

And then we find this curious little entry in *Gwich'in Ethnobotany* recounted by Elder Sarah Peters:

Sometimes if a family had good workers, they had a good life. They made clothes like buckskin jackets with all kinds of different beads on them. The kind of beads I'm talking about were different from the beads now. They

were made of ivory bone and they coloured the beads with different kinds
of berries. These beads were pretty big and you could see on the shoulders
of the jacket the bead work.

Of course! The Gwich'in people from the old days dyed their white bone
beads blue and red and so forth with local plant extracts—but then why
does Mackenzie never mention what must have been a common practice? The answer appears obvious: it seems Mackenzie was not interested
in *those* sorts of beads, for they were not defined as "beads" in his eyes
at all. He was interested in trade beads alone, and seeing none of those,
he was able to report to his principals that the prospects for trade in the
Northwest were very good indeed.

⋮ What does this wide-ranging inquiry teach us? That technology is not of
itself going to save us, if the past is any guide. European tool kits in 1789
were only marginally superior to Aboriginal manufacture in this particular variable environment and were quickly supplemented by Aboriginal
crafts and especially Aboriginal skills.

Arrows filled Mackenzie's pot, and furs kept his men warm. European
men's clothing at this late Contact date consisted of homespun wool
breeches, linen shirts with full sleeves, short waistcoats, pantaloons
(full trousers as opposed to the bourgeois culottes worn with stockings),
leather boots or *sabots*, wooden shoes—most of which were produced
at home for immediate family members, or, more formally, in nascent
cottage industries for local sale. They were adapted for temperate agricultural pursuits, not for continental roving through the vast canyons of
geological time.

Soon enough, the Quebecois voyageurs adapted the Aboriginal practice
of wearing moose-hide moccasins with snowshoes in deep winter; they
came to understand that of all the furs, including the supremely valuable
beaver, only the fox, wolf, and wolverine furs repelled frost and worked
best for parka hoods; they fastened wool blankets around their shoulders

with colourful ties just as the First Nations people did—in effect, wearing one's nightly bedroll decoratively during daylight.

Mackenzie ruefully noted in his journal that his "Men" initially lacked such useful items on the expedition, remarking that they slept pressed together like "whelps" around a fire one chilly evening. The typical voyageurs proudly sported wool felt hats, decorated with ostrich plumes, and a scarf or bandana handwoven in distinctive "arrow patterns." Then they loosed themselves on the land, with many, like Étienne Brûlé, disappearing forever into the mist of historical speculation.

These were the men who transmitted the hard-won knowledge of northern peoples bit by bit to the rest of us, in a process that is not over just quite yet.

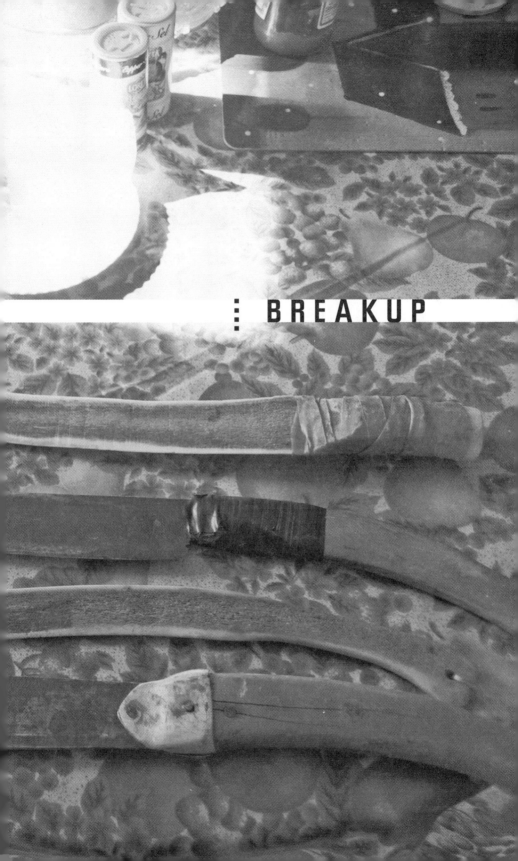

BREAKUP

8 : Willow Flats

THE SEASON AFTER SPRING is called breakup, *Daii*, by the Gwich'in. Breakup in the Mackenzie Delta marks the period from the end of May up to the end of July when the water begins running, high and fast and free of ice. The ducks, geese, and swans are returning in great numbers, and the wetlands are slowly drying out to the point where forest fires will become a hazard. The inland hunters have two options, now that the muskrat trapping is over and the caribou have left for the coast.

In Old Crow, Esau Schafer and Lawrence Dean Charlie mentioned the practice of hunters stalking bears by confronting them in their dens and forcing them to emerge, a exclusively male event that appears to be very old and shows a degree of ritual, as it involves a designated bear-slayer from the all-male party, who, in former days, was obliged to dispatch the beast at close quarters with a spear rather than a bow, like the intimate encounters of matadors in the Spanish *corrida*. This animal growling in its lair is, of course, the black bear not the grizzly; informants say the hunt party has a pretty good idea where a male bear is denned up beforehand, and they make their plans accordingly.

Then, for the cooking pot, migratory waterfowl by the millions fly into the delta, using patches of open water as temporary staging areas, retreating quickly south again should the mild weather get overtaken by a cold snap, and moving by impatient degrees until they arrive at their summer nesting grounds. Mallards, blue-winged teal, Canada geese, snow geese, canvasback, oldsquaw ducks, tundra swans, and sandhill cranes can be seen in mixed rafts on the open channels and nearby ponds before they disperse for the year.

Previous trips with Cree hunters in the Eastern Subarctic (James Bay) have led me to conclude that the waterfowl harvesting technique is pretty much the same across a wide swath of the north. Here in the delta, the hunting families move out in two boats to a local point of land jutting into a bay, or a weedy island fly-past. They heap up stones and brush for low, off-facing, temporary blinds and bend their faces to the ground as they call out to the overflying birds—cupping their hands to amplify the sound—using an urgent honking language that means "Good feeding, join us!" The Cree hunters varied their pitch somewhat between the Canada geese and their smaller cousins, the Brant geese.

Is there a whole language available to direct different types of geese and ducks into shooting range? I have watched local hunters pull back skeins of geese madly flying and directly away, like they were on a short leash; and the combination of clever if rudimentary decoys made of grass clumps or downed birds and expert marksmanship do the rest. The best trick is to knock down three birds with one twelve-gauge shell with Number 4 shot, and I have seen it done enough times to know that it is intentional but not enough times to know where that magic spot might be in a flock at fifty paces. As it is, the hunters can down fifty or a hundred birds in a day, which fills a freezer pretty fast.

Local Dene hunters also shot and ate tundra swans in Mackenzie's day, as he repeatedly notes, and they still do today, although I have not heard of anyone shooting sandhill cranes anymore. Swans are culturally taboo for Europeans, and particularly Britons, not because of their association with the ballet but because hunting them was restricted to royal pageants from the time of Edward I, who feasted on mute swans with 260 new knights just before attacking Robert the Bruce of Scotland in 1306. The new knights must have felt guilty about their rare dish because the subsequent campaign against the Bruce did not go too well. The 1971 Wild Creatures and Forest Laws Act reaffirmed the prerogative the monarch has over "royal fish and swans."

The fact that the water is high during breakup season means that much of the low-lying land is soggy or wet and the shorelines are flooded. Like the caribou, whose grazing changes the texture of the landscape dramatically, these nesting ducks and geese crop at grasses growing around the shores and fertilize them at the same time, which helps to maintain and spread grassy species like *Beckmannia* (sloughgrass) in a dynamic condition called *desclimax*, meaning that the system is stable as a result of repeated feeding, but it is not what the local plant life would look like in the absence of this collective process.

The muskrat, which is not a rat at all but a giant field mouse that has adapted to North America's ice age flood conditions, contributes to the state of desclimax by selectively eating cattails, water lilies, and other preferred water plants. The importance of the muskrat in the delta is such that the Gwich'in trappers can sustain themselves on a long trip across their traplines by eating their daily catch (fried or boiled) supplemented with bannock and tea—in effect, working as human agents of the desclimax process as well, a process they understand fully.

"If no one goes out on the land any more, the game animals will all disappear," warns Gwich'in Elder James Itsi, repeatedly making the point that it is the harvesting that creates the harvest. And this appears just as true of herbivores' impact on plant life as it is, in turn, of humans' impact on animal life. The muskrat's poplar-and-willow-branch *push-ups*—little way stations constructed as breathing points on their underwater sequential travelling during ice conditions—provide an accessible winter food source for caribou, so these relationships are quite complex.

Studies on willows and other low browse in the Finnmark region in the extreme north of Norway show that unchecked browsing by elk and reindeer leads to habitat fragmentation and a decline in overall species diversity. The process of desclimax works in favour of both the browse and its browsers but only if predators are free to crop the browsers. Gwich'in trappers in Aklavik say that recently (2012) wolves have become more common in the Richardson Mountains just west of the community, and that the moose populations are significantly down as a result. When asked about this, Aklavik trapper Peter Ross shook his head over the issue of wolves: "They're getting bolder because no one's trapping them or hunting them. They are starting to come into town looking to kill dogs. We've lost three of four already to wolves, and they're getting into a real bad habit now."

Showing none of the antipathy in his account that some ranchers will display when the subject of wolves and coyotes arises, Peter, a professional trapper in his seventies, knows that wolves are a valuable resource and he has the large Conibear wolf traps to prove it. The issue is about asserting a measure of caretaker responsibility over the cycles of nature by selectively smoothing out the animal population peaks and valleys. Still, globalization has its impact on this process, sometimes in roundabout ways.

In February 2013, North American Fur Auctions (NAFA) sales in Toronto reported sharply rising Asian and Russian demand for fisher, raccoon, muskrat (marketed overseas as "musquash"), lynx, and marten ("sable"). But the trade also saw an 18 per cent decline in beaver pelt prices owing to an "ongoing issue in dressing problems." Wolf pelts are currently in low prestige demand, especially considering their usefully large size and scarce harvesting numbers, averaging only $125 at the 2011 auction in Thompson, MB, and not moving much since. With lynx at $200 prime, marten up 60 per cent to a $150 base price, muskrat pelt prices up 10 per cent to an $11 base price, and raccoon now matching or beating beaver prices at $31, it is changing global fashion that clearly dictates prices—the main reason being that these showy pelts are now used as trim in high-fashion coat designs of composite materials in Asia and Europe.

The net result of these market pressures is that First Nations and other trappers have a greater marginal incentive to harvest low-labour, reliably profitable furs such as muskrat and raccoon, which are easy to trap, stretch dry, and sell in bulk. Beaver still dominates the fur trade by the sheer volume of pelts harvested, but the steady annual rise in the nation's beaver population to an estimated twenty million in 2012, from their historical low in 1900, estimated at 100,000 animals, suggests that the hunting pressure is now off the animal, and the results can be seen in incidents of beaver dam flooding and tree damage increasingly reported by cottage owners across the country.

This conflict can only become more common as demand for vacation land escalates in the north, and the unpredictable whims of the global marketplace selectively impact on the various fur-bearer populations. The question of hunter impact on local populations and ecological systems has long been studied by scientists, if imperfectly understood. First Nations people designate these relations with compound words that identify specific landforms with available resources and also reference a cluster of traditional subsistence and social activities carried out there.

A formal oral study of local, traditional place names conducted by the Gwich'in Social and Cultural Institute in 1994 describes how some such compound biogeographical words belong to their own "Stone Age," and while those names are still in use today, their meaning is now irretrievably lost. For the most part, these relationships relate to historical subsistence activities and strategies.

"No matter where you go, there are still hundreds of place names for every twist and turn of the river," one local hunter explains, "And very few blank spots on the map."

These Indigenous names also convey remembered community and family seasonal uses associated with them. For example, *Nichiitsii diniinlee*, Big Rock, was the scene of a regular communal gathering during breakup. The oral histories suggest that the compound word *chii* ("rock")-*tsii* ("iron")-*diniinlee* ("lined up") refers to Gwich'in geological knowledge, which holds that this set of three big rocks forms part of the same sporadic range of outcrops that includes the Campbell Hills and continues to the Black Hills in the distant Richardson Mountains. At breakup, the local families would take advantage of the good fishing created by three fast-flowing eddies there and net enough whitefish, inconnu, and crooked-back catches for the following winter's entire consumption. The three rocks, according to Elder Harry Harrison, also provided a collective sitting area swept by clear breezes that blew insects away, so the term is redolent with positive and deeply social associations.

⋮ Similarly, the local willow (*kaii* in Gwich'in) conveys a rich, multilevel host of Indigenous associations that the scientific Latin genus name *Salix*, or its cultural referents in English (*The Wind in the Willows*, "Willow Weep for Me"), might fail to match. The willow flats—the intermediate shoreline area between the sedges and grasses eaten by ducks, geese, and muskrats, and the spruce forest proper, a zone specifically called *k'ii chah* in Gwich'in—dominates the landscape of the delta by creating the appearance of a dark and unruly green hedge. The willow flat strikes the outside visitor as an impenetrable, mysterious, and even threatening marginal entity, a single-minded thing with a will of its own and the power to confuse, deny, and obscure.

The dark willow flat is not what one thinks of as part of a classic northern aesthetic, with its regal landscapes set apart by aloofness, visual clarity, and precise scale, but as something murky and foreboding that really belongs to the hallucinatory bayous of the Amazon.

The visitor might also dimly sense that the entire wall of willows, running for hundreds of kilometres along the shorelines of the lakes and rivers, might actually be only a single living maze-thing, an individual super-organism showing itself in the soil as and when it decides, the vegetative counterpart to *Nichiitsii diniinlee*, the celebrated rock outcrop, cited above. This would be a fair assumption to make, because *Salix* propagates itself vegetatively, as well as sexually, and chances are that any one willow plant might take up hundreds of metres of shoreline, if not more.

No one is in a position to say either way with certainty, because the scientific research on this botanical mystery is rather skimpy given its ecological and cultural importance to the local population, a lack of literature that might be caused by the exhausting effort involved in mucking through a buggy, airless, and dark wrangle of lashing branches and tripping roots, with no sleeping princess waiting for the intrepid scout on the other side.

As even the casual hiker will quickly discover, the willow flat is certainly a zone that you must push hard to get through, either on your way down to the open water, or, conversely, up to high ground of the forest, so the idea of investigating it on its own instead of the many, far more congenial places takes a great deal of mental resolve, as well as physical effort. It may also be a matter of the availability and constraints of contemporary research grants: travel in the north is frightfully expensive, and investigation results are required in relatively short time frames. Judging from the complexity and accumulated detail of local lore on the subject, a full scientific study of the willow flat might take an entire lifetime. I initially came to investigate this botanical prodigy after I was told by residents where they found the best Labrador tea (*Ledum palustre*), a local spot that was optimally high in altitude but partially shaded.

Following these directions, a few days later I climbed the highest ridge outside of Inuvik town, and, after admiring the view of the Mackenzie River below and the gauzy Richardson Mountains away in the distance, I ambled down an overgrown dirt road by the vividly green lake that provides Inuvik town with its drinking water at breakup, as the heavy sediment from land runoffs makes that river source unappealing from May to freeze-up.

The day was bright and airy. Not a sound but for unseen birds tweeting rhythmically from the depths of the inner forest. It was late morning so there were few bugs about, as they would emerge when the air got cooler toward evening. Various butterflies flitted by on delicate missions to nowhere, the mountain fritillary (*Boloria napaea*), a fast little flier, and some larger species. A dozen of the latter collected on a rotting log and carefully fraternized like lawn bowlers do, waving their wings ostentatiously but not getting too close to each other for fear of a midcourse collision. A few mushrooms had pushed their way through the topsoil, the product of recent heavy rainfalls.

Of course, I was intent on searching for the promised cache of potent Labrador tea, but what was distracting about this climax foliage on the ridge was the extreme variability of its common members like the spruces, willows, and alders. The crowns on the spruces varied from boxy arrangements that looked like bishops' miters to cactus-like maces that appeared more alien the longer you studied them. The design of the willows was all over the place, coiled like skinny vines, thick as old apple trees, branches upended, branches downcast, big leaves flopping like sow's ears, tiny leaves sharp as new mint. Armed with a close-up camera lens, and shooting away, I found I could not find a "representative" willow to save my life. I was walking on a bench or plateau of the ridge about fifty metres high that appeared relatively well drained and geologically consistent, so much of this morphological diversity had to be an expression of genetic factors rather than environmental stress. The thrusting willows struck me on inspection to be wildly expressive novelties with no resemblance to the sedate park trees lining the man-made ponds back east.

Willows are *dioecious*, meaning they have both female and male reproductive systems in the same plant. They also have high allelic diversity, grow vegetatively, as well as sexually, and because they are adapted to a northern environment criss-crossed by isolating rivers, mountains, talus, and, especially, permafrost, they grow in many separate communities that further increase the opportunities for selective genetic drift. Just as a lack of genetic diversity in some species might indicate a historical population bottleneck, researcher Juan Lin and his colleagues have found that the opposite is also true: higher than expected allelic diversity might indicate *isolate-breaking*, the fresh mix of formerly separated populations when they become rejoined again as the land opens up.

From the height of the ridge, the end of the last ice age twelve thousand years ago was still visible in the vast number of remnant eskers, oxbow rivers, and moraines, a landscape that is slowly rebounding from the removal of a glacial overburden four kilometres thick and now occupied by a human population still struggling to adapt to this novel environment.

What I was really looking for that day on the moraine ridge was not there, and this was a repetition of form and sensation that brought some regularity and rhythm to the boreal hiking experience. What I was seeing was series of unique one-offs, an unending collection of individual vegetative characters bunched together into a thing called a forest or the forest, a thing that further resolved itself into the silence and shadowy space surrounding these plants without actually touching them.

Was this the way that Gwich'in people saw k'ii chah, the willow flat? As a sequence of peculiarities and idiosyncrasies ordered by their subsistence needs? Here is a relevant quote from the text Gwich'in Ethnobotany that must be understood in a subtle cultural context:

A taller, big leaved form of muskeg tea (Ledum groenlandicum) is also common throughout the area; however, it has a stronger taste and is not generally used. Elizabeth Greenland explained, "The big one is strong good medicine, but the small one is better."

The US Department of Agriculture Forestry Service website warns the public that this larger species, called bog Labrador tea, contains alkaloids that might be toxic to humans, and it provides an extensive documentation of the stomach contents from a number of indigenous animals that shows their ingestion of this Ledum species is usually only accidental, and further states that it has very low food value except for its flower nectar for bees.

The above Gwich'in summary avoids words like "toxic" or "dangerous"; polite circumlocutions like "not generally used" and "strong good medicine" both seem to honour the plant's natural being and its generative power, and tell the story we all need to know without giving the plant, as an actor, due cause for offense. We will see how this traditionally circumspect speech also shapes local accounts of grizzly bears in a later chapter.

As I hiked along the trail through the elevated bog, my eyes kept returning (longingly) to the grasses and sedges that grew in uniform patterns by the roadside; I found rest and harmony in the repeated patterns of line and edge. Of course, I was looking at the forest aesthetically, as urban people are unconsciously wont to do, and when something told me to go back a few paces and look again at a patch of mixed plants, it took me a few moments to realize I had smelled the fragrant Labrador tea before I actually noticed it growing in the half-shade amidst the fireweed and wild roses.

The aromatic presence of the plant was unmistakable, evergreen-herbal, like rosemary, and yet our inner language is so deficient in words to describe scent, tactility, and aural sensations compared to visual distinctions that the apparent silence of the forest is compounded and amplified by the sensational silence of our technical language. I was glad to be able to locate the Labrador tea plant by scent, for it made me feel we shared a real connection. I have taken hundreds of photographs of willow flats in an effort to make some visual sense of their enduring botanical mystery, but the contextual language was always missing, an ecological descriptive language that describes the complexity of its environmental and historical relationships, with the same richness of feeling, say, as the language of whale hunting in *Moby Dick*, or the deft appreciation of connoisseurs for their oaky fat red wines. Europeans have long lost our need for a common, practical language of the forest and its offerings, just as First Nations people seem to slowly be losing theirs.

The Gwich'in, for example, retain separate words for the willow (*K'aii*); dry willow twigs for starting fires (*K'il*); young willow shoots that are edible (*K'aii dzhuh*); willow whistles (*K'aii uzhuu*); willow branches used as tent bedding (*K'aii ah*); flexible young willow branches used for stringing fish or for ring toys (*K'ii loh*); willow poultices for insect bites (*K'aii t'an*); willow roots for making cord (*Kaii ghaii*); and so on. This is a working language, a descriptive language rich with human undertones. The importance of the willow is highlighted by the mythic role played by K'aiheenjik (Willow Man) among the Vuntut Gwich'in of Old Crow in Yukon.

As mentioned earlier, K'aiheenjik literally means "Willow Creek," so it is the willow flat personified in a super-powerful male being, armed with both positive and negative qualities—a being who can swallow up a moose whole (!) at one gulp. Near immortal, K'aiheenjik cannot be killed by anyone else—he survives an arrow attack that leaves him looking like a porcupine with quills—but he can be killed by himself—as he does at the end of his story cycle, jumping off a cliff and asking the band of vengeful men who pursued him to declare that he froze to death instead of (shamefully) committing suicide.

Fantastical tales like the Willow Man epic play with, reverse, and distort the expected order of things and so offer a fresh way of examining close relationships: If moose eat the willows, what happens if the willow eats the moose? This same reversal thinking occurs in typical Gwich'in artistic depictions of a caribou with a wolf contained in its belly, where the logic of the reversibility of such relationships is shown to be valid in the wider ecological time frame, as it becomes generally recognized that predation ultimately improves the stock: the wolf "feeds" a healthy caribou herd. The willow bush, in fact, does "eat" the browsing moose, in turn, because it responds to its own consumption, along with other selective pressures, by speciating into new varieties, some of which may prove more nutritious or digestible with further research.

Researchers have already discovered that the willow has developed amazing properties in response to selective pressures, including the ability to produce a hormonal substance that attracts ladybugs to it, which then gobble up the parasitical insects attacking the plant. Research has also confirmed what Indigenous people have claimed all along in their traditional list of the willow's medicinal properties, namely that its crushed leaves and inner bark make useful and safe painkillers and antiseptics. A 2007 medical report written by Hany A. El-Shemy and his colleagues found that when young leaves of willow (*Salix*) were given to mice with cancer tumours, the mice were cured of the disease or survived longer, without any deleterious side effects to be found.

One of the key northern values is respect for the task at hand, which also incorporates respect owed to the teachings of ancestors and Elders who arrived at this corpus of practical knowledge through trial and error at great personal cost. This store of values must be respected as an ongoing legacy, for it was bargained for in the same way that red ochre was obtained through payment in K'aiheenjik's sacrifice, or the medicinal gifts of the willow were originally brokered.

Whenever I have travelled with First Nations people, I have been struck by how they will slip into the forest and immediately fall to their stated purpose, disappearing, as it were, into the very action of cutting wood or setting traps or picking berries. I have witnessed the same thing with Indigenous carvers, weavers, and fishermen. To my eye, they come into the bush with their eyes open to its curiosities and possibilities, and notice other things in the course of their tasks, becoming a moose hunter rather than a berry picker should the opportunity arise. But they have demanding chores that must be carried out, and tasks, like securing enough fish to feed their dogs over winter, are seasonal, demanding intense dedication for two full weeks or more.

This ability to be "swallowed whole" by our chores is sadly deficient in the multitasking universe of modern technological society, with its glitches, breaks, outages, and lost connections. Southern residents view the word "breakup" as interruption and loss, not as expanded opportunity.

Urban ambivalence about cultural diminishment is reflected in the term "nerd," identifying those who are lucky/unfortunate enough to disappear into their work, which, because it is invisible to the rest of us, can have no perceived social value until and unless it is awarded honours in the public sphere. Immediacy, unassailable functional value, and full-blown attention are the great prizes of northern existence; knowing when "enough is enough" and when it is time to quit is an issue that the Gwich'in myths address with tales of studied ambivalence, like the ancient Medicine Man who keeps rabidly eating up entire raw moose quarters—not out of greed, as the audience naturally expects, but because he is eating food for an invisible giant (i.e., his extended and always hungry kinfolk, in all likelihood), as well as himself.

Whether the shaman has somehow ingested the giant, who now demands to be fed from within his belly, or is in some form of reciprocal, distant communication with him, the available version of this strange story does not disclose. At bottom, it seems to signify that the shaman is utterly overtaken by his spiritual task of "feeding the giant," whatever it is, and he is acting far outside the boundaries of normal human discourse. The importance of whole-hearted commitment is underscored in the tale.

The giant might simply represent the demanding season of breakup, which imposes its resounding demands on all. Gwich'in hunters say they can collect and cut enough spruce firewood to heat their cabins over winter with ten days' to two weeks' steady work. They might do this in two or three phases, but either way, "You want to be ready for winter before it comes!" In a land where it will snow in July, it means no dawdling in September, the busiest month of the boreal year. Such tasks must be planned and completed: there is no margin for error. The envy that I feel for them is not for their existential freedom (we all have freedom) but for their freedom of life in action.

One way the forest is conceptually organized by local people can be gleaned from the special ritual practices that attend certain procurement activities. Traditionally, the Gwich'in leave offerings of tobacco, sugar, tea, spoons, and other small gifts in exchange for taking ochre (limonite, iron oxide) cuttings from the tamarack tree (*Larix larcina*) and berries from the juniper or crowberry (*Juniperus communis*). Juniper is a medicine, tamarack is a medicine, and ochre is also a medicine, external, applied to the outside of things like winter gear (snowshoes) or animal skins.

The local rule seems to be that the value of the human gift determines the potency of the plant medicine. There is a hierarchical order or ranking based on such bargained relationships. For example, moose meat is said to be less filling than caribou meat because moose specialize in eating willow shoots, whereas caribou eat reindeer moss (*Cladina*), the same white moss humans can eat and for which gifts should also be left whenever this moss is harvested.

Of all the plants used by the First Nations in the Northwest Territories, it is the willow that is the most prominent, so much so that a northern tradition without the willow as its material base is impossible to imagine. There are two willows. What is called the red willow in the Mackenzie Delta, on account of its deep red branches, is actually the green alder (*Alnus crispa*), a shrub that shares with the true willows (*Salix*) the ability to grow on lands constantly disturbed by frost heaving, flooding, and erosion, such as the river flats habitually experience, and more so these days now that the climate is changing and stressing local vegetation even further. Willow (*Salix*) and red willow (*Alnus*) complement each other in the traditional subsistence kit; and the latter extends the range of creative uses into red dye for hides, sweetly pungent smoke for flavouring dry fish, stomach tonics, and game-butchering mats.

Gwich'in hunters collect red willow branches as convenient and clean mats to field dress their game. The colour red is symbolically appropriate for this blood-draining function, but whether or not a chemical hygienic connection is literally apt in this case (i.e., that the red willow actually keeps the red meat clean), evidently such plants serve a metacultural function in organizing the conceptual frame of the world for Aboriginal people. These two plants help keep the whole working enterprise intact: the willow flat as a whole can be understood as a living constitutional membrane that mediates, protects, and preserves the final processes of subsistence itself (*stomach* medicine). Life is ordered as a series of correspondences—beggared, it is true, by anomalous incidents and dogged by bad luck—but always resisting disorder or breakage with the yielding force of the willow's essential tenacity.

At his end, K'aiheenjik does not break apart in his fatal fall from the cliff: he *melts*, rarefied by the convergent logic of alchemy into a being of red ochre, into a place where offerings of tobacco and matches are to be left in exchange for his powerful blood-dye.

Community travels (*tr'eenjah*) through the spruce forest are experienced thematically in this ritual way; additionally, and, more privately, the traveller will bring to the forest his or her own memories of past travels and experiences that will be encyclopedic and turn this risky wilderness into an unending series of family narratives. Trevor Charlie, a Gwich'in youth whose family was originally from Old Crow in Yukon, recounts how his grandparents took him by dogsled across the Richardson Mountains in the dead of winter. He contracted a high fever on this journey and, to commemorate his survival, they named a small lake they had passed after him.

As mentioned previously, the Gwich'in Land and Water Board in Inuvik has commenced mapping a database using Global Information System technology to render oral histories of land use by Gwich'in and Sahtu and other trekkers. The two-dimensional map models a four-dimensional map of their collective historical pathways through the bush. The resulting coloured scheme, still in its development, shows a spaghetti plate of forest trails loaded with the detail of a road map of L.A. or Tokyo.

Of course, there is some overlap, but what this map shows is that Gwich'in and other Aboriginal hunters and gatherers have their own ideas of the inner structure of the taiga and its accessibility. The chaotic mat of willow and alders we see lining the edge of bush roads in a closed wall of impenetrable thicket is matched by an open mental thicket of ancient paths cut through it—a thicket in the thicket—that reveals the synaptic richness of human relations between nature and memory.

9 : Knife versus Ulu

James Itsi at work in his salmon smokehouse in Old Crow, YT.

THERE ARE THREE basic knife forms traditionally made by local craftsmen in the Arctic: the curved woman's knife or *ulu*; the men's all-purpose hunting knife, called the *pilut* by the Inuit of the Eastern Arctic; and the large snow knife or *pana* used exclusively by the Inuit. Owing to increased communication by air travel, there has been an ongoing cross-cultural transmission across the north of these different forms, along with the arcane knowledge of their manufacture since the Second World War.

Dwayne DeBastien, a Gwich'in from Fort McPherson in the Northwest Territories, recalls learning how to cut an *ulu* from an old saw blade in his Grade 2 shop class back in the 1970s: "I really liked making *ulus*. Our teacher showed us how. I made a lot of them when I was seven or eight and gave them away to family members."

A forest-dwelling people, the Gwich'in historically did not use *ulus* as they had more pressing needs for axes and fish-gutting knives.

But today some families find them highly useful in the kitchen for chopping meat and vegetables. The Inuit use six or seven types, including the basic kitchen *ulu*, which is about nine centimetres wide; the smaller hunting *ulu*; the little, four-centimetre, "personal *ulu*," for shaving and eating; the snow *ulu*; and the larger sealskin-scraping *ulu*. Within these basic functions lie hundreds of regional and individual variations.

As master *ulu*-maker Anthony Manernaluk of Rankin Inlet in the Eastern Arctic says, everyone has a personal preference for things they use every day, and he obliges them with his custom designs. "My *ulus* are all over the world now. People phone me up at home and ask, 'Are you the *ulu*-maker?' I say yes, and they ask me to make them *ulu* as they like. I don't even know these people who buy my knives."

Anthony was born on Baffin Island in 1936, in a remote Inuit community of eleven people, including a fur trader. "No candy, no pop. Just tea and flour." At seventy-six he is still going strong, smiling frequently and showing off a full set of teeth as he switches adeptly from English to Inuktitut, depending on his audience. His well-organized work table holds a dozen *ulu* blade patterns cut from cereal cardboard; a vise; a grinder; a half-dozen handmade chisels, files, and rubber mallets; and sheets of stainless steel. He studies the leftover bits of sheets, frugally working out how to get the maximum number of blades on order from his remaining stock. He also economically shuts his lamp off whenever he takes a blade outside to polish, saying that he can properly see what he is doing only in full sun: "Work is best in daylight."

The first job is to assign the right blade to the right person. As he surveys his stock of patterns, he tells a story about hunting:

You have to get up before the day begins and go out, straight out to where the caribou are waiting. I did this and shot three caribou, a bull, cow, and calf, under the hill where they were waiting. They tell you where you are when you pay attention to the land.

He repeats versions of this enigmatic story three times during the course of his instruction, perhaps indicating a kind of transcendent identity between the macrolevel of the big decisions involved in a hunting expedition and the microlevel decisions involved in cutting a blade. They are one and the same thing: the experiential world is cut by the decisive mind. The resemblance of the *ulu* to the lunar phases cannot be a coincidence; there is ordinary daylight time and the other, more mysterious time.

"This one is most popular," Tony says, holding up a blade about fifteen centimetres wide. This is the kitchen *ulu*; in the old days they were made of slate, or from copper if the Inuit had access to this native metal. He methodically chisels out the blade from a stainless steel sheet according to the cardboard pattern, an operation that takes him about ten minutes. The handle will be hardwood; in former times it was made of caribou antler, sometimes musk ox horn, but "never bone." Tony has an old musk ox horn in his kit, along with a chunk of hard organic material that might be a sea turtle shell—it is hard to tell. The point is that his workspace has the look of an experimental laboratory, and its eclectic inventory shows he is always ready to try out new design ideas.

A strict methodology is also apparent. After watching Tony complete a kitchen *ulu* over the course of three hours, I would estimate that he follows something in the order of eight hundred different steps or procedures to create the final, and supremely functional, product.

It is a very intense experience, watching a knife maker at work. You hear the ringing of steel on steel, the thud of wood on wood as he hammers the handle into its brass tong; you smell the burning carbon as the blade is ground razor sharp in a shower of yellow sparks; and, most of all, you witness the interrogative gaze the old man gives his work, as if he is asking it deeply personal questions every step of the way to its final arrival.

Are you straight enough? Are you firm and secure? Are you pretty?

This last, of course, is an old English word, taken from the iron-wielding Norse, meaning tricky. But "pretty" also conveys the final quality of finish that Tony is searching for in his emerging knife, a kind of seamless merger of utility and aesthetics into which his own human intentionality disappears forever. The knife literally becomes its own thing, perfect and autonomous. At the end of the morning, the new blade sits on the table and the old man sits on his stool, both resting in the calm dignity of their mutual repose.

Making such autonomous things come alive is the essence of magic, of course, and we humans have been at it for fifty thousand years, as the magical bone and antler shamanic instruments of the Upper Paleolithic show us in their purity and timeless freedom.

This is the theme of a thousand European fairy tales, too. The broomsticks that fly, the red shoes that take over the dancer, the puppet who learns to love repeat the refrain: things have their own power and destinies. As we shall see, the Inuit have their stories, too, of things that come alive; and the struggle of this narrative is always to convert those things into human agency and so re-establish proper relations between the two orders of existence, imagination and its expression in materiality. One Inuit word for this quality of formlessness-in-form is *nulajuq*, meaning "he/she grows up suddenly by magical means." The Dene nations of the Subarctic have similar notions expressed in words like the Gwich'in *nagwahdeh*, meaning an inexplicable appearance or manifestation of power that animates things.

George Roberts is a master knife maker based in Whitehorse, YT. Like Tony Manernaluk (whom George knows from various craft exhibitions in the north), he is constantly perfecting his craft, using high-tech powdered steel and Damascus steel for blades that will cut through lesser metals, as well as bone and wood. These joint exhibits have accelerated the transmission of traditional knowledge across cultural boundaries. There is plenty of time at these events to watch other masters at their trade and pick up techniques and solutions to common problems. George proudly shows off a hunting knife that won a design award in 2011. The sinuous curve of the blade shows a deep appreciation for the parabolic shapes favoured by Inuit artists in all their traditional mediums but especially in their carvings, as George is quick to acknowledge.

"Of course, my design is based on Inuit knives," George says, "I like that roundedness, it's an efficient design. You can rock the blade back and forth, using less pressure to cut through things. Of course, at a certain point people who buy my knives don't want to forget them stuck in a stump back in the bush. Knives don't get used when they become too expensive to lose."

George's knives begin at under two hundred dollars and go up to several thousand; he has jackknives with exotic red amber handles that glow like the dangerous jewelry they are, on offer for five thousand. The gleam is the knives talking—in their refinement and polish, the knives insistently demand a deepening skill from their maker, just as they demand a high level of respect and care from prospective owners.

All this technique is, of course, very well, but what uses can a good knife be put to in the bush? What makes a good knife, good? On a bitterly cold day on the frozen Mackenzie Delta, I watched Gwich'in hunter Noel Andre butcher a bull moose with only a short blade mounted on a cheap yellow plastic handle. It was the careful cuts and not machine force that allowed him to methodically trim the meat away from the hide and bones, assisted only by some youths who watched, learned, and helped him roll the carcass from side to side as needed. It took him about three and a half hours to secure all the meat and scraped hide and leave the remnants for ravens and foxes.

Similarly, I once watched two women, also Gwich'in, take about two hours to butcher two bull caribou with short knives with bright yellow handles just outside their home in the town of Inuvik, where, of course, they could have easily got larger and heavier tools if they needed them. One of the women even complained repeatedly that her knife was not sharp enough, but that did not stop her from cutting meal-size portions so efficiently that she kept a third woman entirely busy sealing them up in freezer bags.

I have witnessed other Aboriginal people using versions of this same smallish knife in the bush: the conspicuous yellow handle makes it hard to misplace. Again, a small child was in attendance, carefully watching the entire process. But notice: whether it is a one-hundred-kilogram caribou or a three-hundred-kilogram moose, the general rule is one person, one animal, one knife.

The person wielding the knife is the conductor, the maestro, *the* knife incarnate—while the others heft, and pull, roll, and drag, or, with polar bears or grizzlies about, stand guard. The operation of butchering a large game animal is exactly analogous to the job of making a knife, requiring the same intense dedication to the next step and the next in the process, utilizing the efficiency of a hundred right actions in which sheer human muscle power is subordinated to the all-inquiring eye. It is nothing remarkable to see aging grandmothers and grandfathers hard at this task in the Far North, just as it is common enough to see septuagenarian conductors and violinists at work in the south. Live performances like symphonic music or ballet preserve the archaic role of the interpretative artisan in the privileged art forms of industrial society.

A working appreciation of nuance is now restricted in the dominant society to such elite practices and special occasions: the craftsman, and more, the craftsman's special way of seeing the world, was specifically targeted by the radical programs of early-twentieth-century proponents of industrial efficiency in Europe, theorists like Marinetti and Rodchenko who fell under the spell of the machine. From the first days of the rise of the modern state in the Enlightenment, propaganda campaigns habitually attacked craft and craftsmen, an attack aimed at their working principle of polycentric reality.

The industrial state abrogates for itself the sole right to define reality for us, and, by equating time with security, it justifies the use of bureaucratic violence on its indolent and supinely indifferent citizens. All work is hierarchically monitored; even lottery winners in contemporary government TV commercials are shown busy at collective pursuits with their newfound millions, as if trout fishing in teams is something we would really do with our fat winnings. This monopolistic system is, of course, also present in the north, but it breaks down frequently enough that the competing artisan system still thrives. The reason for this is that people living in the bush need real information to survive.

What I notice with a First Nations artisan is the supreme emphasis put on the interpretation of his or her original material. Butchering a caribou is not simply about getting meat; it is also about getting information on the unique conditions of kilometres of terrain that the caribou met in its long-distance travels, information that the entrails, stomach contents, fat levels, skin quality, etc., will reveal to those who can read them.

It is industrial practice that has warped our humanist perspective on work and craft, for the idea of a thousand necessarily separate and repeatable tasks is not carried out in traditional practice. The autonomy of action is always reserved to the craftsman himself, not to the plan. Always missing from the plan is the variation of local conditions that a modern clinical culture, based on standardization, dismisses as "anomalous" or "anecdotal."

It is in anecdote that all life begins. Tony Manernaluk carries with him family *ulus* that are forty and sixty years old. Undoubtedly, they, in turn, carry histories with them, histories of their manufacture and ancestral use through the years. In the Inuit community of Arviat in Nunavut, Mary Mikiyungiak was pleased to bring out a sealskin bag of family heirlooms, including old *ulus* of even greater vintage, but unlike the silverware of middle-class Europeans, where the histories are confined to recitals of proud ownership and testamentary recovery, her items invoke the memories of those who made them, used them, and survived with them. They are proof of fate's favour.

Tony and George, like all artisans, would certainly recognize a knife they made decades ago because it is imbued with a unique relationship and individual character from the start. George gives each one of his knives a personal name suggested by the specifics of its inner nature; he calls a twelve-centimetre hunting knife with a laminated birch handle the Evil Hunter after the red knot that suggests a glaring eye. Note the difference: it is not the Evil Hunter *model*.

Of course, we recognize that cars and even computers have idiosyncrasies that undermine the ideal of standardized units (at least mine always do). But we are not encouraged to recognize what lies behind the fiction of standardization. The foundation of scientific thinking rests on the repeatability of results, and without repeatability, the whole Western edifice crumbles to dust. All failure must be logical, explicable, and so, correctable— this is so whether we are talking about moon rockets or marriages.

In traditional, usually nomadic, communities of approximately 20–100 individuals, such as humanity lived in before the rise of agriculture and herding, the recognition that we are unique individuals, down to our fingernails and daydreams, is impossible to avoid. There is no opportunity to abstract human relationships and every reason not to do so, for one needs to know the precise psychological and physiological limits of everyone else in one's community. The idea that things must be repeatable to be true is alien to such societies, for it is precisely in variation that the truth of our being is sought and tested, as the Greek epics assert.

A perfect illustration of this divergence between a culture of singular happenstance and a culture of avowed repetition happened one sunny day in early July, when a Gwich'in group invited a dozen executives from the south to an outdoor feast at their wilderness camp on the Mackenzie River. Debarking from their boat, the executives milled about the cook fire, surreptitiously checking their watches despite the plain evidence that a spread of snacks was available and the whole meal was presented as open and extended, not fixed to a start and end time. Only when the meat and fish were cooked did they sit down and eat, and when they were finished, they retreated en masse into the main lodge, as the meal was now over in their minds.

Yet for their Gwich'in hosts the meal had just begun. For what is better than to sit on the banks of a wide river in July, stomach full of good food, watching the bald eagles and ospreys soar over the treetops? What was dead, directionless time to the executives was rich, creative time to the First Nations people. Two things impressed themselves on me that afternoon. One was that sitting around in the bush apparently aimlessly is the key to understanding the power of the bush in its infinite variability and perpetual play of nuanced messages. A family of semipalmated sandpipers (*Calidris pusilla*) made its nest only a few metres from where we sat; watching the intensity of their antics was better than a Woody Woodpecker cartoon, as the parents faked a broken wing every time someone approached too near. The summer breeze whispered through a clump of red willows and an unseen brook gurgled within them, sending messages about the health of the land and its capacity for renewal.

After some reflections on these dancing surface events, the mind becomes aware of deeper notes emanating from the ground itself, a kind of resonance or upwelling of energy that was there all along, and which you start to feel with your whole body. You look around, silently taking measure of the phenomenon, and you realize that your companions are feeling it, too, and, more, they seem to be drawing physical sustenance from it directly.

We have all experienced variations of this earth force in alpine hikes, or on a breezy day by the ocean, or at a sparkling waterfall; we give it a scientific explanation that negative ions produced by the friction of air and water work to lighten our mood. The forest—the living, naturally intact forest—has its own subterranean presence that underlies all the green and growing things and the penumbra of animal life—the insects, birds, and game—that feed off it, and each other.

To become aware of this force requires that we empty ourselves of the noise and clamour of our social preoccupations. To just sit and listen is extremely hard to do for urban people, who are raised from birth to pursue activity and demonstrable results as the *summum bonum* of civilized life. How many camping treks into the bush are led by hikers who need to beat some previous record, birders with their competitive lists, organizers who insist on a schedule of events being followed to the letter? It never occurs to them that these attitudes are merely the historical products of ancestral cultural responses to eighteenth-century technologies like the mechanical clock and the factory work team. Readers may recall the proposal of Jeremy Bentham (1748–1832) for a *panopticon* or circular surveillance system, where the inmates are housed at the perimeter and the guards stationed in the centre. The French critic Michel Foucault made much of this imaginary clock apparatus, a metaphor for modern society governed by bureaucratic policy as much as it is by law and might. The panopticon is, of course, simply a clock made of human beings: the clock masters at the unmoving centre are scarcely more privileged than the workers shuffling around the rim, for they are constrained to sit tight and grow old in the vacuum of events they have imposed on themselves.

Two contemporary films from Aboriginal perspectives show us that they witnessed how the mechanical clock ruled the Europeans of the first Contact far more than their distant kings and queens. In *Black Robe* (1991), directed by Bruce Beresford, a French timepiece set up in the Jesuits' wilderness quarters becomes a kind of ritual altar for the Hurons, who sit patiently around it waiting for it to strike the hour: it is already affecting them far more profoundly than the priests' sermons about Jesus. In *The Journals of Knud Rasmussen* (2006), directed by Inuit filmmaker Zacharias Kunuk, a Christianized Inuit organizes his growing band of followers around the same centripetal model, withholding the camp's supply of food until everyone has performed its hymn singing to his satisfaction.

The contacted Hurons (Wendat) speculated that a little man operated the Jesuits' clock; or, that the clock *was* a little man. The truth, as we have learned, is far more improbable. What operates the clock, what operates all clocks, is an agency or force absolutely divorced from all human feeling and, unanswerable to its original makers, reanimates itself in the innards of atomic bombs and in the spectre of merciless Darwinian selection.

There was more to be learned on the river that day than the operative distinction between the urban workers' jumpy time sense and the Gwich'in relaxed observance of Time's arrow. There is an easy lassitude shared by the people sitting on stumps and old chairs watching a river go by, as the cumulus clouds formed themselves into polar bears and plump ptarmigans. This speculative play soon extends itself to words and memories: Ruby the camp cook recalled how a trapper named Elijah had got himself a new pair of glasses and promptly forgot them on a stump because he was so used to seeing the world slightly out of focus. He went back, but they were gone. Just fresh moose tracks.

"Maybe the moose came along and got them on his head!" someone suggested. "Yes, then he'd be seeing things differently, this moose with Elijah's specs!"

Someone recounted another story, this one about a woman who lost her new dentures on a canoe trip because she threw out the tissue in which they had been wrapped for protection. "She only realized what she'd just done from the splash it made!" There was a general pause to reflect on her misfortune. Then: "Maybe some whitefish is swimming around with a new set of teeth!" Laughter. Someone else chimed in, "That moose with his new glasses better not go swimming, or he'll just see that whitefish is going to bite him on the ass!" Huge laughter; the series of abrupt reversals ended in a comic image that commented on gender power relations, aging, science versus nature, even the prospect of a political upset.

Soon enough, the executives emerged from the darkness of the lodge, blinking at the bright sunlight reflecting off the water. They were ready to go. The day was over.

A few days after this outing, I had an opportunity to see and handle an assortment of George Robert's new knives. What struck me was a great divide between his modestly priced hunting knives and the flashier models that commanded all the prizes and public admiration. One knife had a simple fifteen-centimetre blade and a bright orange synthetic handle. I was drawn to it; it felt right at home in my hand.

"That's the Arctic style," George said. "No metal bolster, so it won't freeze the skin off your hand at forty below." I hefted it and realized that my knife had found me.

: SUMMER

10 : Berry Picking

Overleaf: A pair of sandhill cranes near the hamlet of Tsiigehtchic, NT, delicate in flight but raucous in song.

Diane Baxter and Sheila Vittrekwa picking blueberries they find immediately adjacent to their buckets, no (male) meandering required.

FROM MID-JULY UNTIL SEPTEMBER, the Arctic regions of Canada produce a variety of lowbush berries and other edibles that are high in sugar content, minerals, and vitamins, owing largely to the intensity of the long summer sun. According to Robert Charlie, a Gwich'in resident from Fort McPherson, high summer is also the best time to pick Labrador tea (*Ledum palustre*).

"It has more flavour in summer," he says. "We like to pick off the mountaintops where it gets more direct sun, it's stronger. We freeze it, and mix it half and half with regular tea for flavour." In addition to its vitamin C content, Labrador tea so made is said to have a calming effect on most people.

The Gwich'in Social and Cultural Institute guidebook, *Gwich'in Ethnobotany*, combines traditional Aboriginal knowledge of each local plant with scientific nomenclature. It lists no less than eleven different species of edible berry plants that grow in the Gwich'in

153

Settlement Region, essentially a lowland taiga environment punctuated by remnant treeless mountain ranges averaging 1,700 metres high. These include common plants like the blueberry and the cranberry.

Drinking Labrador tea is a prerequisite for berry picking, as anyone soon learns when picking with local people. One summer evening, three Gwich'in women, Diane, Charlene, and Martina, took me out to their "secret" picking location by a creek about thirty kilometres from the town of Inuvik after work. They were intent on picking blueberries from 6:00 until 11:00 P M, when the Arctic sun of late July was still high. At a certain point, the lengthening shadows make it unproductive to pick. Either way, one must keep changing one's plane of view from a squatting position because the berries grow in vertical and horizontal layers, the bulk of which are invisible to people looking straight down from a standing position.

Within a few minutes of arriving at our destination, the women had chopped up spruce logs for kindling and got a fire going, put on a blackened teapot filled with one loose handful each of Labrador tea and regular black Chinese tea, and had corn on the cob with onions and fish baking in foil wrap—all without five words exchanged among the three of them. It was still hot at 6:00 P M, so there were few flies about to bother us despite our proximity to the waterlogged willow flat surrounding the creek. After the meal and a smoke, the women took out a heap of rubber boots from the back of the pickup truck and tried them on for size. They were obviously all too small for me.

"You're going to get a soaker," one of them said, shaking her head at my hiking boots. "The water is over a foot deep in places." "Go that way," another told me, pointing out a rabbit trail that followed a line of dry ridges. "The berries won't be as juicy but at least you'll keep your feet dry." The third one weighed in: "Well, it really doesn't matter if you get your feet wet. The water's nice and cool. Sometimes I like walking around barefoot in it. We will even sit down right in the water if it's a really hot day."

I finished my Labrador tea, a half-litre in a big thermos cup, and, then, without thinking about it, I opened the litre of bottled water I had brought with me and drank half of it, too, at a single go. I was extremely thirsty, although we had not been out on the land for more than a half-hour. I had forgotten how dehydrated one can get, exposed to the direct elements in a wilderness environment where you are constantly walking about in full sun and facing drying breezes without the constant shade and windbreaks of town in otherwise identical weather conditions.

The body must eventually adjust to these sudden shifts from an ameliorated town climate to a harsher, full-weather, wilderness climate over the seasons, as my friends began discussing how exactly the men they knew could stay out in direct sun working physically all day at their cash-economy jobs without complaint. In fact, earlier we had passed two men they knew who were standing about in a freshly dug drainage ditch, wearing full work uniforms with hard hats and safety gear and showing not the least signs of fatigue after eight hard hours on the sweaty outdoor job.

"I could never do that," one of the women had commented, and the others murmured concurrence.

"But they are no damn good at berry picking," one of them said with a snort. "Always wandering off to look at something."

"Oh, yes," said another to general laughter, "*Any* excuse will do them just fine!"

Sadly, this gender-biased comment soon proved true in my case also. I should like to report that I diligently picked a full pail of juicy fruit and handily refuted these presumptions, but the fact is that a hundred paces into the forest, with strange little birds calling out, and any number of unusual biological sights demanding my immediate attention, it proved impossible for me to sit in one place and just pick. I was restless and unable to resist the novel attractions of the immediate landscape, much of which—as I knew from previous forays into the woods—would successfully resist my photographic efforts, as well as my powers of literary description. A photo of a highly interesting boreal site looks like nothing but a lumpy collection of common weeds and bramble when one returns home, berryless except for the few hundred you managed to stuff into your mouth as you rambled about the forest, fulfilling your companions' expectations of male uselessness in the picking department.

Diligently, I slogged through the bog, chose a promising spot where the berries showed themselves to abandoned perfection, and squatted down, miles away from all thoughts except for my subvocalized determination to keep on picking. Competing cues in the environment soon overcame these pearls of glossy blue and proved impossible to resist: I kept moving to a "better" berry patch. Each time I turned to reorient myself to my friends' position, they were sitting exactly where they had been five minutes earlier, engrossed in this business of separating the berry from the plant and their minds from the cares of the week. They were visibly happy, in total communion with the ground (sloshy and lumpy though it was), and at times they appeared so at one with the land that they were nearly invisible. It was as if they had knowingly succeeded in fading into the green and shaded background, reducing their exposure as separate creatures to the barest outlines by taking up a position beside a concealing bush.

Only a spot of red wool mackinaw or the flash of a metal pail gave their position away as the evening shadows advanced. This strategy of personal concealment, conscious or not, is universal in the northern forest. Unlike the urban south, where the squirrels and songbirds are habituated to a predatorless environment and openly bask exposed on tree limbs in the sure knowledge of their domestic security, northern wildlife flits from concealment to concealment, never staying in open view for more than a few seconds.

The birds and animals of the boreal forest deliberately put as many branches and shadows as they can between themselves and the onlooker; even the fat town ravens, living high off fast food refuse, have not forgotten their old ways, and, when approached, will immediately change their flight path downwards so they are silhouetted against the broken patterns of streetscape and not exposed in the open sky.

Tweet-tee-whoo!

Summer birdcalls were ascending from everywhere around us. But where were they? The little creatures stayed hidden, yet they sang out with mighty voices a hundred times bigger than their bodies. Warblers, song sparrows, wrens: the whole Aves class was out here somewhere in the bushes and I could not see a single one because they did not want me to see them. I loped out through the cool bog and returned to the road (the Dempster Highway, the infamous gravel heap that runs four hundred kilometres south to the hamlet of Dawson in Yukon) and amused myself by watching the shadows grow obliquely from the bare hills to the west. In former times, the Gwich'in, like many Indigenous peoples, significantly altered their landscape with large controlled fires to increase the yield of berries, and to provide new browse for moose and other preferred game animals like the ptarmigan.

As it happened, this summer (2012) set a regional record for forest fires, most of which had been started by lightning storms. There was also an unusual amount of rainfall, which put out most of the local forest fires, a natural stalemate, as the Inuvik Fire Office manager confirmed: "But then all the lightning bolts set off new ones!"

Lightning is a friend of the berry in another way, as Diane recounted when she and her companions finally emerged, sweaty and happy, from the bountiful forest with silver pails loaded with blue fruit.

"Lightning creates free nitrogen that the berries and other plants can use," she said, pulling her boots off and admiring her haul. "It's been a good year for berries because of that—hey! Where's your pail?"

"The lightning bolts didn't strike where I was," I said regretfully.

The amount of edible plant life available in a boreal environment in summer is staggering. The women had come to the same spot three or four times already in the past month and apparently stuck to their patch about fifty by fifty metres in size—less than an acre. What would a full acre produce in total available fruit over five weeks? Easily a hundred gallons of berries, probably much more. But it requires patient work, and more, the careful calculation of one's own array of resources to derive the maximum amount of nutrition from the taiga.

On this occasion, the three women had collected four, one-gallon pails of blueberries in over two and a half hours, including travel time. Using the calorie rate of 120 calories for a cup of domestic blueberries gives an approximate value of two thousand calories in one imperial gallon of wild fruit. It may be less, because the sugar content is lower in wild fruit. As the women prepared to return home to freeze their berries, one of them asked another how many "bags" (meaning gallon pails) she had already picked that summer on her outings.

Her answer was seventeen bags. It would not be unreasonable to assume that by the end of the summer harvest about forty gallons of blueberries might get bagged per picker, for a total of eighty thousand calories obtained from a high-value crop. The other two women said they had already collected nineteen and twenty-three bags, respectively, to be used for "pancakes, trifle, jam, and tarts." Again, as discussed in earlier chapters, the "practical belief" among local harvesters is that the very act of picking itself substantially increases berry yields, so this might explain the ladies' preference for their repeated visits to the same site. The apparent wildness of this secret location hides its role as an intensified production field, and, perhaps more importantly, as a collective site for renewing social bonds among women who respect and admire each other in a context far removed from their daily household concerns.

There is a preferred berry, called the yellowberry or cloudberry (*Rubus chamaemorus*), which is sweeter, larger, and more rare than the blueberry, and it is usually eaten fresh because it bruises easily. Wild cranberries also take to freezing well; the latter berries are still edible on the bush throughout the winter and are dug out of the snow by people who remember where they grew back in summer. Pussy willow buds are also eaten like berries in the spring and provide a high vitamin C and zinc content.

What is called a blackberry up in the Far North is not the same fruit as the hairy bramble berry in the south: it is a smooth black berry, like a cranberry, from a low-lying bush and somewhat hard to spot. It is also known as crowberry (*Empetrum nigram*). If the local food preference rankings are any guide, it would seem that cloudberries have the highest nutritional value, followed by blueberries, followed by crowberries, and then cranberries, without forgetting what was said about the wide range of values within the same plant species at any one location.

As an illustration of this latter phenomenon that has been documented by researchers, we can look at another common, long-lasting northern fruit accessible from local terrains, the rose hip (*Rosa acicularis*), which I nibbled on in the company of my friends, secure in the knowledge that it is known to be much higher in vitamin C than other local berries.

"Better spit out those rose seeds or you'll get an itchy bum," Charlene said to me, laughing. It is actually fine hairs wrapping the pit of the fruit that cause the itching, an academic point if you have nibbled too far into the bittersweet fruit.

What is interesting about the rose hip is that it was studied scientifically in Britain during the war, because it was used then as an alternative domestic source of vitamin C when restricted shipping made imported citrus fruits unavailable. The rose hip's measured plant-to-plant content of vitamin C was found to range over a factor of ten, far more variable than domestic oranges or apples.

Everyone who harvests plant foods in the Mackenzie Delta has their special places and preferred seasons for picking "the best fruit." Local people attribute this random-seeming variation of potency to the individual plant's power, or to its elevated setting. As mentioned, I was directed by an experienced Gwich'in harvester to pick my year's supply of Labrador tea from the top of the highest hill near town in the first week of August, after the sun began setting again, and to freeze my harvest immediately. There must be a good reason for all these salutary precautions, but I cannot discover it (although I did pick my Labrador tea at the approach of sunset).

⋮ Across the Richardson Mountains, near the mouth of the Bluefish River, trapper Stephen Frost is admiring his wilderness garden, a ten-by-three-metre raised bed with potatoes, carrots, tomatoes, and onions growing very well indeed in the middle of an absolute pristine forest clearing. There are no deer (Virginia whitetail) this far north, so he has few concerns about pilfering except perhaps for rabbits, and his berm is unfenced. It is made of logs with a few planks, and the earth is simply scraped up to a height of forty-five centimetres and deposited in a heap from the surrounding forest and raked even with the twigs removed—"No special fertilizer, nothing," Stephen says, brushing off the soil from some potatoes and healthy yellow onions. "This valley land is extremely fertile. It is just the permafrost that keeps it locked up."

The proof of Stephen's commentary is in the boiled potato, which, served with butter and salt along with some caribou stew, is excellent, a meal unto its own, for it is the simple boiled potato that reveals the treasures of the earth's mineral nutrients more than any other dish from the home garden.

What is interesting about Stephen's cabin, and about James Itsi's cabin eighty kilometres away up the Porcupine River, is that the areas around both places are loaded with different kinds of berries coming ripe at the same time, as if they are contestants in an international beauty contest. Stephen Frost's acreage had the blueberries, crowberries, cranberries, and cloudberries—and another one I have not mentioned so far called a bearberry (*Arctostaphylos rubra*) because I personally find them rather sour and lacking the clear morning snap of cranberries.

James Itsi's acreage had a different mix of fruit, but it was also very profuse—one evening at dusk, James picked a large bowl of cranberries in less than ten minutes to accompany our dinner of caribou chops, but other kinds of berries were waiting in fat rafts behind the woodpile to be taken as well. I say this because there was another plant crop growing at these locations that made me think this whole profusion is not coincidental, and this is the so-called wild rhubarb (*Polygonum alaskanum*). At least, that is what Stephen Frost called it in his yard; I suspect it may have been the domestic species, *Rheum rhabarbarum*, in the same family, gone feral.

Stephen's father, Harold Frost, was an RCMP officer from Ontario who was sent to the remote Northwest Territories in the 1920s and was immediately let go when he married Stephen's Gwich'in mother, as was the official practice back then in a less liberal age than ours. Harold Frost became a successful trapper in the 1930s and often told his children of the amazing sights on the Ontario farm where he had grown up—the big black-and-white animals called Holstein milk cows, and the bright orange pulpy balls called pumpkins from which a hearty sweet pie could be made.

It is conceivable that the elder Frost was able to secure seeds and planted rhubarb by his cabin, as the fruit is both hardy and ready to eat early in the spring, so a good choice for a winter-driven locale. The common rural practice in eastern Canada at that date was to dip the raw stalk in sugar and give it to children as a treat. This tradition derived from Britain, where rhubarb growing has a special and ancient place in the lore and cottage gardens of country folk.

The word for wild rhubarb in Gwich'in is *ts'iiggyuu*, and the local textbook *Gwich'in Ethnobotany* gives recipes for puddings made with fish eggs and mashed wild rhubarb that further indicate its traditional use in these pemmican-style dishes. Like the domestic rhubarb, the wild version becomes tough and inedible after it goes to seed, so it must be harvested in a window of two weeks and frozen for future use, easy enough when the deep freezer sits a half-metre under your feet across the north.

At Bluefish Camp, Stephen Frost was pleased to show off his homemade cold box to us, a shallow pit dug into the iced soil covered with a wooden box about a metre wide. The temperature at the bottom where his packaged meat was stored is steady year-round at below freezing, perhaps -5°C. It must be remembered that deeper soil in this region does not get as cold in winter as shallow soil, where the air temperature might hover at -45°C.

His two local antagonists competing for this boxed store of natural bounty would be wolverines and bears, and Stephen mentioned that one effective trick to avoid the depredations of bears was to write them a foolscap note nailed to the front door, asking them nicely to desist: "Dear Mr. Bear: please leave my camp alone as I put a lot of hard work into it. It is my home, yours truly," etc.

A grizzly bear that had started coming around was persuaded to leave the Frost premises for good by this method, but Stephen had some doubts about wolverines, which are "harder to bargain with."

As it was, there was enough fruit in a few acres behind the Frost cabin that a guest picked a gallon of blueberries in an hour while I wandered about, sampling all the other varieties on offer. Again, the total berry yield, if fully picked, would be staggering. Stephen meanwhile had caught some foot-long grayling, casting little spinners with a rod "for amusement," and that made for a tasty lunch along with black tea with honey and fresh-baked bannock. Very satisfying.

The archeologists who found the old trade beads mentioned earlier also made careful note of wild rhubarb growing in association with some of the Mackenzie Delta habitation sites they had excavated, and it seems that this propensity of harvestable plants to grow in close proximity to human settlements speaks to an interim form of subsistence between wild gathering and dedicated planting, and whether these conditions for improved yields of certain species happen by design or accident, the design or accidents are slight, incremental, but sufficient to be noticeable.

My point is to consider what minimal effort might go into ameliorating growing conditions for such "natural" (low-effort) northern crops and calculate what is the average outcome in increased productivity. Logging and fire, with ashes being spread about, and the dumping of natural waste materials like fish bones, might all play a part in this apparently offhand process. But one can see from the unequal ratio of the limited amount of berries harvested, to the enormous and essentially limitless size of the available crop, that the allocation of labour is really always the paramount consideration.

It is not the food resources that are limited in the north; it is the limited quantum of human effort that must be carefully allocated among competing demands, and, as the ever-practical Stephen Frost showed us with his trout rod, one of these competing demands is personal entertainment. I am reminded by his angling action that day to include in this summary of Indigenous plant uses some fanciful but *socially useful* items, like toy whistles made from the stems of willows (*K'aii uzhuu*) and a ring hoop made of stripped willow that is floated downriver for a children's game.

The larger question today is about local cultural flexibility to the variability of climate. The history of the southern Dene speakers like the Navajo show us that it was possible for a hunting people to take up gardening before Contact, where it became feasible to do so as emigrants in their sunny new territory in New Mexico. What happens in an inter-mediate maritime coastal region like the Yukon River valley system if the mean weather fluctuates incrementally to the warmer side of the long-term climate chart? Do marginal opportunities for plant husbandry arise? How quickly and efficiently can local people respond to opportunities with new subsistence patterns? At what scalable points do the seemingly casual efforts at local gardening become full-blown wholesale efforts?

It does not seem to require a huge shift in consciousness or perspec-tive to begin pursuing a more intensive agricultural base if the changing climate encourages it, for the simple reason that northern people are, to varying degrees, already plant experts who have explored the uses of so many plants in their domain. The Gwich'in have been more than quick to take up new invasive species and add them to the traditional larder, such as this entry in *Gwich'in Ethnobotany* on the imported fireweed (*Epilobium augustifolium*) makes clear:

> As food, the pink flowers of the fireweed plant are edible and can be mixed in with jello and salads. In the spring, the new shoots can be cooked like asparagus, chopped and eaten as greens, or mixed in with salads. As a medicine the whole plant can be boiled and the liquid rubbed on the skin for rashes. A poultice is made from the leaves and applied to burns, bee stings, aches and swelling caused by arthritis.

The wide range of these identified Aboriginal uses can only have come into play since the main thoroughfare, the Dempster gravel road, was built in the 1970s, allowing such roadside plants to spread north. It raises the ques-tion of who and how such innovation proceeds, given the small population and the many competing demands for its day-to-day living needs since the cash economy took hold. Even if I am wrong on my dates and this plant is an older resident of the region (which its lack of a local name argues against), it begs the question: Who boils the plant, who tries it on their wounds, and who first puts it raw and sliced into their curious mouths?

It's one thing to have an inquisitive mind, to direct experiments on a trial-and-error basis, and another to be the brave one to bell a possibly fatal cat.

Again, one hears the resounding First Nations answer: *The plant told us what its uses are.* What level of intense awareness is predicated on that notion? Still, it is a different thing to sleep outside in a tent, whether canvas or caribou skin, surrounded by whispering plants that, like dogs, people, and the starry sky, take on a new aspect at night. Maybe they speak to us through our dreams and we wake up a little wiser, with entrepreneurial neural connections rewired by dawn.

Just to restate what may be obvious to many trekking readers, sleeping in a tent makes one aware that the forest is cyclically exhaling and inhaling over the course of the night. From midnight on, there are peaks of humidity and valleys of colder air that come and go as regular as a heartbeat, for the living forest breathes as one presence.

I once stayed with two companions in a Fort McPherson white canvas tent while visiting Stephen Frost and found the experience radically different from sleeping in a spruce log cabin in the same region. The ambient light from the moon and stars washes gently, hypnotically, over the tent walls in time with the swaying of the black trees, becoming fixed and still at certain moments as if anticipating a major announcement from Creation itself, and the feeling comes over you, dozing bodiless, open to suggestion, muffled with woolen Bay blankets, that a presence is out there, clarified by the sudden silence, bathed in awareness. Each night around 3:00 AM something wakes me, not a thing but an event—perhaps it is the respiratory end of the *vegetative* night, for there is a stillness in the air that was not there five minutes ago.

You reluctantly get up out of your warm bedroll, hoping you don't step on someone as you grope for the tent flap, and of course your companions are all blinking awake, too, for whatever it is that woke you up also woke them, and you poke your head into the unbelievably sharp air that smells nothing like the air of twilight (the pollens asleep, the pheromones are different, mushrooms and fungi broadcasting their wares, for, like animals, some plants become more active at night)—and you find the green luminescent aurora borealis crashing silently overhead, big as an undiscovered continent from a science fiction movie.

The white reindeer moss glows in patches around you, odd lumps of photo negative imagery everywhere you look, a living thing suddenly made prominent as if it, too, is coming awake, rousing itself from the dark patches of substrate. You recall that the sphagnum moss, the dark green moss, was once used to make moss houses and is still used today to insulate the chinks of log houses. It seems to be holding this whole little meadow together, binding it fast to the earth.

White moss and dark moss, light and shadow. Cold green astral fire above, sparking red campfire below. What a curious world this boreal forest is, unendingly thorough in its exploits, spreading itself deeper into one's imagination and reaching up for the stratosphere with uncountable fingers.

11 : King Bear

The polar bear that tried to attack me by floating
downstream with only its eyes showing above the waterline.

Sudden movement triggers the animal.

— PETER MIKIYUNGIAK

IN EARLY AUGUST, I took a Beechcraft
Turboprop to the hamlet of Arviat on the western shores of Hudson Bay. I had arranged to
stay with an Inuit hunter and guide named
Peter Mikiyungiak and his wife Mary.

Every day the three of us, Peter, his adopted
thirteen-year-old son Uli, and I, would get into
a small motorboat and head out into the sparkling waters of the bay. We would check the
family's nets for Arctic char and turbot and
chum salmon, make ourselves a shore lunch of
sweet black tea, raw fish, and fresh bannock
baked that morning by Mary, and, fortified by a
short nap, we would cruise all afternoon along
the coastal islands in search of big game.

Peter had a battered .30-30, and Uli his .22 rifle and a handmade harpoon. Sometimes their hunting partner Leo, a bearded younger man, joined us.

Late summer is a good time to be out on the land at the edge of the northern sea. The days are long and mild. The Bathurst caribou herd is beginning its annual fall migration to the coast, and whales and seals now appear in growing numbers in the shallow waters near shore. Molting snow geese run awkwardly over the tundra, chased by determined foxes and snowy owls; ravens croak and burble from creaky plywood rooftops. Cheerful villagers play nineteenth-century reels on their fiddles at night and Elders tell stories of heroic pluck and power.

Everyone was happy. Everything in Arviat seemed strangely familiar. My own ancestors, too, had not so long ago lived in remote villages, told tales of lucky men and resourceful women and powerful shamans, and strode across a sea of wild grass in search of their life's fortune. In fact, Peter looked a lot like my great-grandfather, a Cossack named Osyp Kupchenko, whose Tartar ancestry showed in his high cheekbones and jet-black eyes, and in his disposition for broad humour and long-distance travels.

When I returned from the Arctic, I wondered about all I had seen and heard: the huge polar bear that had brazenly circled our canvas tents on the tundra all night; the uncanny coincidences between the old story the shaman's daughter recounted and the killing of his first whale by young Uli; and especially the way a stark landscape of granite boulders and crimson mosses suddenly transformed itself into a living thing right before my eyes.

All you had to do was sit there, bathed in the crystal light of the seashore, listening to the Arctic terns wheeling overhead, thinking of absolutely nothing. And a Presence would unfold...

There was something powerful lurking below the surface of things, something at the core of the chanted folklore and the handmade bone charms and the ritual observances. As a boy I was warned by my Carpathian grandmother not to whistle in the kitchen or the Devil would enter.

I had watched as Uli gave his whale a drink of fresh water and then hand out every last piece of its butchered meat and blubber, the villagers arriving at the boat at dock with plastic shopping bags to relieve him of the guilt of taking the creature's life, transforming his bloody transgression into a selfless act for the communal good.

There was something dangerous out there, something common to both peoples, a shared vision of a dark power lying just outside the bounds of daily perception. It seemed to me this dark world was bound up in the figure of the shaman, who, like the stone *inukshuk*, always pointed to a world crushed and remade anew by forces too large for us to see with ordinary eyes. It was Angie Eetak's cryptic tale that opened my eyes to the truth; that we lived in two worlds, the world of life—and the world of death.

It is often the beginning of winter that sets a shaman's tale: the moment of truth, revealed by a sudden change in the weather. How was it that I happened to be here, out on the tundra, sitting by a driftwood fire and eating fried *muktuk* with black tea, when the weather changed? Even at the height of summer, a lone shadow lingers across the glowing Land.

But the sunlight, too. Forget the coming shadows of long night! Breathe in the blue skies of August! The joy of the tundra, endlessly unrolling its fusty red carpet of bloom-covered mosses just for you. Look at these tiny wildflowers—the yellow draba, purple saxifrage, and white cottongrass—each jewel-like petal more precious than the last. Trembling with anticipation as you bend to sniff them...

The people of Arviat love telling jokes. "He was firm as that slick brown seaweed," was a satirical line that drew more laughter that summer with repeated telling. I heard a lot of funny anecdotes, hunters recounting how they were squatting in a convenient depression in the tundra, trousers down at their ankles and their gun out of reach, when a bull caribou poked its nose over the hillock to see what rival was making those funny snorts.

But I never heard a funny story about polar bears. A poster put out by Arviat's Department of Environment cautions:

Minimize bear conflict at your camp! Choose safe campsites. Keep your children in sight.

Surrounded by treeless tundra and a vast inland sea, Arviat is a little vessel in a sea of light and darkness with white bears bobbing in and out of focus. The nearest other community is Churchill, twelve hours away by big motorboat on a good day. A community of white bears shares the immediate region, huge predators whose presence you must always keep uppermost in mind the precise moment you leave the house.

We saw four bears close at hand that first week; one was a nine-footer that watched us closely in return. Peter studied them in his binoculars and made a firm identification at a distance of three or four hundred metres, carefully noting their psychological disposition, as well as their likely trajectory across the tundra islands.

"Young male, maybe two years old. Hunting on his own now, no mother."

"That one has maybe eaten. Big meal, he's sleeping it off."

There are few places on earth where four-hundred-kilogram predators roam freely across your line of vision every day, and the psychic impact is terrific. You must always stick close to the person with the gun and watch the mottled rocks you are trekking through for signs of movement, terrible eyes blinking, or a twitching tail that you thought might have been a dry leaf.

On the weekend, Peter and Mary decided to go camping on the Maguse River. We got in the little boat and headed north along the coast after the tide rose, to give us plenty of bottom to navigate the rocky mouth of the river. A large raptor with a white head flew overhead as we entered the river; like us, it was headed upstream in search of game.

"Snowy owl," Mary said uncertainly.

"American bald eagle," Peter said. "We never used to get them here before."

Moose and red foxes were also becoming more common on the western shores of Hudson Bay. And, for some unknown reason, so were polar bears. It was Peter's hunting partner Leo who recounted how a local hunter had killed three polar bears with an ax on the Maguse River, the same river whose effervescent rapids we were now negotiating in a seven-metre motorboat at high tide.

This hunter had just shot seven caribou, Leo said. He was reaching for his butchering ax when three white bears appeared out of the sea mist, snorted, and hunched down to dine on his kill, a dozen paces from where he stood still. Leo said,

He tried to get to his gun on the ATV, *but the mother bear got up and followed him. So he stopped, and froze. Sudden movement triggers the animal. He waited. She and her grown cubs began eating the caribou again; he slowly moved sideways, and got his ax. He tested the handle to see how long his swing was, exactly. He knew he had only one chance. He had to hit the bear in the centre of the skull. Hard as he could. He slowly drew the ax far back to increase its momentum, and smash! The bear collapsed! He hit it three times to make sure it was dead, then he killed the other two. He rode to his father's camp and told everyone to come, he had lots of meat!—seven caribou and three bears!*

Leo's summary sounded like the title of a manic Broadway musical. As if reading my mind, Peter began singing a country and western tune, pitching his voice high over the low staccato of the 50 HP Honda kicker.

The afternoon sun magnified the emerald shoreline into sharp relief. We saw rafts of molting snow geese, running comically over the tundra in tight, self-protective team formations; eider ducks, croaking like old card players; predatory jaegers, wheeling in pure liquid sky; and a snowy owl, sitting on an ice age rock like a Viking earl on his throne, satiated after feasting on an endless supply of voles.

But no caribou in sight.

Peter scanned the horizon while thirteen-year-old Uli stood at the bow, probing for hidden rocks with a paddle.

"They are late this year," Peter said. He began humming an old Johnny Cash hit.

"Maybe that new mine at Baker Lake is scaring them away," Mary offered.

"*I walk the line,*" Peter crooned the chorus, as if wooing the herd to come out of the distant eskers.

The Inuit depend on caribou for their subsistence. As one resident said, "It's not killing, it's our *food*." But the annual migration of the regional Bathurst herd is affected by many random factors including weather, always unpredictable on the maritime coast.

We continued upriver for about ten kilometres, set out a gill net for char, and made camp on a grassy point. Their little bear dog trotted at my heel as I went for a hike, scaring up a hare that was improbably purple. The evening was bright and clear and endless; our white canvas tents glowed like jewels in the Arctic twilight. Mary proudly unpacked a thick white fur and handed it to me for a sleeping mat.

"Polar bear hide," Mary said. "You won't feel all our sharp rocks in your back."

"Oh, there's one," Peter said, not taking the heavy binoculars from his eyes. "*Nanook*."

"Where?" I said groggily, thinking about sleep after a long day out on the water.

"He's walking along that esker. Just over the other one that's lying down."

"The *other* one?"

I could see the first bear without the glasses, a white sugar cube dissolving in the brown tea of the distance and then reappearing as he passed masses of land.

"That round thing like a big white boulder?"

"Yes," Peter said, handing me the glasses. "And the third one, left, a mile from them."

I could see the second bear but not the third. Maybe I didn't want to see it.

"How far away are they, exactly?"

"Maybe four miles. But that one, he's coming closer."

Peter picked up the twelve-gauge and began loading it with flares; it was wrapped in scarred duct tape, but it looked serviceable enough.

"With bears you got to fire three times, so they get the message: *We got plenty of ammunition and we use it.*"

Bang!...*KAPOW*!

The flares exploded over the tundra like Victoria Day on a low budget. The bear glanced our way and seemed to veer off, but otherwise he kept ambling toward the river. Peter now turned his attention north and let out a delighted whoop.

"There they are. *Tuktu*! Four...five of them, a big bull in the middle! And behind them...at least a hundred more! *Tuktu*, caribou! See? Right against the horizon."

"How far are they? All I see is smoke or something."

"Ten miles. They are headed into the wind; they could be on the coast by tomorrow afternoon." Peter was happy. "Look at that big bull!"

I could see only indistinct movement, even with the big binoculars. A *suggestion* of movement, actually. I handed the binoculars back to him and glanced behind us. The little white things that were actually almost three metres long with claws were still out there, moving in the twilight.

"Well, we got three polar bears. All we need are Leo's seven caribou now."

Peter grinned; even their little dog ran around in tight circles, smelling the coming action. I went to my tent, hunted down a dozen giant Arctic mosquitoes that had sneaked in with me, and fell into beautiful sleep on the bear rug, feeling strangely immune to attack despite the periodic gunfire blasting through the night.

At about 3:00 AM I woke to a barrage of rifle bullets.

Beeeow! Beeeow!

I knew Peter was now firing live rounds *at* the bear—under a magnificent display of northern lights, as he told me later that morning—but I did not care. I went right back to sleep. I had sufficient beauty, adventure, wisdom, and purity for one day. I could feel such things slipping away with every .30-30 round exploding like giddy fire in the darkness of my growing rapture.

When I finally got up the next morning, Mary had made fresh bannock and tea in her tent, while Peter snored away in the full light of an Arctic dawn.

"He only got fifteen minutes of sleep all night," she explained. "*That bear* kept coming."

The morning sun was as warm as my steaming bannock. Warm enough that I felt like a fresh swim. I took my tea to the riverbank and squatted, testing the temperature and looking for a smooth patch of sand to launch myself over the slippery underwater boulders.

I heard a snort.

The oddest thing. A white head, floating by itself.

A big white head floating downriver. Fifteen metres away. The head turned its black eyes to me as I stood there, thinking logically that there *had to be* a polar bear's body attached to that head that was so visibly enjoying its free-floating trip.

"*Nanook!*" I shouted over my shoulder as I edged slowly backwards, remembering Leo's story.

"*Nanook! Nanook!*" No confusing English words from me! "*Nanook!*"

Peter appeared in an instant, rifle in hand, took aim and let off a volley of live shots that exploded about three paces from the swimming bear.

Beeeow! Beeeow! Beeeow...Beeeow!

The polar bear scrambled to the far shore and ran upriver, dodging big stones but sure-footed and rocketing fast as hell over the rough terrain despite his bulk.

"*That bear*, he keeps coming!" Peter shook his head. "How did you notice him first? You see him or you *hear* him?"

"*First I* heard him snort; *then* I looked up. I don't know where he came from because I was looking right at the river there that whole time."

"When they snort they are getting ready to charge," Peter said quietly.

"Good to know," I said, remembering my tea getting cold on the shore. "We going back to the coast this morning?"

"We have to wait for high tide at three this afternoon, to get out of the shallow mouth of the river. Maybe we fish this morning. Try and catch some grayling for lunch."

The family's hunt cabin was another thirty kilometres upriver, on the shore of meandering Maguse Lake, but we were going only as far as the Forks, a favoured fishing site. About five kilometres later, we turned a big bend—and there was *that bear* again, suddenly a few metres from our boat, swimming alongside us, he was going upriver, too!

"Hello, *nanook!*" Peter shouted a warm greeting, playful and serious at the same time. Now we had caught *him* out.

I took some close-up photos—as the bear seemed to sheepishly admit, showing us a good set of implacable big teeth—then we veered off and spent the morning anchored in midstream, casting for grayling. Nothing. The pretty little trout proved scarcer than bears. After a lunch of sizzling *muktuk* grilled on an open fire and black sweetened tea, we headed back to the coast.

Peter fretted about the change in the wind direction.

"Maybe they went inland again? Going into the breeze blowing the *other* way?"

He needn't have worried. When we reached Austin Island, there were four caribou on the beach, running madly back and forth to escape the flies.

The fifth caribou, last of the same group Peter had spotted the day before, was walking behind us on the sandy point. We landed our boat and crept silently ashore. Peter dropped the young bull at 250 paces with a single shot.

We dragged it to the water's edge to the boat, so we could skin it on a deserted rocky islet far out in the bay.

I had been here long enough now that I didn't have to ask why.

"That bear," I said to Peter Mikiyungiak over breakfast when we returned to Arviat town. "That bear tried to trick me!—Floating down the river! With just his head showing, like a piece of white driftwood!"

"That one, yes he kept coming!" Peter shook his head. "Full of tricks. In winter they put their white paw in front of their big black nose to hide it."

He chewed on the hot bannock Mary had just baked over the twig fire, both of them watching their little bear dog scout the living room for interesting trouble.

"They're so good at hiding you have to watch out always. Be careful no matter where you are. Lots of stories of hunters who only see one strange little movement that isn't right. A funny little swishing back and forth. Is it a little leaf blowing in the wind?—No, it's a little tail belonging to a big bear, he is getting excited as the hunter is getting closer.—*That* one? You're lucky he snorted! No tail wagging to give him away in the water!"

The Arctic world is a mighty trick, full of tricks. Several times when Peter, Uli, and I were out in the bay exploring the gravel islands around Arviat, they pointed out large stones that had been labouriously moved, one atop another, including a massive granite boulder on Sentry Island that had been carried sixty paces uphill by "a shaman in the old days."

These constructions are not *inuksuit* ("copies of a person") in the usual sense, as there is no attempt made to suggest a human form. Rather, they appear to be demonstrations of a particular kind of artistic prolificacy. And while the big boulder might have been rolled into its chosen position in winter, over an icy bridge made expressly for that purpose, still, it's a massive undertaking. Examples of this cryptic exercise pepper the coastal landscape for many kilometres around the village. These moved rocks jump out at you from the background if you know *how* to look, turning the tundra into a Zen garden, only vaster, wilder, and stretching to the horizon.

The local explanation given is that such repositioned stones serve as reminders of specific historical incidents, so that the scale, colour, and type of rock and its emplacement constitute a kind of mnemonic language understood by those who have learned to read them. The roughness of the shaman's boulder on Sentry Island suggests (to me, at least) the monumentality of the private incident commemorated—perhaps an epic tale, if not a full novel of life and death.

It's not just shamans who ponder and move rocks. Hunters like Peter and his hunting partner Leo spend so many minutes carefully choosing the perfect beach stone as a suitable weight for their daily fishnets that some of its ideal sinker qualities are subtle indeed.

Either way, a stone metalanguage is generated over the tundra every day, a living arrangement that expresses the full range of human experience, ranging from idle, playful experiments to full sagas, using all the tricks of narrative, starting firstly with the trick of remembering itself.

Arctic visitors will spy tiny pebble pyramids everywhere, heaped in hard-to-reach crevices, and much larger rock structures, balancing delicately as flowers set in a granite vase of opposed counterforces. The trekker receives the inescapable impression that the Inuit landscape is actually a detailed, three-dimensional map of the local collective mind, its sensory workings and emotional history, a chessboard with a thousand pieces, a walk-in physiognomy of local society's otherwise obscured historical face.

Each new addition to the manufactured tundra bears an intimate relationship to the whole, adding a detail to the ongoing conjecture in the round but never complete nor authoritative in itself. Finally, this stone map appears supplemental to the oral tales, wall hangings, bone carvings, and, now, written texts—with each of these other formats following their own sovereign rules of composition and articulation.

In other words, the physical world of the humanized tundra is wholly *incidental.*

There is another stone that has been transported without artistic alteration from its past life in tents and igloos into contemporary houses, and this is the *kaugavik.* It is a smooth rock used with a hammer for breaking dry caribou meat, and so on, into edible portions.

One day, we visited the Arviat home of Phillip Kigusiutnak. The celebrated dogsled musher offered us dry caribou meat he had broken on the smooth *kaugavik* in his otherwise modern kitchen. It is the same *kaugavik* he owned as a married man before his wife passed away, smoothed by decades of daily use. This is the thing that "breaks other things," and turns the land's produce into comestibles. Phillip wanted to show us his dogs out in the pound by the ocean. They were massively powerful, blue-eyed, malamute huskies, endlessly courageous dogs that had taken him crackling across the frozen sea ice for seven decades of hunting trips, as well as four-hundred-kilometre Hudson Bay Quest races from Churchill, MB, to Arviat.

Through Peter acting as interpreter, I asked this legendary man what advice he had for long and good life: "Always keep your breath warm," Phillip replied without hesitation, pointing to his chest. The surface meaning was clear: protect the vital functions. A glance at Peter's awed face showed that Phillip may have meant something deeper. About connecting to a vast power, an inner spirit perhaps.

Later that day, with a high wind rocking the bay and confining us to shore, Mary brought out her collection of traditional Inuit items made by family members. There was a walrus ivory *iggaak*, or snow goggle, which Peter put on his eyes to show how it worked; a *qulliq*, a charred stone oil lamp that every young woman had to maintain before she could marry; four handmade snow knives, two of which had been painstakingly carved from bone; a long rope made from a single caribou hide cut concentrically; two small handmade woman's *ulus*; a collection of seal-scapula scrapers and other bone tools, which I will return to shortly; and that curious skill game called *ayagaq*, consisting of a bone minispear the size of a pencil tied with a hide cord about thirty centimetres long to an elaborately carved ivory target in the shape of a Zeppelin the size of a male organ (average).

You were obliged to swing the target in the air and stab one of the holes drilled in it with the little spear. It is a variant of the "target game" called *nuglugartuq* in the Western Arctic, where three hunters stab, in turn, at a suspended carved target, and it is a mainstay of hunters' gambling practices throughout the Arctic, although it transpired that Mary was the best player that day.

Very simple game, very good training for hand-eye coordination— and very frustrating for the non-Inuit in the group who provided the real amusement that afternoon, especially when he voiced the opinion it was more of a trick he hadn't figured out rather than a skill he hadn't mastered. I eventually got it in, but "the seal had already bled to death and sank into the sea!" according to my grinning onlookers.

It was the family's collection of unmodified Arctic animal bones that really caught my attention, and, if they didn't trigger the sudden shift in my consciousness that afternoon, they certainly marked my passage into another realm of awareness, which the eating of raw char, the days spent drifting effortlessly across the crystal clear waters of the bay, the primeval sense of danger occasioned by omnipresent polar bears, and the sense of being immersed in the present minute had already precipitated to the tipping point.

As it was probably designed for, the deft concentration required for the "target game" brought my mental focus down from the scale of about a minute to the scale of 1/60 of a second, perhaps even less. This recalibrated time sense changes the overall look of things outside. I can scarcely believe I would have seen anything but a bunch of bones in my former state of diluted urbanite concentration, and now I was noticing details upon details everywhere: first, those large boulders on the tundra that had been repositioned for some human but obscure purposes, and now these bones, which seemed to have a life of their own that went far beyond their traditional function as hide scrapers, awls, and burins. Were they more alive from long use?

Western culture lacks the language to describe this idea of an object suddenly coming alive. There is the Greek word *aura* (which means "breath"); the anthropological term *mana* from the South Pacific, referring to the residual power of objects and select people; and the Japanese *wabi*, the quality of the familiar in an item of long and treasured domestic use.

None of these words adequately capture what I saw in the Mikiyungiak family collection that day, nor in a subsequent exhibit of sea-animal bones from the Eastern Arctic by an Inuit artist. The latter collection of bones was artfully chosen and arranged on a simple stock poster to represent whole animals of other species—loons, whales, polar bears, char salmon, etc.—mimicking them all without any alteration. The stark white shapes showed at a single glance the universal correspondences of all living things and their renewal in the frozen moment of bone. I would call this attitude *winter consciousness*, the basal current that flashes between concrete things at their most primal level, with this living, universal, electric current remaining at one with, and inseparable from, human consciousness.

The nearest word to it I found in the Arctic lexicon is *qunbuq*, the Alaskan concept signifying "the glint of light on sea-ice boundary in the horizon," which is always a welcoming sight for hunters looking for game out on the frozen sea. *Qunbuq* marks the transitional fracture between landed certainty and the potential of the unknown.

It is the shaman who specializes in exploring this fracture, and to whom we must turn now for enlightenment on its mysterious power.

12 : Powers of the Fantastic

Fifteen thousand years after the first Paleo-Americans hunted here, the region remains as wild as ever (wolf track, Bluefish River, YT).

IT IS OFTEN the beginning of winter that sets the shaman's tale...and one afternoon in Arviat, with the northwest wind running high on the bay, and the hunters confined to their kitchens, snacking on fried tidbits of caribou and cleaning their motors, I went looking for the beginning of winter and found it in a local shaman's story.

"Blind Boy and the Loons" is an oral story belonging to Angie Eetak of Arviat. It was first written down in Inuktitut in the 1980s when Mrs. Eetak began promoting her work as a professional visual artist. She translated it into the English version given here. Angie's father was Keeyuyovtik, a well-known shaman who died in 1956 just before Angie was born.

Significantly, or so it seemed to me, when Mary and Peter Mikiyungiak introduced me to the artist, they did so by telephone and told me to make my own way to the Eetak house.

I set out on a windy, overcast day through the tumble puzzle of unmarked plywood and frame buildings that make up Arviat town. Two thousand people and hardly anyone around. I had to ask directions twice from lone passers-by to find the place; it was a smart-looking cottage at the edge of town, surrounded by wild sedges, and immaculate.

The two households could not have been more different. Peter and Mary's house in Arviat was casual and rambling; a steady stream of relatives showed up on dusty ATVs to gossip and watch TV. The two jars of Niagara honey I brought as visitor's gifts disappeared in a day, thoroughly enjoyed by carefree children who decorated their pet bear dog with watercolours and drove their own quads like speed demons.

When I knocked on the door and entered the spotless Eetak house, I found myself in a living fairy tale. The walls of the living room were decorated with Angie's dazzling mosaics of polished sea stones and mussel shells. They showed dancing figures walking on their hands and a blue sea alive with mythic creatures. The sun was a skin drum that made life dance to its rhythmic beat.

More—and as a visual artist myself, I was aware of the utter sophistication of it—Angie Eetak had painstakingly collected artifacts of early industrial culture, like 1940s cookie tins and branded flour sacks, and artfully displayed them on her kitchen walls, not as nostalgic collectibles but as an authentic expression of a lost culture that she has endowed with a second life. She had collected and displayed urban artifacts!

To comprehend the material life of one's society is to command it. Angie's late father was a "white" shaman as opposed to a "black" shaman, practising beneficent magic like spiritual healing in the 1950s, a time when people still wore sealskin parkas and used large dog teams; and many Inuit needed healing in the post-war era as tuberculosis (TB), polio, influenza, and other maladies ravaged Arctic communities.

In her journal, Angie recounts how she was confined as a child for treatment for TB in Ninette, MB, getting "eighteen pills and two full needles" every day. There's an image that needs nothing more than a few words to conjure up: a beady-eyed nurse in a starched blue pinafore; a large needle waiting on a metal tray; a five-year-old away from her parents for months; and an institutional clock on the wall saying it's that time again.

Their family story is an account of the shamanic healing quest in which supernatural vision and holy blindness are key motifs in advancing the narrative of a battle between the individual and the materialized thing-ness of the world. This is a special kind of vision, that allows the traveller to usurp the claims of chronological Time, to travel freely across the boundary of life and death, and to witness the frozen and unyielding subterranean psychic landscape that exists below daily experience. The "moment of truth" converts the story into pure action that is at once earthbound and transcendent, freeing us from the realm of thing-ness—always the hero's sacred task.

The world of the Inuit is a world of active *things*: the *ayagaq*, a game of manual dexterity played with a pointed stick, string, and a wooden ball with small holes in it; *pookak*, good snow for making igloos; *aviagianik*, a fork in a river, where one part of the river goes another way; and the *kaugavik* stone that sits in the middle of the traditional hunter's kitchen floor and is used to break up dried meat, a thing that breaks other things, and so turns the land's produce into comestibles; and, finally, the shaman stones, which remind the traveller that the Arctic world is a mighty trick, full of other tricks.

The repositioned rocks, examples of which pepper the coastal landscape for many kilometres around the village, deftly succeed in turning a stone map that appears only supplemental to the power of the oral tales, wall hangings, bone carvings, and, now, the written texts—with each of these items following their own sovereign rules of composition and articulation.

Similarly, the Eetak version of the widespread Arctic tale "Blind Boy and the Loons" is peopled with concrete things: tents, ropes, tusks, *amatiuks*. Their common object is the elucidation of power, power of a special kind. It is the power that the material world exerts over the living relationships of a world in which humans are central but not exclusive actors, sharing the stage with other creatures, great and small, and with each set of players given its exclusive props. The material world is setting and actor both.

We see such power openly if briefly manifesting itself in luck, both bad and good, in accident and coincidence, and in the unusual and the unexpected. Some people are more gifted than others in detecting its presence, and, as artists, musicians, and shamans, interpret and negotiate its irruptions into our plane of existence. The fantastic is the glimpse of this *other* face of reality—its antithetical, fluid, perverse, contrapuntal, magnified, and inverted face. The thing in "Blind Boy and the Loons" is the mother who will not feed her son:

> *Once there was a family who lived in the northern tundra...One day the father got ill and died. The boy was old enough to hunt for his sister and mother, they always have plenty of country food. They would share to the other that needed country food.*
>
> *One day the mother so tired of doing all the work, so she planned to make her son blind. Early one morning his mother took a blubber oil and rub it on her son's eyes. The boy awoke and notice that he's blind. The family got deficiencies of country food. The mother would give him the filthiest water and unfortunate food.*

"*Unfortunate food*," yes! Who is she, this monstrous mother?

The Eetak family story is, on one level, an allegory of winter. Nature, who gave us our very being, inexplicably turns hostile and withdraws; she must be somehow coaxed or tricked into becoming provident once more. At the same time, as Angie Eetak confirms, the "mother" is really a *step*mother.

"This is a mother-in-law story, yes!" Angie enthusiastically agreed, "It is like Cinderella, even though my mother never heard of the fairy tale like this Cinderella one. It is the same! The stepmother wanted the boy to go blind as she was tired of doing all the work for him when he brought food home from his hunting."

Now the mother plays a second trick on the blind boy: she denies his value and efficacy as a Hunter:

One morning the mother heard a polar bear growling outside the igloo. She woke up the boy and gave the boy an arrow and let the boy strike it to the polar bear.

Even though the blind boy knew he killed the polar bear. The mother told a lie that the blind boy missed the polar bear and the arrow was struck to the caribou skin. The blind boy wondered why his mother lied.

The mother kept on giving the usual filthiest water and unfortunate food. But his sister would still give him the polar bear meat to eat.

Contemporary Inuit eat polar bear meat, but it is not their preferred country food. "For me, it's below ring seal, caribou, Arctic char, walrus, and *muktuk*," is how one Arviat hunter ranked it. The bear is a fellow predator, above all, a dangerous competitor that sometimes must be killed, especially when it makes a habit of seeking out children who cannot fight back. Bear meat is a survival food.

The stepmother has (privately) rejected the natural order of the world—denied the truth that life requires life for its sustenance, denied the necessity of sharing, mutuality, taking responsibility for others—she has secretly committed to preferring the individual mask that disguises her cold aggrandizement over the social existence of a revolving community of men and animals.

Significantly, the boy's blindness is not his own, it does not originate with him or from some internalized moral lapse. It is her blindness, projected onto him—a product of their unequal domestic relationship that has become grossly exaggerated. She is nature *as a* stepmother, *pretending to be* a real mother but inimical. The thing has entered the social order at its weakest juncture, in late winter when Inuit people are hungry and vulnerable. And it takes over the parent and child relationship, turning it from a living truth into a bare object, a burden. The thing is always opportunistic.

In late winter, the sea ice becomes soft and risky for travellers, and game is distant. Even polar bears grow more aggressive and dangerous from starvation. Trickery and mimicry is the meaning of this world, the hidden face of this world.

Mimicry and trickery are constant ploys in the everyday life of the Arctic hunter. Hunters in the field use thier quarry's perceptions against itself, and so do wild animals as well. One Arviat hunter placed the skull and antlers of a bull caribou on his head and strolled over the top of eskers with it, hoping to fool its living relatives into coming over for a closer look. During the spring goose hunts, the Inuit hunting parties position them-selves in relation to lines of stone heaps that act as scarecrows, diverting the flying birds toward their guns, while calling them down with imita-tion feeding honks to visit with their clever decoys made of dry grass.

Not to be outdone, the local polar bear is aware that his nose is black and therefore stands out against the snow. So he approaches his quarry while covering the offending organ with his white paw. The Inuit hunters who recounted this technique saw it, they said, from the perspective of its intended prey. Prowling bears like the one in "Blind Boy and the Loons" are always testing humans and keenly learning new tricks.

By 2010, after only a few seasons of use, the huge predators had fig-ured out how to crash through the electric guard fences erected by field scientists around their Hudson Bay base camps. The male bear that had been trying to invade our Maguse River campsite resorted to the almost-successful strategy of concealing his vast bulk into what seemed to be a piece of white driftwood, bobbing closer and closer—until the driftwood snorted. The plot of "Blind Boy and the Loons" hangs on just such trickery:

The blind boy asked his mother if he could tie the harpoon rope to his mother's waist. His mother didn't mind so he tied the rope to the mother's waist.

Characteristically, as soon as the mother is ensnared, the boy stops hear-ing her voice: "And her voice started to fade." The mother's internalized voice has finally exited his life: she is objectified, the thing goes back to thing-ness.

Arviat hunters, like other coastal Inuit, use floats attached to the harpoon head by a length of rope; in former days these floats were made of seal bladders. Angie Eetak's wall hanging, the wool-felt *nivingagunguaq*, shows the mother floating in the ambient sea in the second of seven descending scenes, suggesting her return to nature as a fetus attached by an umbilical cord to the whale. The artist has used the mother's long braided hair to repeat the motif of the thrown harpoon and gives us five visual declensions of action flowing into the narwhal's male tusk: harpoon, rope, umbilical cord, woman's hair braid, male tusk.

Again, these separate things are really the same thing, seen from different perspectives and only looking separate according to the tricks of seasonal light. Seasons colour and shape us, disguising an essential unity. Our strength lies in taking action out of the deceptive realm of relative time, both literally—throwing the harpoon to where the whale is headed, not where it is, and adjusting the aim for the water's distortion of light—and ritually—learning to be patient and letting things ensnare themselves in the constellation of purposeful action.

The truth is a trick. One recalls those misguided attempts of Contact explorers to debunk the magical actions of Aboriginal shamans by spotting the palmed objects they "removed" from the patient's body. Such eighteenth-century Enlightenment rationalists were unaware that it is precisely in such deft and disguised actions that their own society survives or fails. It has not changed with industrial society.

We learn from earliest childhood that adroit tricks will save us, whether it is overhearing Rumpelstiltskin's secret name or stealing fire from the Greek gods or playing the rigged financial games of global banking. Tricks rely on secrecy and timing. Sleight of hand, unsurprisingly, derives from *sly* and the German *schlagfertig*, "quick-witted," and literally means "ready to strike."

The lucky hunter deals out the card he needs to win. He uses "animal sight" to see down to the truth of things amid their secret relations.

Animal sight appears to be directly related to the power of winter consciousness. Winter consciousness is the awareness of time's moments, strung like beads waiting to be plucked, opportunistically and without hesitation.

Arctic loons are harbingers of spring, because they dive into the newly opening sea to hunt in the murk for fish, and so are not dependent on new grass like the geese. The loons have the power to see what lies beneath the surface, and they help the blind boy restore the natural order. They are his spirit helpers, allowing him to travel across the boundary of life and see the thing in its unnatural state of desolation and lifeless immobility:

> The loons said, "We are going to dive you under the sea, and, if you are getting short of breath, please shake your body and we will rise you to the land."

The loons take the boy diving under the sea three times. The first time, his restored sight is just blurry, but the second time produces significant changes in his perception:

> The loons asked the blind boy how his sight is? The blind boy answered, "I can see the smallest rock on the other side of the shore."
> The loons notice he has animal sight, and the loons thought it's not good for his humans' vision, so they wanted for the last time to take the blind boy, so the loons dove the blind boy once more.

The tidal waters of Hudson Bay in the many narrow coves about Arviat are exceptionally clear to a depth of about four or five metres—clear for a northern sea, of course. On calmer days, one can see every detail of its mottled bottom, an unending plain composed of smooth boulders and gravel bars, a wavering moonscape that, apart from a few strands of slick algae, is eerily empty and yet somehow also mysteriously full of Arctic char and sea mammals. It is the common practice of boating hunters to look down at these wavering rocks and shifting depths through the course of the day, from pure interest's sake as much as for navigational need.

So, on one hand, this *other shore* exists as a real place of speculation and daily rediscovery, a place on the other side of the living waters, both as the bedrock located vertically below the sea and also horizontally as the horizon of collective knowledge, i.e., Hudson Bay's other shore, one thousand kilometres east.

It should be recognized, however, that the boy's newfound ability to see the "smallest rock on the other side of the shore" may also refer to a metaphysical conundrum, a place where mental concepts and physical things all merge into one: What is the smallest rock? The smallest rock on the far shore in this esoteric sense only exists as an object of the shaman's special vision; in the ordinary sensory world of human, as opposed to animal, vision, this thing remains invisible—only its effects can be seen, as distinct entities when they come into play on *this* side of reality.

After his third dive, the boy recognizes that the loons are "kayak size," giant spirit helpers. His sight is restored to human sight, and the first thing he does is feed the giant birds a few fishes they politely ask him for, in recompense for their help—once more, the sharing of food restores the surviving community of people and animals.

Toward the end of my visit, we went out on the bay on Peter's boat again, this time to Sentry Island, a place charged with historical significance for local people. It had been a good place for hunting walrus in former times; now Peter was on the lookout for seals, and, of course, whales.

Uli sat in the bow of the boat, sharpening his handmade steel harpoon tip. Scanning the sea for signs of life, Peter said they would take the larger bearded seal, which provided hide for a strong rope in addition to meat, and the much smaller ring seal, which provided clothing material. They would not take the ranger seal or the harp seal.

"The ranger seal never gets fat," Peter explained. "They always sink to the bottom when you shoot it. It moves pretty quick, like a cat, so we don't eat it, myself, or my family."

We cruised for an hour. Another polar bear appeared on the shore of the island, and in the absence of visible game in the water, my companions enjoyed watching it, making careful note of its condition and actions and storing that information in their encyclopedic memory banks. Peter had not only been able to tell me how many caribou he shot the year earlier (twenty-nine) but exactly where and precisely how he had shot every one. Their recollections are so precise because their survival depends on informational accuracy.

We were alone in the sea by Eskimo Point when Peter saw the herd of white beluga. He counted them in a few seconds.

There were sixteen of the massive sea mammals, about four hundred metres away. Uli cleared the rope of the harpoon around his feet and took up his rifle.

"Got your camera ready?" Peter asked me breathlessly.

"Yes, yes." I set the mode dial to high-speed action.

We closed the distance, two hundred metres, one hundred metres. Peter kept a steady course toward the middle of the pack and then at fifty metres he accelerated the motor and roared toward a big male, as the other whales scattered to the left and right of us.

"Okay, Uli!"

Uli fired his first shot.

"—Too low, Uli! Too low!"

His father saw where the bullet had gone; it had missed the animal completely.

The whale descended under our boat, leaving a trail of large bubbles in its wake. A flash of blue-white: the seven-hundred-kilogram animal was running right below us.

Seabirds cried above. The two hunters stood up in the rocking boat, scanning the nearby waters. Silence of the windless sea. Uli leaned at the prow, his harpoon at hand.

The August light danced on the waves and played its endless sea tricks on us. But we stared beyond the surface of the simmering water, arms at ready, and waited breathlessly for the moment of truth we knew must come.

FALL

13 : Thinking like a River

The author's camp on the tundra, Maguse River, Eastern Arctic.

*I could tell you many things about these dots
I made on this piece of paper.*

— MARY MIKIYUNGIAK

I HAVE BEEN LAX in my use of various Aboriginal terms, incorporating words like *qunbuq* from the Iñupiaq of Alaska's North Slope when talking about Inuit hunters far across the continent in the Eastern Arctic. Worse, I have probably got a lot of my informant details wrong, despite my two digital recorders and copious field notes scribbled down in the canvas tents and sitting on rocks facing one river or another. *Details*, there's the rub.

Did Peter Mikiyungiak really say he killed twenty-nine caribou last season? Or was it my misshapen 28, or even a 39 with a dead mosquito smudged over my penned note? Maybe I didn't even hear him right in the first place, over the sound of rushing water...

I could blame the clouds of black flies and the Arctic's other natural distractions for my laxity, not the least of which is a visceral awareness of the ebb and flow of imminent bodily peril throughout all its variable seasons. Arctic summer, ha!

Freezing fog to 25°C and back down again overnight in early August without warning. Twenty hours of sunlight still beating down in midsummer, yes, if that gray oceanic cloudbank doesn't sit like freshly mined pure lead overhead, applying its funny acoustics to distant noises. There is also the constant basal fear of starvation or fatal injury, which comes to the fore despite your cheery excitement at being off the grid at last. It seems like scaredy-cat nonsense, for do you not have two full boxes of canned goods in the boat? And are you not travelling only eighty kilometres from the nearest hamlet?

So what could possibly go wrong? Meanwhile, your body is asking you—calculating survival machine that it is—exactly how long will those two boxes of groceries last two people, or three people plus a dog, at the edge of the known world, unless a fat fish is caught or the timely innocent caribou appears in the sights of a loaded and well-aimed rifle?

But these are more blackflies, these sharp little concerns, not the real problem. The real problem is that you are posturing: you have no intimate knowledge of this bush or that one. You are abysmally ignorant about your circumstances, despite your sharp hunting knife and waterproof boots. And more, you have no intimate knowledge of intimate knowledge itself, the kind of hypervigilant attention for detail that Indigenous people like Peter or Mary appear to maintain as naturally as breathing.

I asked Mary one morning to draw me a map of their hunting territory, and she did, posting it on the refrigerator and looking at it intently as if investing it with all the historical information stored in her head like someone downloading a chunk of data into a computer drive.

"Here it is. I could tell you many things about these dots I made on this piece of paper."

We got to talking about events that happened in her father's time, based on the pencilled dot marking the location of his old hunt camp, so this new map of hers was layered with both her personal memory and her family's oral history, an X-ray of a living, ongoing, extended relationship.

Similarly, Peter kept two chest freezers in the back room of the house; one was filled with frozen fish and the other—as a precaution against home burglary—was filled with his battered collection of rifles and shotguns. Certainly, Peter could have told me a novel's worth of detail from the hunting history of each of his half-dozen guns, but what was even more telling was that when he reached into the other freezer to pull out a char, he stared at the fish with the same intensity his wife had displayed studying her map.

Peter was studying the two-kilogram char, dredging up the memory of the circumstances of its catch, and, as I believe, also monitoring his own mental facility to recall such distant events when and as needed. *Metacognition*, it's called, and some behavioural scientists such as Leonard Mlodinow think it is one of the few universal mental operations privileged to the whole human race.

I have seen this same acute cognitive ability in farmers for their fields and their tools: their working knowledge of the peculiarities of uneven terrain extends to the individual characteristics of trees and rocks and the tilt of the fields, memories of past storms and their impact on crops, and the whole mysterious interplay of groundwater with different soil types that is constantly changing and mostly unseen. Does the *uniform* exist anywhere except as an admission of ignorance?

It's the same, as I have previously mentioned in another context, with my Gwich'in fly fisher friend Earl, who uses his large and growing collection of hand-tied flies in a delicate interplay with grayling trout to map out their preferential feeding pattern, one that takes into account dozens of local environmental factors (creek outflows, water temperature, hatch times of prey insects, sunlight intensity, etc.), discovering along the way how exactly moose-hair flies work better than deer-hair flies as an element in the practice, and, more, speculating as to why this should be so—which is the great cognitive leap, to find the structure that all these factual, field-derived details point to, in their occasional, but always thrilling, unison of thought and action.

Moose-hair trout flies! The beautiful and strange delivered truths of an insect decoy! Aristotle must have been a fly fisherman, too, for he initiated the whole testable-results inquiry.

Buried by manufactured detail, most of it spurious, we residents of industrialized society seem to have lost this cognitive ability, a loss sometimes signified by the irritated marvel we feel when confronted by the abilities of the eidetic wunderkind who tells us exactly what suit we wore to a wedding three years ago, contradicting our attempts at spinning a slick personal narrative of social mastery with the implacable assertion of our less-than-satisfactory fashion choices. Details are, in fact, despite Mies van der Rohe's architectural aphorism to the contrary, the enemy of moving forward in a society that produces them so effortlessly. Don't these prolix details crowd out *real thinking?*—Not quite so deterministically, apparently.

Real thinking has a real purpose and that is to allow the thinker to survive his or her environment, whatever environment that might be, and however quickly it might change from day to day or season to season. It has even been suggested by radical sociologists and contemplative religions like nondualist Buddhism that the thinker is only the stream of thoughts themselves—we are merely the thinkee, the physical housing for the flowing thoughts over which we exercise little if any control. I am posing these questions, because I am concerned with an issue that I hope is pretty clear in its general outlines at this point in the book—whether Aboriginal people, confronted as they are daily by the consequential, by the what-it-really-is realities of their every waking moment in the bush, see an aspect of existence that we city folk can only glimpse at from time to time.

Or, more pointedly, do northern people see what-it-is more directly and fully because they often do not have the motley luxury of being able to dream their days away in symbolic pursuits, i.e., reading texts and watching flickering images on a screen that the grid delivers to us, along with its uniform food, air conditioning, and chlorinated water? This book is not about how to trap rabbits in winter and catch fish in summer. It is about the type of thinking that goes in to how to trap a rabbit, which means how to think like a rabbit thinks, how to think like a caribou thinks, how to think like a spruce tree thinks, how to think like a rising river thinks, and how to think like winter thinks.

Our urban environment has two aspects that militate against its residents' need to retain such localized details as Aboriginal hunters do routinely: (1) the global city is a fast-changing *conflicted* environment because of its role as a field for contesting technological advances, and it is increasingly irreconcilable with any coherent narrative structure; and (2) much of this urban landscape is deliberately made trivial and disruptively incomplete by ubiquitous advertising and industrial signage.

Grounding in any transcendent values (if even possible today) must be fabricated internally rather than sought in external details of this patchwork social system by its navigators, we put-upon individuals sentenced to postmodernism for a crime we don't remember committing. And now we are obliged to deride or discount our very existence to the extent it is implicated in this constant stream of dubious commercial fiction.

Each day, we globalites knowingly encounter a swarm of digital mosquitoes, importuning lies masquerading as *valuable offers*, microdramas decisively resolved in the feverish pitch to *buy now*, and this inveigling arcade demands a certain proactive aggressive-critical-editorial stance from us. This stance locates itself on a spectrum ranging from ironic detachment, through deconstructive activism, to outright public rage. We see it every day in coworkers joined in the fray over our diminishing store of public truth, whether they want to engage it (as serious questioners of the system) or not (frivolous beneficiaries of the system). Let me say this: it's a relief being bitten by blackflies who only take blood, not your spirit.

The need to detach oneself from the fictive realms of modern society is a paramount survival tactic. The steady rise of what is called "critical thinking" from the time of the French Revolution merely tracks and anticipates the parallel rise of manufactured commercial and bureaucratic publicity, dating from the original print era bursting with its agitator's pamphlets, snake-oil handbills, lithographed girlie posters for semitoxic wormwood spirits, political lampoon cartoons, and thunderous war-seeking broadsheets, to our own not-so-soft era dominated by corporately branded public buildings, spin doctors, and Internet cookies.

The famous experiment of the German criminal psychologist Franz von Liszt in 1902 showed that a roomful of law students exposed to a scripted scene enacted with live actors and a blank-loaded pistol made up to 80 per cent mistakes of memory in fourteen categories of questions. The legal bookworms couldn't remember what they just saw happen in front of their faces. They even got the 9mm *bang!* wrong. Most of them couldn't count to *one*. How did Christopher McCandless die alone in the Alaska bush? He misread a botany text.

The unreliability of the Western mass audiences was described at length by Walter Lippmann in his book *Public Opinion*, and was cited by him as the reason for creating an elite cadre of public relations experts to guide these twentieth-century fusty masses to a consensus policy set by the executive branch. But these were industrialized *print readers* we are talking about; and it is probable that early rote training in group class-room reading produces more malleable and gullible audiences than ordinary illiteracy or private tutoring does, as Jacques Ellul argued at length in his seminal work, *Propaganda: The Formation of Men's Attitudes*.

Ellul points out that twentieth-century dictators all promoted class-room reading as a way of making their populace more susceptible to the media the regime controlled, and they ferociously attacked their peas-ants (who knew their land and the concrete facts of a stoutly rooted life) for being backward and even counter-revolutionary. Wasn't this precisely the same impulse behind our own Indian residential school program in Canada? To reform children's attitudes in a wholesale and receptive man-ner for the convenience of the state and its policy programs?

One day, out on the Arctic sea—let me tell you about this one ordinary day that stands out in my mind more than any other, despite its lack of singular adventure or specific incident—we were motoring on our way to

Sentry Island, rifles at the ready, watching for seals along the way. Coming around a rocky point, Leo and Peter happily spotted the large ocean freighter that periodically delivers supplies to Inuit communities in the summer months, and Peter immediately turned the little boat around and headed for the prow of the anchored ship.

As we slowly circled the *Camilla Desgagnés* from bow to stern, both men keenly watched the sailors' modest work activities aboard the vessel. My companions might have been inventorizing the ship's entire cargo as well, for it was stacked on deck in wooden crates with stamped lists of contents, all awaiting transshipment by smaller vessels to shore.

"It still looks in good shape," Peter said proprietorially, staring up at the steel hull with a practiced eye. "Should last a few more years, *Camilla*."

We approached to within twenty paces of the ship. Looking up at its high steel walls from my wood bench, I experienced an anxious moment of vertigo. We rolled over the choppy waters of the bay, the silent ship enigmatic and unreal in its vast improbability—and here it was again, the monumentality of the inaccessible civilization that every summer kept re-enacting its original appearance in the New World back in 1492.

I turned and concentrated on the Inuit hunters studying the supply ship, two men in a tiny craft confronting an ironclad colossus from the south, and I realized that hunters hunt for global information as much as they do local game. What information the men took away from this encounter, and what use they eventually put it to, I can only guess.

Either way, the commercial instinct is still alive and well in a people who traded with the Vikings soon after the latter landed on the eastern shores of North America around A D 980. A close reading of Inuit stories like "Blind Boy and the Loons" shows that traditional art and storytelling can, and do, enter the global commercial domain just as quickly and purposefully as my two hunter friends did, who (loaded rifles sitting on the bottom boards) circled the freighter as they might have circled a giant bowhead whale in years past, wondering whether they were up to the task of doing anything more profitable than merely admiring its vast bulk.

In Angie Eetak's case, she has successfully fostered the transmission of a traditional oral account into a written story into a commercial, multiple-edition artwork. At the same time, she has examined the inner processes of commodification as closely and with as much attention as any other aspect of the full landscape of Inuit subsistence opportunity.

The theme of "Blind Boy and the Loons" is not only widespread in the Inuit-Inuvialuit-Iñupiaq cultural region but seems to have migrated into Gwich'in folklore as well. This process of assimilation and appropriation is ongoing and makes a mockery of academic efforts to find the original or pure or authoritative version of such tales, precisely because they have no social value unless they can be traded, commodified, appropriated, and even *stolen*—as the stories themselves explicitly explain.

Such stories both reflect an awareness of closely bargained exchanges and are themselves exchanged as articles of commercial value. In "Blind Boy," for example, the hero's ordinary sight for things is exchanged for a privileged sight of the thing. The blind and wounded are especially esteemed in these supernatural tales. Their lack of an important sensory organ or physical ability confers on them *qunbuq*, winter consciousness.

Obliged to substitute hearing for seeing (in the winter dark), and immune to the external prettiness of surface detail, the blind necessarily avoid the contagions of flesh (as do monks and nuns), and, by heroically entering a different sensory realm through the evident-to-all cracks in consciousness, they bring us direct news of a shifting subterranean reality.

The blind boy hears a polar bear growling and shoots it with an arrow. The growling can be interpreted cosmically, as the roaring sound of the breakup of sea ice in spring, a process the blind boy's arrow ritually initiates. In league with the loons, he has defeated Stepmother Winter and brought Sister Spring back to life, a seasonal theme emphasized by the caribou skin his arrow allegedly hits, anticipating the skin tent the Inuit move to when Mother Summer arrives again.

Angie Eetak's depiction of the blind boy in her felt wall hanging, the *nivingagunguaq*, emphasizes his large eyes, connecting them to the rising spring sun through repetition of the red rays set around both. Moreover, what he first sees with his restored sight is the unexpurgated raw fact of generative sex—his mother, bound bodily to the whale she soon merges with—a whale he has "harpooned" but not killed.

How is this a shamanic tale? It is a sleight-of-hand transformation carried on before the audience's eyes. The trick we get to see is the role of the artist herself in the public act of transforming a traditional oral tale into a fixed and special type of metacommodity, an invoked thing that both openly acknowledges and promotes its role as a privileged marketplace item (valuable Inuit art), while simultaneously commenting on the irony of its paradoxical status as "the only thing that opposes demonic thingness." It might feature the *Camilla Desgagnés* as the evil stepmother in some future version of this story. Angie's *nivingagunguaq* itself is an arrow loosed back upon the global art marketplace.

Recently, I had a long discussion with a twenty-one-year-old West Coast First Nations artist who told me about the difficulties in bridging the rigidly maintained official gap between Aboriginal art as a commoditized, if sacrosanct, genre and high art as a purposeful exploration of modern existence, freed from ethnicity and the dictatorship of the local:

> *I got to UBC [University of British Columbia] on a full three-year scholarship but just over a year into it I'm already thinking of quitting. The problem is I do a sculptural piece like this one, [showing a red-and-silver sculpture of a male head on his cellphone] where I used red Coke cans, cut and flattened to make tin feathers for his War Bonnet, and the professor refuses to mark the project—or even to consider it as a submission on the theme of appropriation.*
>
> *He says he won't mark it because it's "First Nations art," not something I created. Which I did! It's very frustrating. Meanwhile back at home on the Island [Vancouver Island], I am working on carving a traditional cedar totem pole, with other people from my mother's clan. That's Aboriginal art! It's social, sacred, really traditional, right?—Who gets to say what Aboriginal art really is?*

For that matter, who gets to say what high art is, too? Who controls the discourse? Provocatively, the classical scholar Jane Ellen Harrison broke this conventional mold almost a century ago in 1922, when she controversially opined that the Titan generational war myths actually express shamanic rituals of the Early Bronze Age.

Harrison's larger implication is that the claimed rationalist basis of high Greek culture is an eighteenth-century invention of early industrial society, which promoted the exceptionalism of Greek democratic history (in contrast to the alleged ritual mania of the monolithic Egyptians, for example) as a reflection of its own claims to historical transcendence, an attitude that imbues the prototypical modern European philosophies of Hegel, Marx, Nietzsche, Tolstoy, Jung, and de Chardin (as well as post-Darwinian millenarian sect founders like Mary Baker Eddy of Christian Science) with the colouration of a high Western destiny. High art is exceptionalism for white walls.

If the Greeks really sustained their civilization through shamanic rituals for 1,500 years, what does that say about the real prospects of our industrial civilization, which is only just over 550 years old (since Gutenberg, c. 1460) and has been racked by cataclysmic sectarian wars since the first printed page of the Bible came off the blocks?

⋮ The metacognitive issues of a gold key to the questions of cultural appropriation and cultural transmission and cultural loss and cultural revival and cultural change (the holy grail of a social metascience) are things we all have to negotiate in global society, which uproots people and their cherished ideas much faster and farther than before.

We worry publicly, of course, that the Elders' store of traditional knowledge ("TK," as it is called in anthropologists' terminology) will be lost, and lost for good; fifty-thousand-plus years in the making, come to naught in a geological instant called the twenty-first century.

But what if it is *relational* knowledge generated by the Land itself, rather than, let's say, a *proprietary* knowledge, such as the technical know-how involved in formulating a lasting type of lime plasterwork once used by master builders in ancient Uzbekistan, the chemical secret of which has eluded modern archeologists since? Does one have to be Aboriginal to comprehend the land in a uniquely intimate way?

I would have thought so, marginally, at any rate, because we are talking about an accumulating relationship forged in intimate experience over millennial time, in which both parties affect each other directly, the people and the living land cocreating something new in their ancient partnership.

But then there is the plain historical fact of the Quebec voyageurs like Étienne Brûlé (b. 1591), who very quickly learned the language of the Wendat (Hurons); adopted their customs; worked as a guide and interpreter for anyone who could pay the price of his services, including French Jesuit missionaries and the English army; and ended skinned, killed, and eaten by his former Wendat allies in the village of Toanche on Georgian Bay, ON, in 1633. Colonial authorities such as Samuel Champlain were abhorred by Brûlé's cultural promiscuity ("vicious and a womanizer") and shocked at the ease of his transition from petty bourgeois French immigrant into *"un sauvage"* in ochre-painted buckskins.

The boundary-breaking explorer Brûlé was the forerunner of the voyageurs who peopled the north along with the Metis nation, estimated today at 400,000 self-identified constituents whose existence makes the prospect of identifying a distinctively Aboriginal ontology daunting—if it ever existed in the first place.

The sophistication of Inuit artists like Angie Eetak requires me to revisit the original premise of my book research. Where is the core of the Aboriginal knowledge of the bush to be found? Is it in the accumulated experience of their Land, or is it embedded in the discrete forms and productions of specialists such as artists, storytellers, and shamans, whose metacognition of their own society's deep structures ought to be taken as serious philosophical inquiry that examines this very question itself, as well other critical questions?

Would these Inuit specialists agree with Immanuel Kant's position that "objects must conform to our cognition," or would they side with empiricist David Hume that our necessary skepticism can only be relieved by reliable but typically intermittent observation of the "necessary connexion to be taken into consideration" whenever we observe things that appear to be causally linked? Observation, in other words, is hardly foolproof in Hume's opinion, but it is absolutely required nevertheless to make sense of the world.

I attempted to leave Arviat on a foggy cold August morning three times in a row before the prop plane was finally able to lift off, flying low to avoid the thick pea-soup ceiling at two hundred metres, the ruddy-faced young pilots flying by sight without instruments, cheerily at home with the unmarked blue waves and mossy red planet below, grounded in the air as it were. The scattered islands of Hudson Bay appeared like pieces of a puzzle left behind by an absent-minded giant child who took the box of instructions home with him.

The sea fog lifted at one point, revealing a brilliant speckled ocean of magenta and turquoise bounded by foamy little whitecaps; then it closed up again, reminding us that reality dances and never stands still just because we need to examine it. As we broke in and out of the frisky clouds, I recalled a trip I had taken with Cree hunters some years earlier in northern Quebec, and how we had foraged for several days, trekking the land without a specific end in mid-May after the other guide with the food pack went missing.

Our main Cree guide was not worried; it was late spring and we had fishing line, matches, knives, etc. We watched like good students as he showed us a surprising variety of local and easily procured foodstuffs from the mixed northern Quebec hardwood forest—tiny wild strawberries, cattail stems that contained starch, bullfrog tadpoles that offered some needed fat, and a pleasant and stimulating tea made from pipsissewa (*Chimaphila umbellate*), a sort of low-growing wintergreen. Pipsissewa is a *mycoheterotroph*, meaning that gets part of its nutrients from fungi in the soil.

Who knows what was really in the tea one makes of it, in other words.

Pipsissewa tea has the advantage of suppressing the appetite, a good thing since our efforts to catch fish met without success for three days running. I estimate we were getting 500–600 calories a day in picked tid-bits, which a meatier item like a roasted rabbit or baked trout would have supplemented into the 1,500-calorie range. We also learned that every-thing in the environment gives off a certain *glow* when you are fasting, whether by choice or not. More, we learned that stillness does not exist in the bush. Everything shifts, stretches, suggests. Late at night, curled up by a small twig fire for warmth at the edge of our spruce lean-tos, I waited for the forest around us to quiet down. It never did. No wind was blowing, but everything moved and rustled determinedly on its own.

After hours of drifting in and out of sleep, with strained senses attuned to unusual effects, and possibly approaching creatures of the night, I heard an unseen bird perched in a nearby tree. The pitch of its plaintive two-note call kept changing. Or did it? Maybe the repeated cry was chang-ing *my* pitch? The bird seemed to be drawing nearer as the hours rolled by. Was it a bird? Focusing on the cry, which grew bolder and larger, I began to lose the certainty of things, of position and perspective. Now it was inside me, and the hypnotic cry took over the shapeless shadows. I fell into its unseen lair beyond midnight.

A few weeks later, I flew west to Old Crow in Yukon, returning to the hamlet in time for the annual migration of the Porcupine caribou herd. This time I had different questions to ask.

Harder ones, this time.

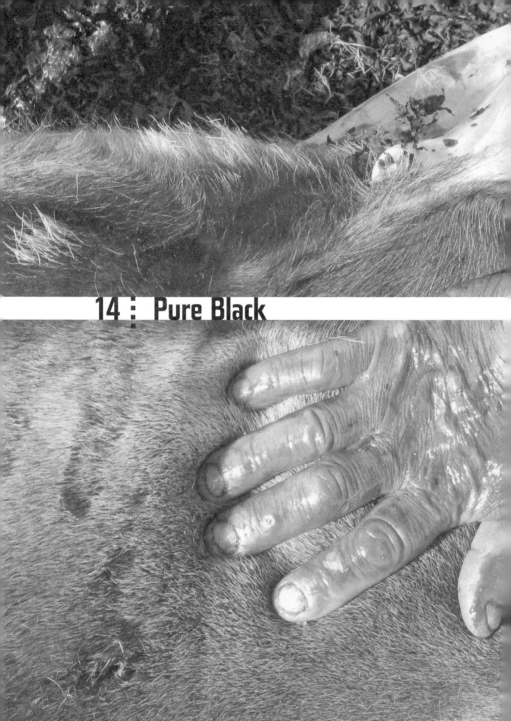

14 : Pure Black

Peter Mikiyungiak with his first caribou of the great fall migration.

Grizzly hears us when we talk about him.

—LAWRENCE DEAN CHARLIE

IT WAS LATE AUGUST when I flew into Old Crow, YT, in an unheated propeller plane that reminded its passengers that the Arctic fall chill was already well in the air before we landed on a gravel runway, cut from a thick forest of yellow birches and black spruces. The little airport had glass cases containing examples of local art for sale.

A few of the more striking pictures belonged to a Vuntut Gwich'in visual artist Lawrence Dean Charlie, who used black, red, and white inks to dramatic effect. Wondering how the visual arts might differ as between immediate neighbours, Gwich'in and Inuit/Inuvialuit, with ideas encountered from Angie Eetak's work percolating through my mind, I looked him up.

211

A handsome and serious man in his thirties, Lawrence invited me into his spare but light-filled modern cabin in the east side of Old Crow hamlet. It was clear that an artist lived there: a battered desk with paints and brushes, works-in-progress pinned to the walls, and a large fresco of a Gwich'in warrior surrounded by a flock of ravens sketched directly on the plywood panelling. As we watched the teakettle boil, I asked him about the utility of Gwich'in art in the bush. How did artwork serve a hunting people?

"Our art all comes from making practical things we need to survive in the bush," Lawrence replied. "It's how we make our snowshoes, toboggans from moose hide, birch bark canoes."

There is a taciturn, otherworldly, and almost monastic attitude to people who spend a great deal of time in the quiet but always rustling boreal forest, patiently observing the unending variability of its natural phenomena, and Lawrence, for one, maintained this reflective attitude indoors. He began our discussion by sorting through the mix of items on his desk, considering which ones might have the most relevance to my stated research interest.

There were three different cultural items that we ended up discussing in detail, each more amazing than the last: an old mythic family story in its original transcribed form; a series of related pen-and-ink artworks of recently painted ravens; and a necklace of grizzly bear claws.

The "Chit ta ho khei" Manuscript

The papers on Lawrence's desk included a family history and handwritten versions in English of various Vuntut Gwich'in myths and cycle stories. As described earlier, in 2009 Lawrence discovered his late grandfather had left him a sheaf of a half-dozen mythic accounts, handwritten and typed, much of it on lined yellow notepaper and translated into serviceable English, set down some years before his death in 2008. One of these tales, simply entitled "Chit ta ho khei," a variant spelling of Atachookaii (as mentioned earlier, also spelled Ch'ataiiyuukaih), is the primal Vuntut Gwich'in folk hero whose peripatetic hunting adventures transform the fierce Northwest wilderness into the land of the men. Chit ta ho khei performs this task using just his natural wiles and a thin willow stick to kill a collection of man-eating giant predators: Eagle, Bear, She-Otter, Mosquito, and Dog Salmon. The Charlie family's version of Chit ta ho khei's exploits is told in six typed pages of concentrated action and begins straight away without introduction:

CHIT TA HO KHEI

This man he fix all the bad animal that animal eating human. The first thing he started make bow and arrow. He ask for where he could get spruce gum and person tell him where he could get spruce gum where spruce gum were always boiling when he got there he push down with his hand and stop so he take some and then he ask where he could get feather. Man tell him on top of bluff where eagle nest that eagle also eat man...

Lawrence Charlie pointed out that spruce gum is medicinal, traditionally used as a practical and easily available antiseptic for cuts, so it offers a cure for the bloody wounds the great hero suffers in discovering its secrets from Wolverine. This is Lawrence's oral account of that section of the Chit ta ho khei myth, told from memory:

Chit ta ho khei travelled up and down the rivers and killed giant animals that were killing people. Lots of people were killed. He killed Wolverine and chased his two young ones and chased them up this tree. He was trying to get them down so he could kill them.

They made a deal with him that they would share medicine with him in exchange for their life. So he agreed and they came down and shared with him the spruce gum, pitch...You can eat it, it's good for your stomach and you can also put it on your cut so it will suck out the poison from you.

The highly useful spruce gum is invariably linked with stories about Wolverine, and the wolverine is, in actuality, a particularly tenacious and solitary predator. Some Vuntut Gwich'in hunters go so far as to say a wolverine will always bring you bad luck, even if you merely see its tracks. It is the creature's abject solitariness, coupled with its voracious single-minded appetite, that draws the attention of the numerous myths to its troubled relations with human society: even the feared grizzly bear is sometimes sociable, and can be seen occasionally in family groups fishing for salmon or feasting peaceably on a downed moose.

Lawrence Charlie could not say how old his family's version of the Chit ta ho khei story is, but there is no reason to think it is not ultimately hundreds of years old if not thousands, because the events it enumerates are related to the prehistoric arrival of the Gwich'in to their homeland, an area stretching from Yukon and Alaska into the Northwest Territories that is roughly contiguous with the migratory range of their principal prey, the boreal caribou (*Rangifer tarandus caribou*).

Linguistically related nations like the Dogrib, Dene, and Hare live to the south and east. The unrelated Inuvialuit, who arrived in the Canadian Arctic much later, perhaps as late as the eleventh century AD, historically lived in the treeless tundra and concentrated on hunting sea mammals, as well as the migratory barren ground caribou. They began making forays into Gwich'in territory in late pre-Contact times, according to both oral traditions, seeking lumber, flint, ochre, and caribou.

The "Chit ta ho khei" manuscript does not mention internecine warfare directly, but it strongly hints at it: the six-page account ends with two antagonists, Chit ta ho khei and Giant Fish Man, both in the guise of giant fish, competing over a historic-named watershed.

From somewhere on the coast he started to come over the divide to Crow River but he hit Johnson Creek which Indians call Attri njik. That mean Bark Creek because Chit-ta ho khui [sic] make birchbark canoe when he hit the creek. He throw birch bark and spruce tree bark in creek. He want to know which one would float but birch bark was floating on top of water while that spruce bark was just about sunk....From there he started down river and when he was close to New Rampart he knew somebody is there.

Was another giant name is Tshe Choh [i.e., probably Shii Cho in contem-
porary spelling, meaning Giant Dog Salmon, Oncorhynchus keta].

He was sitting on the beach watch of fish he got big fish spear. So Chit
ta ho khui land this side where Tshi Cho [sic] wouldn't see him. From
there he left all his gear and canoe so he turn into big jack fish and then
he went down river other side or across the river where this man sitting so
he wouldn't know. From below this man he started up stream so this guy
could try and kill him.

And that is how the "Chit ta ho khei" manuscript ends: with the hero
seeking to dispose of an enemy armed with a spear by swimming underwater in the guise of a prey fish himself. This might represent an incident
of small-scale fighting over salmon fishing grounds, as these encounters
were still common with the Inuvialuit in early historical times.

The manuscript reveals two things about the Gwich'in understanding
of their earliest history: that there was indeed a historical entry into this
post-glacial land by their ancestors, and that this entry was a hugely difficult and dangerous enterprise requiring great cunning and skill to carry
out. Reminiscent of Hercules and his club, and Samson and his jawbone
of the ass, the Gwich'in hero Chit ta ho khei uses a sharp willow stick to
domesticate the wilderness that threatens men at every turn. After dispos-
ing of Eagle, top predator of the sky, he goes after She-Otter, top predator
of the region's rivers:

And then go down Mackenzie [River] and run into female otter. She stay
there when people pass her. She treating people nice and she take them for
her husband and while her husband sleep with her, she kill man that way.
That way she lives on that, and even tan man skin.

When Chit ta kho khui [sic] get there, mouse was stay with otter. When
Chit Ta ho khui come in, otter started feed him while that mouse kept say-
ing man pemmigan [pemmican] so Chit ta ho khui pretend he eat it but he
put it inside his coat, never eat it. She started giving Chit ta ho khui water.
Chit ta ho khui tell her I never drink river water, just creek water. He tell

her I see creek other side the bend, so otter start go for water where Chit ta
ho khui mean.

While that, mouse tell Chit ta ho khui everything what otter do to
people and she eat man. That why she so nice to [them] when she see
somebody. So mouse give Chit ta ho khui some food, give him root pemmi-
gan. He eat that and he take off while otter not return yet with water. This
is in Mackenzie delta. He try to go away so he paddle till late round noon.
And Chit ta ho khui kill beaver. He started camp he skin beaver, throw
beaverskin and he went to bed. While he was sleeping otter get there while
he go to bed before he put long willow in hot ashes so when he woke up
otter was sleeping other side of fire. She show he[r] inness that way Chit
ta ho khui could do something to her. But when Chit ta ho khui get up that
beaver skin was tan already was hang up on a pole. So Chit ta ho khui
take that willow and he stick in her inness. Stick go right through her and
kill her.

When she dead mink come out of her mouth and Chit ta ho khui put
charcoal all over mink. That why mink is black. And then weasel come out
of her inness. Chit ta ho khui hit end of tail that's why weasel got black tip
on his tail. That's end of otter. And that beaver skin was turn raw again.
From there he start off again.

From somewhere on the coast he started come over the divide to Crow
River.

Chit ta ho khei re-enacts the First Great Hunt in each of the five realms—
sky, river, land, air, and, finally, the open water by the sea—and identifies
the relationships and dangers of Gwich'in culture and nature. First, the
hero becomes a predator's predator, killing eagles, bears, and otters—the
three kings of the air, land, and freshwater realms, as noted. King Eagle,
King Bear, Queen Otter. Three royals and a despoiler, Wolverine, whom he
must bargain with rather than destroy because the wolverine is a trickster
like himself. Then Chit ta ho khei becomes a game animal himself, whom
Tshii Choh, Giant Mosquito, relentlessly pursues through the forest.

A King Fly! The fourth king, the whole animal kingdom is covered: bird, fish, animal, insect!

The hero now plays with the whole notion of trapping in a passage that would be incomprehensible to a person not familiar with northern trapping culture. Chit ta ho khei realizes that he cannot elude the needle-nosed monster forever. When Giant Mosquito sets a rawhide snare for him, Chit ta ho khei uses his enemy's own canoe to set it off. The single-minded monster thinks the hero has turned into a canoe—in other words, that he has become, or is, a *thing*. Giant Mosquito is so intent on his own bloodthirsty efforts, on the workings of his own device, a snare, that he cannot help but confuse the means for the end, the game for the game animal itself. He cannot see that his quarry Chit ta ho khei is still hiding in the willows, waiting for him to starve to death. Means, techniques, two-way snares, of themselves they are nothing. They can trick *us*, too.

It is the killing of the She-Otter that provides the climax for the Charlie family's version of the Gwich'in tale, for the giant predators are now all reduced in size to the little mink and the smaller weasel, who exit the dead otter's mouth and vagina, respectively, while a skinned beaver is simultaneously restored from tanned back to raw, converted to human trading needs from animal carnivore needs. The killed She-Otter is not really "dead," as she continues to spawn water animals: she is dead as a man-eating predator. Again:

She show her inness that way Chit ta ho khui [sic] could do something to her...So Chit ta ho khui take that willow and he stick in her inness. Stick go right through her and kill her.

By rejecting her sexual advances, Chit ta ho khei refuses to generate more monsters. In killing She-Otter, he domesticates sex itself, substituting a charred (i.e., cooked) willow stick for his penis, for, like the male member, the willow, on which so much of traditional Gwich'in material culture depends, keeps springing to life after it is used up—cut or burnt in forest fires. The willow twig also represents the beneficent side of fecund nature—usable, reliable, resilient, pliant to men's needs.

As we saw previously, in Chapter 8: Willow Flats, the fact that the willow shrub can reproduce asexually pits it as the logical opposite of She-Otter's wantonly needy vagina. The remorseless biological hunger that underlies both sex and food is contained and overcome. Chit ta ho khei uses the willow's charcoal tip to paint the mink black, and then he applies the leftover bit to blacken the weasel's tail, marking his pioneer triumph with an artist's signature touch. This might be read as Chit ta ho khei triumphing over nature as the first Gwich'in artist.

The Raven Drawings

Like the Gwich'in hero, Old Crow artist Lawrence Dean Charlie also uses black ink for his animal art. Blackness is a prominent feature of the Gwich'in regional landscape, an almost pure black owing to the special qualities of northern continental light. One sees pure black as an *interruptive* element in the constant presence of ravens, as a transitional element in the moving shadows of the spruce forest, and as a fixed element of the mud of the riverbed.

To defeat Giant Mosquito, Chit ta ho khei covers his naked body with river mud, pretending to be a lifeless chunk of waste, detritus, or worse, not breaking out of character even when Mosquito sticks his hand up the hero's anus to test his resolve: "Smell like man. How come he never even smile?"

Chit ta ho khei is the first Gwich'in Actor, as well as first Artist, making himself into a black artwork then carrying out the silent role of "Pure Black" to its successful conclusion.

The influence of this boreal landscape is deep and abiding on the psyche of its inhabitants. Lawrence Dean Charlie credits his unique graphic designs to a sudden inspiration that "just pops" into his head, a form of communication from the elemental forces governing nature, and perhaps mediated to some degree by inner voices of counsel belonging to his forebears. The artist has decorated the plywood walls of his Old Crow cabin with images of a powerful Gwich'in hunter surrounded by six flapping crows, using the suggestive curves of the wood grain to emphasize the subjugation of life to powers that bend and shape our reality. And, as he says, he prefers to use pure black ink for its primal starkness:

I use black ink with a little red ink for circles in the eyes. There's a man named Willow Man, K'aiheenjik, he was a giant, he killed his own people, so he didn't want to do that, so he committed suicide by jumping over the cliff in Bear Cave Mountain. They believed that red ochre was his blood, they began painting their tools and weapons with red ochre. I use red now because that's what they used in the old days, red ochre.

A feature of Lawrence's ink-drawing art compositions consists of reverse imagery and symmetrical doubling, such as *Black Crow White Crow*. One might suppose that the cracked lines around the two ravens are artistically rough abstractions, perhaps representing lines of spiritual power, but if we examine the contemporaneous photograph I took of wolf tracks in dried, cracked mud near the Bluefish River, we could argue that Lawrence has also faithfully rendered a plain geological fact of the local landscape and skillfully applied it to his design. That he seems to have incorporated natural cracks in his drawings, and ensured that the ravens flying around the shaman on his wall drawing are also pierced with irregular absences, suggests an ongoing thematic concern with the duality of formal presence versus unpredictable absence.

Lawrence Dean Charlie draws the founding animal figures like Raven and Wolverine by using parallel sets of holes to signify, for want of a better term, their conditional existence in human consciousness, absences highlighting their otherworldly effervescence and utter self-possession.

As discussed in previous chapters, northern boreal animals are extremely wary of humans and are highly adroit at camouflage and concealment. Few local creatures of the spruce forest allow themselves to be seen by humans for more than a second or two. Even mergansers and other small ducks fly off at a boat's slow approach. Divisiveness, doubling, duplicity, and darkness figure in the Gwich'in cosmos as much as clear truth and plain talk. Random and dual apparitions play out against a vast backdrop of monumental stillness.

The Porcupine River runs pure silver, an elemental quickening as seen from the height of the Crow Mountain plateau overlooking the hamlet where I am writing out my notes. I have hiked here alone, eager to bask in the late September sunshine. From a certain elevation the duality of the Land resolves itself into a blue grandeur that goes on and on and on. Below me lies an embodiment of various kinds of dual social truths. The Gwich'in divide themselves into two exogamous clans, Crow and Wolf: Crow must marry Wolf. Up here there is a steady alpine breeze, and no compulsion. Rollicking sky, flowing firmament. I am not alone, however. There is something moving through the scrub, a fox. It sees me and keeps coming without pause. What kind of fox is this? Not a red fox, not an Arctic fox. A cross fox? It has a dark red body and a black heavy tail, black oversized ears. It keeps coming toward me and I think I will take out my hunting knife from my backpack, but before I do, the strange fox veers off and skips into the clutch of jubilant buttercups and disappears.

I am relieved, but I take out my skinning knife in any event, stop thinking about art, and think about rabies and spirit signs instead. I finish the transcription in my rented cabin back in town. I was glad of the rare animal's disruption but left mute as to a zoological explanation. I make a mug of black tea, add powdered "nondairy whitener" to it, and hold the steaming drink close to my face as I muse over the little mystery. Another day spent negotiating rocks and water, strange things and unknown energies. Not the first time, either.

I was hiking along the gravel Dempster Highway one morning when a sweaty jogger approached me and breathlessly warned there was a cougar up the road. Dubious, I took out my camera and proceeded with chills-in-the-back caution. Soon enough, a large animal raced across the road and into the bushes; it also raced across my pixels, leaving only an undecipherable digital blur. It's good to heed strict mental categories: wolf, cougar/dog, big housecat. Like stout walking sticks, classes offer solid companionship, even if—especially when—such spontaneous oddities and anomalies threaten your sensory integrity. It comes down to identity, defining yourself in relation to the improbability of being.

Lawrence says that his late grandfather, Charlie Peter Charlie (1920–2008), a Gwich'in hunter originally from the Tukudh band, was renowned for running down whole herds of caribou on foot, in snowshoes. He firmly advanced the view that there was a historic migration to the area by their Gwich'in ancestors. The Gwich'in were obliged to fight other tribes to the south, as well as assorted giant animals, before they gained control of their present territory.

"The Gwich'in are warriors," Lawrence says. "We fought to take this land and now we fight to keep it. We are a tough people."

His recollection of his grandfather's version of Gwich'in genealogy differs from some of the published accounts in the professional literature, starting with the Nantsaii, which is usually translated as "First on the Land":

The Nantsaii means the Toolmakers who first learned how to live on the tundra, how to track animals that were here at the time, the habits of the local animals. They did not have stone weapons, but only used horn implements. These Nantsaii later became the Wolf Clan. The Ravens were the Chi'ichyaa, who were the second people on the land; they learned about living on the land, all about the plants. When they were coming here, back then, babies were being born, that's where they got the name, it means Babies Being Born. They got their tools from Wolf Clan, and were considered to be "the Helpers."

Lawrence acknowledges the anomalies and controversies raised by this account. Like the mud-covered Chit ta ho khei who successfully pretended to be a large turd to fool the monster, the Gwich'in are also good actors. In command of themselves.

It is these characteristics that one sees echoed in Lawrence's *Shaman and Crows* mural drawing. Again, these artists are highly aware of the expressive aspects of their own cultures. I found it interesting that both Angie Eetak and Lawrence Charlie, living 2,300 kilometres apart, elaborated evocative scenes directly on the walls of their respective living rooms, and I mentioned this to Lawrence. He nodded, as if absorbing the information, and I wondered aloud how much cultural traffic ran between these different nations, noting that I did not see much evidence of cultural borrowing in his drawings. In response to this query, Lawrence showed me a thick workbook, which he was engaged in producing as a kind of catalogue of animal subjects in the Gwich'in style, making it clear that the inspiration for the body of work came exclusively from the inner life experience of his people.

The traditional hunting life produces in its followers an aristocratic manner in bearing and disposition. There is a lordly manner, a quiet invocation of noblesse oblige, in the way Lawrence Charlie offers me an open tour of his house and his contents, without inquiring as to my purpose, a self-contained and patrician attitude prevalent among other local hunters like Stephen Frost, Esau Schafer, and James Itsi.

The Gwich'in are also relatively tall, *think* themselves tall, and act tall. If the greatest acting consists of a studied silence, of inner awareness signified by gesture, then the Gwich'in have developed studied silence to a fine degree.

Tallness is as tallness does.

The Grizzly Claw Necklace

In a case of life following art, Lawrence had a recent deadly encounter with a grizzly bear that followed the general outlines of the battle between Chit ta ho khei and Grizzly (*Sheh*).

In the "Chit ta ho khei" manuscript, Grizzly drinks up all the water in the lake where the hero is submerged and hiding, and the hero instructs Snipe, with its long pointed beak, to puncture the belly of the bear— which causes the bear to rupture all the water and die. It is notable that Chit ta ho khei does not kill this creature directly here, unlike his other foes, but uses an emissary: for the grizzly has enormous spiritual power, as Lawrence's following account makes clear, a power that is never easy for humans to overcome.

Lawrence's grizzly story also calls attention to a singular act, the hunter's supreme act of doing nothing in the face of everything, the power of silence in the face of greatest danger. To not show yourself, to not bolt or cry out, takes enormous resolve.

We have already seen in a previous chapter how trapping is the essence of hunting, the key discipline. The traps are logistic and sensory. Successful trapping requires utter stillness of intent, the absolute suspension of the needy, historical self. The trick is to disappear, to get the game animal to follow its own perceptions into the camouflaged killing zone. This requires careful observation and merging one's consciousness with the prey's point of view. And staying there, with that identity, until the prey is taken.

In the hunter's version of a timeless triad, the sovereign is a powerful bear who uncannily hears everything said about him; the prince is a lonely hunter distracted in his chase by family obligations; and the demure princess is a tempting offering from nature, who, untaken, quietly fades from earthly sight as her season changes: bear-king, hunter, and dryad. It is this elemental triad that comes alive in the following hunting stories, the first in an account about killing a marauding grizzly, as told by Lawrence Dean Charlie:

People have a lot of respect for them up here, such a powerful animal. They say that if you even talk bad about them, it will hear you, and you'll have bad luck with you. It will wreck your camp. People have enough respect for it not to talk ill about it. If you ever see one twenty feet away you'd shit your pants. Especially up here, when they have never seen a human before; down south, they are different here, you have to watch them. I shot two in my life.

First one I shot, I was about 24. I shot that one about ten feet away. It was at night, in the moonlight, I couldn't even see my [gun]sights. We are in a cabin up on the mountain there. We were watching a movie with the electrical generator outside. I was trying to sleep, so I went out to shut the generator off. All the dogs were barking, and I knew it was outside. Soon as I opened the door it came on the road. I knew it was outside. It had tore up someone's meat cache in town, down here.

The night before it had come to the cabin, and stood up. I only had a .243 then, not enough. So I got my grandfather's .270 out, ready, in case.

As soon as I opened the door it came out from the mountain road. Before I opened the door I cut out all the lights so it wouldn't see inside. I still had the porch light on to blind it, so it wouldn't see inside. I opened it up, it heard the door opening, so it started walking towards the door.

But this kid that I was supposed to look after, it was a youth camp, and this kid never seen a grizzly before. I was in the process—I was going to shoot it, but this kid kept talking to me, and he was pretty scared, freaked out. He was telling me not to shoot it and I basically told him to shut the fuck up. Every time you're talking he hears you, and now he's walking straight towards us.

It got about ten feet from the door, as best I could I aimed for his head, and I got it in the neck, it went through his ribcage. It was pretty intense. I used a .270, one bullet. After I shot it, I couldn't stop shaking for an hour, a huge internal rush, it was too late to cut it up, so I left it overnight. A conservation officer took a tooth sample; it turned out to be a 23-year-old bear. I cut it to save the fur but there was a big bare patch on the side. Someone had shot it, and someone snared it. It was old, hungry. There was nothing but garbage in his stomach when we cut him up, plastic in his stomach, probably starving.

When I am in the bush I try not to lose my composure, not to get excited. You make lot of mistakes when you get excited, my grandfather taught me. He just told me, settle down. When he saw a bear far away he'd act like it wasn't there, he'd say, "Settle down, he can't harm you. Watch him, but don't be afraid."

It's true outside the bush, too. You always have to be cool, and mind your own business.

The grizzly must be shot because, explicitly, it is no longer a true bear and no longer acts according to its right nature; its stomach is full of plastic bags and junk. The belief that grizzly bears can hear bad things said of them, and will take their vengeance accordingly, is supported by naturalists' observations that the specie's acute hearing is an adaptation for hunting underground prey like gophers and voles. Its senses are stronger than any human's.

The grizzly bear taken by Lawrence Dean Charlie, as he takes pains to point out, was shot in self-defence as the culmination of a series of escalating nightly provocations. In fact, in the end Lawrence only took the long claws from the aged carcass, and respectfully made a ceremonial necklace of them, which he flatly refused to wear, although he was content to allow the necklace to be photographed—and seemed to modestly turn his head away from the visitor's camera when the shutter snapped.

Gwich'in storytellers have appeared to discover an antidote to the seductive artifice that masks itself as reality. Lawrence Dean Charlie recounts a hunting incident when his grandfather told him to break with local tradition:

My grandfather used to run down caribou with snowshoes till they can't run anymore. There were only two people in town who could do that. He'd run a small herd of caribou right down, and he'd shoot the whole thing. The rest of the hunters would catch up and give him their bullets and take what they needed.

Some of the things he did when we were alone in the bush, it was his intuition. He'd see certain weather coming, and seem to know what would happen the next day before it happened. Some of these instances I can't explain. But he really knew the country and he knew, like supernatural things, that I can't explain.

There was this lone morning, there was this one lone caribou 'way out on the ice, and I grabbed my gun and I jumped on the skidoo and went up to it. It was a cow caribou. I came back and told him it was a cow, and we don't usually shoot cows. And he told me to go back and shoot it. He said *that it put itself there for us to get it, so, he said there was going to be bad storm tomorrow and we are going to have something to eat. So I went out and got it and the next day it blew. There was a snowstorm for like three days and we had fresh meat to eat. Stuff like that. I was ten when that happened, in Crow Flats. It's different up there than on the river.*

As always, whenever rapid social change adds its novel demands to the old pot of long-cooking manhood, a pressing demand arises as to how to find a proper life between obediently following ancestral traditions, or, trusting to the plain evidence of one's heightened senses against the seductively lovely grain of the revered past, striking out alone on the rough and trail-blazing path to independence.

Lawrence's revision of a traditional hunting practice invokes the higher authority of a benign ancestral spirit for its resolution: the cow is taken, as offered.

The ghost of the father haunts the contemporary Gwich'in hunter as in *Hamlet*. At least, that's how I read the artist's drawing of the shadowy shaman on his cabin wall.

15 : Crow Never Dies

Ravens in Old Crow, YT, bolder and bigger than ravens elsewhere in the north on account of the abundant local pickings.

> *You should always go moose hunting with a partner.*
>
> —JAMES ITSI

ANOTHER CLEAR SEPTEMBER DAY in the village of Old Crow. The river edge is busy with activity. James Itsi has got a new boat, new to him at least. It is a gray, wooden, eight-metre scow with a 30 HP Honda motor. Perfect, he said, for going up the relatively shallow Porcupine River in search of game.

About 4:00 in the afternoon we proceeded upriver on a day trip to check his fishnets. James brought his old Winchester .30-30 and a newer .22 rifle. A few hunters like Johnny Kay had already shot moose in the past week, but the big Porcupine caribou herd had yet to start moving south on their annual migration. They were two weeks late; James said it was the unseasonably warm weather that had slowed them down. Ten thousand deer were three days away, but the first ones should reach the river any hour now.

Still, the moose were plentiful this year. Elders Esau Schafer, sixty-two, and Stephen Frost, seventy-five, had got their moose in partnership with their grandsons. "He saw it and I shot it!" is how Stephen's grandson David Frost, twenty-six, described his partnership. The latter pair had bagged a three-year-old bull moose. Echoing the belief of other local hunters, David said the bull was wandering the no man's land of the Porcupine River shoreline because it had been chased out of the deep thickets inland by a mature bull in full rut.

"We have the only migratory group of moose in the world here in Old Crow," David said. He had offered me a piece of headcheese made from the kill: the bull was already entirely processed into a score of different meat products after two days' intense work inside the all-important food cache, a wood shed about three metres by three metres, equipped with drying racks and a cutting table, and a small wood stove for creating smoke to keep the flies away. The moose headcheese tasted like traditional beef meatloaf, only sweeter.

"We've got ordinary moose that stay put for the winter," David went on. "They find themselves a little spot to hide from the wolves and stick to it. But then we have the bigger moose up in Crow Flat that stay by the marshes and eat and eat all summer, stuffing themselves. They grow quite huge and then they start heading west off to Alaska in the fall, where the local guides are just waiting for the giant moose from Old Crow. You get a lot of younger bulls moving in the fall because they get pushed out during the rut by the bigger ones. That's why you get them at the river, looking for a place to go."

David had spent the last few days butchering the three-hundred-kilogram animal while his grandfather Stephen rested in his house, recuperating from a recent surgery that hadn't prevented him from going moose hunting. A single moose equalled about four full-sized caribou, and its meat would keep a family of four going for most of the winter.

"You need two guys if you are going to shoot a moose," James said, as the town disappeared into the distance, looking speculatively at me. The old motor was working nicely. It was too nice a day to spend it getting bloody and sweaty heaving moose body parts into the boat, so it was pleasant to see that not a thing stirred along the shoreline—except for some ravens that inevitably attached themselves to departing hunters in the hope they would produce a meat feast for them.

We entered a series of yellow sandy bluffs. They marked a gigantic beach that was the edge of a vast inland sea or freshwater lake: Beringia, the ten-thousand-year-old refuge filled with exotic Pleistocene animals that had collectively escaped the last ice age.

The time-polished remains of mastodon tusks and the teeth of giant beavers, saber-tooth tigers, and even wild horses had been found here in quantity by hunters, but the animals themselves quietly disappeared at the same time the Clovis big-game hunters showed up in the archeological record. The Clovis hunters were armed with distinctive, large, projectile points designed to take down the megafauna like mastodons they found in the New World. Would James Itsi have shot a mastodon if one suddenly showed up? Almost certainly he knew exactly what it was because he had seen its fossils first-hand.

Stephen Frost maintained a whole collection of Pleistocene fossils washed out of the Bluefish River. The Gwich'in tales of giant beavers and man-killing monsters are founded on the incontrovertible physical evidence of their existence. One of these monsters was a bear larger by half than the grizzly, the giant short-faced bear (*Arctodus simus*). How would early hunters, armed only with stabbing lances and the tricks of fire, deal with a predator that stood about 1.5 metres at the shoulder (three metres when standing upright) and could weigh as much as 1,000 kilograms? *Very politely*, as the old joke about the escaped gorilla says.

As if echoing my silent speculations, James added to his unfinished comment five minutes before, "One guy has to keep watch while the other guy cuts up the animal."

Perhaps he meant that a number of "interested parties" might show up at our kill site, drawn by the circling ravens or the smell of blood. He was afraid of grizzlies first off, and asked me to stay in the boat rather than wait on the shore as he pulled his fish out of the two, fifteen-metre, gill nets. He painstakingly took whitefish, suckers, chum salmon, and grayling trout from the frayed mesh, an eclectic catch weighing about forty kilos in total. The fish were silver and red, purple and indigo, amazingly beautiful even in death. Unlike the Inuit, however, James did not immediately cut off a few chunks to eat raw.

When I pointed this lack of culinary adventure out to him, he looked at me speculatively and repeated, "Muk*tuk*, eh...? Hmm, *muk*tuk."

James apparently liked the faintly lewd sound of the unfamiliar word more than the idea of eating raw fish, although he did allow to seeing the exotic practice on TV once.

"*Muktuk*, yes!"

"Wolves could come by, too," James went on, unhurriedly. "Not right away, but later and usually at night." But he was just as worried about moose that showed up with *their* partners, and then recounted a story, called informally, "Turning Your Back," but which he later repeated, consistently following the same rhythm and key points in the second telling.

I was using a .303 with a magazine for the shells and a bolt—you have to make sure the bullet goes high enough that it gets into the chamber when you work the bolt, otherwise it will get stuck. So I was hunting and I saw this bull moose and I fired, and I hit him, and then I used the bolt to move another cartridge into the barrel, but it got stuck—and the bull charged me. He comes right at me—and I was trying to get the bullet into the chamber and I tried so hard I turned my back on him to concentrate on what I was doing—so he ran right past me because I turned my back on him! He kept on going! When I got the bullet into the chamber I had one good chance to hit him again, and I shot and he went down.

But I was all alone and I had to move this big moose to bring home, so it took me a couple of days of going back and forth to carry it out by

myself. The next day when I went back there were fresh moose tracks
around the carcass. I think it was his partner, come to see what happened
to him. I was thinking what would have happened if his partner showed
up, and there I was, cutting up meat, with nobody else with us to look out
and watch to see what might come out of the bush.

That's why you should always go moose-hunting with a partner.
Caribou, it's different. But with moose you are at the kill for a longer time,
and things can happen.

The next day we head out again up the Porcupine River, this time further, up to his camp. The slight tinge of nostalgic melancholy persists in darkening James's mood, all despite the fine morning sun. It is on this trip that he makes a key distinction between his present home in Yukon and the ancestral village in the Northwest Territories.

"See those sunny mountains there?" he said, pointing east. "Those are Richardson Mountains, they are always sunny. The Yukon is always dark and gloomy, cloudy, rainy from Alaska. I always like to be headed into the sunny NWT."

Of course, his statement (recited like a mantra or dedicatory verse) is based on the stringent facts of climate. Yukon gets the western heavy weather, the rain clouds from the Alaskan coast, and they do fade out as they reach the drier interior. But there is also the fact of a large family, unaccounted for in the distance. Dispersed, some lost, unreachable. James's mother Doris was still alive in 2010, and she was now over ninety, but his father and his own wife had passed away years ago. And unlike many men in the north, James had never remarried, although he was only forty-three when his wife died of cancer in 1984. I was brooding, too, for whose life was this river?

More than most rivers, the Porcupine keeps its larger surprises around the next bend and the next. As a metaphor for life, it best suits those persons whose exaggerated dramas pull the semblance of a plot into a catalogue of special effects. I mean, the Porcupine River doesn't repeat itself. You start off your river journey motoring down the middle of a silver river, travelling gently alongside an open vista of yellow alpine meadows and gravel beaches, divided and accentuated by innocuous rows of black spruces.

This soon gives way to the strangely overpowering staccato of sand hills, peppered with twisted and sinister trees that corkscrew off at wild angles from their centre of gravity and fill the traveller with a sense of black foreboding and sheer futility, despite the clear and unchallenged air of midmorning.

What was this bleak desperate area? Had this swampy mishap triggered James into a funk, this disturbed patch of faceless multiclawed limbs, tearing at the sky? Bad emanations, you can feel it.

A kilometre or so later, we come to a series of soaring cliffs, great chunks of solid yellow granite. Ospreys fly one way, golden eagles the other. The world becomes epic, monumental, empyrean. Even triumphant; one can almost hear Berg or Mahler coming from those cliff tops, trumpets and French horns, a chorus of coloratura sopranos, everything in crescendo.

This stereo majesty does not last either, however. This is me, the writer, of course, struggling valiantly to read the unknown landscape unfolding before us; I carefully watch my guide watch the shoreline, but I cannot appreciate or even guess at what readings the experienced hunter is making of it all—this lucid water, the miscreant trees, the eagle-broken sky, the caprices of wind, passage of treetop birds. And my disability is apparent, both in interpreting the telling wealth of detail of individual signs, and in reading the faint suggestions that come pouring out of every corner of the woods. More, I am stuck in deciphering the greater cryptology of our inexorable elevation into the overwhelming dimension we call "nature," which local people call, with absolute neutrality, "the bush." What was that splash? What was that bird? Is that a mountain or a cloud?

In the absence of signposts, I necessarily fall back on the familiarity of the classics. Painted landscapes by Thomas Cole and J.A. Turner, and even the Group of Seven, but none of them have come within a thousand leagues of this place, with the exception of the Canadian transcendentalist

Lawren Harris, who might have come within 999. Soon enough, the granite cliffs give way to jet-black stone faces; possibly, we are in a new crosscut of competing Precambrian geologies because we have turned a long bend without the engrossed writer noticing it, and now we are headed east again, or south, or north, some direction or other. The water glitters like black diamonds under this new unyielding and brocaded mineral that darkens our faces and cloaks the water and our boat in glamorously formal, if austere, shadows of rigid and watery quartz crystals. This spectacle quickly yields, in turn, to a line of purple mountains that were wholly invisible half a minute ago, a dreamy range framed by picturesque tall spruces that appear to have been transplanted from an old villa in Lombardy, accompanied with bowers of bright yellow poplars and lavender willows in a forest understorey that has suddenly gone Impressionist after a brief flirtation with craggy Romanticism.

All of these changes of scenery, I hasten to add, were accompanied by a seen and unseen parade of wild animals that wandered freely across the wide horizon, undoubtedly encountering and investigating the same jigsaw shifts in the local environment that we were, simply boating up the river.

We saw them and they saw us: golden eagles, bald eagles, and a shrieking hawk that also appeared to be fishing like its larger brethren; loons; old squaw ducks; salmon and graying bolting straight out of the water; and, in late afternoon, a creature that seemed to be a large housecat, but it had a black hump and a large silvery stripe: a wolverine.

⋮ The wolverine was sitting on its haunches on the sandy beach. It waited until we were a hundred paces off, then it ambled up the shelf and into the wood with that peculiar hunchback, shuffling gait it shared with grizzly bears and horror-movie monsters. This one was dead-black, except for a streak of silvery fur, and I kept taking photos of it from the rocking boat, even after it apparently fled into the woods.

Ah, but the wolverine didn't go anywhere, as my photos later revealed. No, what it did was position itself behind an impenetrable thicket of dry spruce from which it could study us at its glowering leisure. The picture showed its feral eyes, eyes that were disturbingly aware, and alarming— even though it was a few days later when the photo was downloaded and examined for the first time. The wolverine was clearly watching us with more than animal curiosity, for it displayed a studied malevolence that said it was biding its time while it took in every detail of our behaviour.

The only other occasion where I felt such an uncanny sensation of malice was in the Mongolian city of Ulan Bator, where a gang of market robbers began moving in for the hit in the crowded arcade, and gave their game away by broadcasting their thuggish intentions with this same look of bloody-thirsty menace.

One has to trust one's instinct in these situations; back then, I had escaped the robbers' clutches by quickly exiting the square from a warehouse back door, but today we were going only another twenty kilometres upriver, and the wolverine would easily trek 150 kilometres to steal something to eat, like all our camp food. The same thought occurred to James.

"I never saw a wolverine before," I said cheerfully, unaware at this point that the wolverine was still intently watching us. "That was a rare thing."

"I didn't know you wanted to take a picture of that one," James said carelessly, as we motored down the deeper, middle channel to his hunt camp.

"They are very rare; few people from the south have ever seen one," I replied. "Lucky for me, no?"

"You ever see a moose screwing?"

"Me?" I thought about it. It sounded like a bar joke, so I played along. "I think I saw some *pictures* of moose screwing." I was not sure if it was actually two elephants coupling, but James went on with his dissertation.

"It's bad luck if you see moose screwing, you are not supposed to see it. There are four things that are unlucky. To see moose screwing; a whisky jack; a crow's nest—and wolverine tracks. All of these things you don't *just see*."

He paused, letting the import of his words sink in. His eyes blazed. He looked clearly unhappy.

"You know? These things are not like seeing an eagle or a caribou in the forest. Those things are supposed to be there. But if you see wolverine tracks, it means you are going to have things stolen. It means he is on your trail."

We came to a wide expanse of water where a brusque little creek ran down with a short final gush into the steep north riverbank. The wet beach hereabout was jammed with bleached logs and branches. Some of them, judging from their great length and friction-smoothed trunks, had been carried down from a high timberland deep in the interior. The logs dwarfed the spindly local trees, which barely reached ladder height. James's dark mood lifted as he contemplated this perfectly dry treasure of thirty or forty cords. He built a healthy fire on the wet silt, warming his backsides against the shooting flames and then using the embers to boil black tea and make up a hot lunch of beans and wieners. Then he sketched a map of the land ahead of us into the beach soil, contemplating each stroke of the charred willow stick.

The day was mild and windless. We sat on the biggest of the great white logs and cooked our hotdogs on sharpened willows and watched as a raven flew overhead, landed a few hundred paces upriver, and strutted out of the foliage to peer at us from around a clump of pussy willows.

"That one?" James pointed with his wiener stick. "He followed us from town!"

Was it possible? There was nothing remarkable about the black bird; he was not even a particularly large raven, and as we had seen no other boats but one so far that morning, we were the only real game in town for the scavenger.

"Where do you think these big trees came from?" I asked. There was a spruce log over thirty metres long. "There must be some tall forests far upriver, no?"

"These trees came from all over, from far away," James replied. "See how the ice breaks off their branches, makes them nice and smooth. The river is like a big washing machine, freezing and thawing, and bringing all the trees together, then sending them off again, one by one, to some new place. Now they are together, and talking to each other, telling what they were doing before. It is like a little town of old trees. All mixed together, happy to meet up again. Lots of this came from beaver dams, you know. Old beaver dams that got busted up in the spring by the flooding water."

He walked over to the high heap of logs, pulled out a stout limb at random, rolled it around his hands, and handed it over for inspection.

"See the tooth marks? The beaver chewed it up pretty good."

The plain stick suddenly resolved itself into an artifact with a history and a context. You could see that it had been gnawed off at its root at the thicker end, and that all the bark had been determinedly chewed off in shallow scrapings along only one side. Were the nutrients in the willow bark asymmetrically distributed?

Its botanical secrets were there to read by all those who could see the significance of small signs. It is not enough to call this early, and lifetime, training "keen observation," for it deserves its own proper name like literacy and numeracy—ecoloracy? Biologism? Whatever it ought to be called, it is distinguishable from the practice of the people we call naturalists.

Now fed and loaded with heartening hot tea, we examined the animal tracks running down the beach in a series of more or less straight and parallel lines.

"Calf moose," James said, indicating the splayed hoof prints that were only ten centimetres long. "Running separate from the bull and the cow over here. A big bull too. Look at how deep his tracks up here are!"

"And these wolf tracks? They caught something?" A little heap of soft white fur was embedded in the wolf track.

"That's rabbit," James said, putting the fluff ball into his pocket. "But maybe an eagle came and scooped him up, not the wolf. Sometimes there's nothing left if a wolf takes a moose. Once I was hunting on my snowmobile in winter and I followed these tracks of a wolf and moose, just one wolf— and I was surprised when I got to where he killed the moose. All I saw was lots of wolf tracks and some blood. You'd think he would leave a haunch for someone else. But this wolf, after he ate, he took off every piece of meat to different places and hid them all. All that was left of a whole moose was bits of fur. The wolf had picked off all the fur with his teeth because he didn't want to carry the fur. It was no good to him, right? Too much for him to carry. Then he chewed off the pieces of cleaned-up meat and dragged them away to eat later. He was a big wolf, that one. Big and smart."

"Maybe the ravens got some of that meat, too?"

"You got to watch ravens, they might make a commotion, telling you there's a caribou coming or a moose in the pond. Something like that. They help wolves. They even help eagles to locate some food so that they can eat the scraps. They tell the eagles what to kill."

"So the eagles actually work for the ravens!" This seemed to be an amusing conjecture, but James was describing a general pattern of co-exploitation among various predators.

"It is same with a wolverine. Say, if the wolves are sleeping. The wolverine knows this, and what it does is keep the caribou restless. Tiring them out. He knows the caribou can go four days without sleeping, then at the end they fall into a deep sleep automatically. It is hard to wake them and you can easily hunt them now. Wolverine keeps them up, so the wolves can hunt them better then if they are all rested up."

We walked further along the beach. A small clawed animal had made an appearance, and then, standing in isolated splendour, there was a fresh print that looked like a fat human foot, but stubbier.

"Grizzly," James said without inflection. "A small one. He comes along here, looking for his meal, too."

"Did you ever hunt bears?"

"When you are a young man, you want to try everything. You are ambitious, you want to experience everything that there is, out there. But now, when I see there is a grizzly in the area, I go away and leave it alone."

"What if a grizzly came out of the woods towards you? What would you do?"

"I would see what its intentions are, from the way it was acting towards me. If it was going to leave me alone, I would leave it alone, and go about my business elsewhere."

Significantly, there were no caribou tracks on the river beach. James had said the ten thousand caribou of the Porcupine herd were only a few days away, but apart from a few local deer, there was no sign that any had begun to cross the river in their fall migration.

"When they start coming," he said, "You'll turn a bend in the river and suddenly there will be sixty caribou standing on the shore, looking at you. You can hear their hooves knock against the beach stones like musical notes, and they eat up everything as they pass through, moss, berries, everything—like a swarm of ants. You see the naked land marked up with so many hoof marks it looks like that white stone beach, just a bunch of holes in the ground, not a space between them."

Although it was unseasonably warm for late September, about 16°C, the restless air over the river was chill and immobile. I was glad to be dressed in a heavy, windproof, and hooded coat, long underwear, and insulated boots. We had been travelling for over four hours: What men were these who once paddled these same rivers in flimsy birchbark canoes against the icy current? We were now fifty kilometres from the hamlet, and we had passed a dozen hunt camps belonging to other Old Crow residents. These were invariably located on bluffs overlooking creeks or streams, offering themselves to the steady breezes as protection from flies and providing a view of passing game, amplified by miniature "moose lookouts"—rough, split-rail ladders that allowed the hunter to see animals over the treetops, a structure that may rank among the earliest architectural innovations of the north.

Some of these bush camps were fancy, some rough, and all but one were empty. It was the middle of the moose season, the arrival of the caribou was imminent: Where were the hunters? James's camp was another half-hour away, located below a famous old Gwich'in site called Driftwood by the White trappers. James, who was not born in the Old Crow area, did not know what its original Gwich'in name was. He had taken over the abandoned cabin only a few years ago.

It seems that the mirror-like surface of the Porcupine and its changeling shoreline had perhaps contributed to the inner creative life of the local people, impressing on them a strong feeling for the spiky symmetry of an indifferent nature, stillness duplicated in rushing water. It was exhilarating, this passage upriver, as if we were floating over the treetops.

Here the Porcupine River averaged about two hundred metres wide, stretching and refracting by turn, with numerous arms, shallow bays, blind junctions, musical gurgles, and sibilant sighs. We were obliged to keep to the deeper water, a polished channel lacking shoals or deadheads, but even James slowed repeatedly and pulled out his water stick to test the depths whenever he reached the limits of his own knowledge and needed to confirm that the motor was safe from unseen rocks. Our course upriver was becoming more tentative, deferential; the broad expanse was insistently registering this strangely hypnotic view that more ordinary rivers obscured from sight.

Everyone has seen, of course, this precise spikiness and twisted symmetry in woodland art, and most of us have wondered at its strongly delineated outlines and lack of tone and gradient. The work of local artist Lawrence Dean Charlie evoked the mythical aspect of real animals whose power lay in a precisely defined array of functions and existed in splendid isolation, as if detached from all other influences or relationships at this higher level—excepting, of course, the relationship with the viewer. So it is a direct and unmediated thing that confronts the onlooker with its own abstracted awareness of the onlooker, in turn. It is rather like, if not exactly like, the wolverine that was looking back at us from the camouflage of its deliberately broken outline.

It seems that what these northern woodland pictures of mythical creatures represent, then, is the *animal's consciousness of its relationship to us*. There is a human dimension to all animals (some of them perhaps stronger, or deeper, more intimately connected to us, like that of dogs, and wolves, and ravens), an experiential realm that they alone inhabit and which occupation elaborates or extends their own being. What this art recognizes is an unfinished and hungry identity that burns in all living things, multifaceted, contingent to some degree, and variable over time and incident—and context.

Of course, we are different people to our spouses than to our dogs, but do we ever take time to consider that the dog also experiences himself differently with his master than with his mistress? I am a thing that exists inside my dog's mind—I am also a thing that has been hungrily appropriated by the wolverine, which was looking straight at me.

Sure, I've got him in my camera, but he's got me, too, caught in his devious and cunning and powerful wolverine mind. Yikes! Likewise, when blown up, my photos of Old Crow ravens (which have jet-black eyes, and so, are difficult to see against their jet-black bodies) show they are keeping a beady eye on the photographer, who, one assumes, would show up reflected in their avian pupils if the picture were blown up big enough.

It is the same with all northern animals: they are serially aware of us on some mysterious level. Some wild creatures (certainly crows and ravens, again, and perhaps the clever and opportunistic raccoons and coyotes of the urban south, as well) will even get to know us rural householders as idiosyncratic individuals. It is this ongoing and particularized social knowledge that extends their general animal consciousness into the independent order of myth, which is, at base, a map of all human animal consciousness.

And it works the other way around, too. There are maps, and there is darkness and confusion. One could not help thinking about something James had said, about *things that you just don't see*. It seems that the Gwich'in hunters understand, like most people, the broad technical workings of their environment, about sex and disease and population crashes and the variability of animal behaviour within individuals, the natural science of their hunting and fishing and berry picking, and they know perfectly well that their caribou have their collective and time-honoured calving grounds under the Brooks Mountain Range. Still, the river of life is unaccountable and murky in its broader outlines.

The caribou, this year like any year, will inexplicably appear or they won't. Animals present themselves to us, seemingly out of nothing, and go away again. Technology—motorboats, planes, snowmobiles, guns, nets—may prolong the point of contact if there is one, but these deuces do not of themselves make the royals appear, or even guarantee their eventual appearance in the card player's hand, a state visit that ultimately, and exclusively, derives from that special quality called hunter's luck and which imperial quality in Gwich'in culture is closer to God's throne than we all are, men and animals together. (It may very well be the same thing as grace; food for further thought.)

Let it be said, though: animals are not privileged in the Arctic any more so than men; only *individuals* are. You can lose your luck by taking wrong moral action, or by simple, idle misfortune. Seeing things you are not supposed to see, like moose coupling, might, one supposes, happen to any good hunter. Then again, these sightings are gifts and omens, clear signs that you have taken the wrong path earlier in the journey, a rough path that you alone chose to take. But hunters can also, according to James, become self-destructive and do things they know to be wrong and dangerous out of sheer willfulness, as the following story he recounted on our journey upriver sharply illustrates:

> *You heard this story about this guy from town? He got mad one day, being out and bothered by this crow that kept flying over him, and he was getting no game. So he shot the crow, thinking it would stop and he could get some peace, at least. A few minutes later, the crow comes back, flying overhead. Alive again.*

I didn't understand the point and asked James if he meant it was the same crow. Had it come back to life?

> *It was a different crow, but the same crow, you understand? There is only one crow, that's why they all look exactly the same. Because there is only one Crow. God made them all black and identical-looking because there is no reason for them to be different birds. That's why you can never kill a crow, because it lives forever. Crow never dies!*

I understood: "So this guy couldn't kill the crow?"

Right! But he was really mad, this hunter. He shot the second crow, too. And what do you think happened?

It seemed an easy question: "Another crow showed up, right away?"

Two crows showed up now! And they flew over him. Now he was fixed, he tried to shoot them, and pretty soon a whole flock of crows came over him and wouldn't leave him alone, and he went crazy.

The hunting story made complete sense, especially in view of the fact that our town crow was still very much with us. What makes ravens so special in the world of North American myth is that they never really die. It is not that ravens steal, or play tricks, or that they live by scavenging, as categorical intermediaries between the living and the dead. The larger reason for Raven's supreme importance in ritual, dance, and Origin stories came in a flash of insight from listening to James Itsi's account: it is that ravens tell each other their memories, so they live on forever in the memories of their kind. They are exactly like humans; they tell themselves stories, too.

James acknowledged without comment my response to his crow story, and then warmed up to his favourite theme, the loss of the special relationship the true hunters once enjoyed with the land, a loss in which even Crow had suffered in tandem with his human fellows:

You see these town crows? [Here he jerked his head back, indicating Old Crow downriver.] They are fat and lazy, got no reason to go hunt for their meal. They eat garbage, junk, just like the kids do with their junk food, their chips and pop. Crows, real wild crows, have to be smart. They die out here if they don't make the right decisions, watch everything. Town crows are like town people, they get lazier and stupid and pretty soon they give up and just wait to be fed handouts from the government. They don't know anything anymore, and they don't even know what they are.

All this was well and good, but when we returned to the dying campfire on the beach James became incensed. His hot dog was missing from his stick, a hot dog that had been slowly cooking over the red-hot embers two minutes ago.

"Goddamn it! That goddamn crow! I never saw this before! The little bastard pulled my hotdog right out of the fire!"

He turned and spotted the blue-black bird, waddling behind a distant log, looking at us with what must have been a smirk of triumph, although it was too far to tell for sure. Maybe it was affection.

We got back in the gray scow and continued our voyage. James's memory for terrestrial detail was colossal. There were always abrupt changes to the river's passage to be discovered on every trip, of course, and these had to be read closely against the huge store of information from other trips. The scraggly water stick came out again, more frequently now, and a few times James stuck me with it in the back, as if testing my changing emotional depth, too. We passed a half-dozen places where the clay cliffs had collapsed, that process called *slumping*, a problem the people back in town had attributed to the incidence of heavy rain that fell in the past summer, but James muttered that this theory was sadly mistaken.

"The river is not the same river as before," he shook his head. "People keep cutting trees too close to the shoreline, and there's nothing to hold up the earth together when they do that. Lot of people cut wood when they don't need to, too—there's all kinds of good wood at the town dump, you could build a whole home out of stuff people throw out."

There was a surprising anomaly that any visitor might notice about these riverside spruce trees. The highest trees always grew along the edge of the cliff. A metre or so behind them, the forest was stunted, twisted, and spindly in comparison. So the problem was that the best lumber was to be found at the worst possible place for good soil conservation.

James readily agreed that this observation was correct; we speculated why this must be so—and played with the idea that the trees along the edge of the bluff received more sunlight than the trees in the interior, or that the soil was more friable, or that the subsoil all along the cliffs was deeper because the permafrost had melted to a deeper level on account of its steady exposure to the elements. We finally decided that the trees on the edge were straighter and taller because they took more risks, growing out on the edge: they were wilder.

It was a satisfying conversation, even if it was entirely open to correction by a qualified biologist or forester, who, at any rate, was unlikely to interrupt our colloquy by suddenly showing up in the Yukon bush to register his or her objections. We had this Land to ourselves. No smoke, no planes, no machinery. The river's silence was delicious. We were entirely free to divvy it up into categories and associations of our own choosing.

It so happened that I agreed with most of James's assertions, and this may have been because his reasoning was perfectly and colourfully argued, and that it derived from basic premises that we shared—such as the assumption that these straight tall trees on the shoreline were the same stunted species that grew inland. This assumption, in turn, derived from our shared preference for holding the power of nurture over that of inherited characteristics, which view itself emanated from a personal conviction that heroes are made, not born, and great people like great trees need to root themselves in the best soil they can find, and cling to it with all their might.

Apparently, James believed the modern world was an acid bog, and the individuals who accepted its limitations were misled fools who had failed to realize their full potential from laziness or indifference.

"Yes, you see how *short* the people are getting in Old Crow? They're shrinking, year by year. They don't think like us. They just watch TV and get smaller."

It seemed he meant that the two of us had grown up tall in different forests, different times. We were here, on the edge, and his camp was just ahead.

⋮ We reached Driftwood at 6:00 PM. Set on a sandy bluff above the narrow beach was a classic spruce log cabin with a rent, and jerry-built, tin roof. It faced a broad stream on the far shore, which stream was presently occupied by a golden eagle fishing in the shallows for trapped trout and salmon. It was idyllic, isolated. There were ripe berries everywhere underfoot, cranberries and blueberries and rose hips. However, a few minutes' inspection of the cabin's interior put James in another sour mood. He came out of his cabin, cursing.

"Those little bastards! You see what they do, useless assholes! My blanket! They took my blanket. Tracked dirt in here, didn't take their shoes off. What else is missing?"

He looked around the weedy yard. They—whoever they were—had, of course, also used up his firewood without replacing it and taken a mug or two as well.

"At least they left my hammer and my axe!" he grumbled. "You can't survive on the land without an axe."

Whoever they were had long since gone back to town. The fire was cold. There were no boats moving on the river at this distant point and the immense silence of the forest must have frightened them off before we arrived. James made a pot of tea outside on the open fire pit and watched the pine siskins flit about a reddish willow shrub a few metres away, describing it as a unique tree.

"I can't figure out why they eat upside down," he said, regaining his composure with each sip of tea and enjoying the antic moves of the little feathered acrobats. He pulled off some buds. "These kernels are dry as toast, nothing in them."

He kept rubbing the willow husks until they were dust, but the answer remained elusive. There was only an hour or so left of daylight. It was time for a little exploration.

The beach was marked by a few old caribou tracks and many fresh wolf tracks; it became necessary to remember that just because there were no grizzly tracks here, it did not mean that one could not suddenly appear out of the nearest bush. The caribou tracks were distinguished from moose tracks by their curvy, elliptical shape and lighter impression in the mud. A caribou might weigh a hundred kilograms as against four times that for a moose. Additionally, the caribou's hooves were designed for long-distance trekking.

The two thousand kilometres that these caribou typically travelled in their winter migration is the longest animal migration in the world. It may be for this reason that caribou hunters put up a pair of raw caribou hooves in a high willow tree near their cabins. They say it's cached in the tree as a traditional winter emergency food, that one can make a nourishing soup from hooves if real hunger requires it. But it is also true that a caribou travels through winter on these specialized and superior hooves, and that getting through winter requires every effort a hunter's family can muster: these hooves may symbolically promise that another spring will be reached at the end of the difficult human journey.

Wolves, as James noted, preferred attacking young moose, whose ability to crush their ribs in response was unperfected. The caribou's main defence against wolves was to run far away on these hooves, and keep running. According to my companion, they could run for four days straight. Despite their evident tracks on the beach, James thought that the chances of seeing caribou at this hour were too slender to warrant the minor effort involved. He wanted to pick berries instead.

The forest behind his cabin was mossy and wholly entangled in itself; one had to take a short step or two at a time or lose the whole world to an unyielding knot of lichens and roots and stumps. The cabin disappeared from sight after five or six paces into the bush, and if it were not for the smoke and sparks rising into the sky, I would have been quite lost in what James called his backyard. And what James called the caribou trails were either old, or the caribou that made them were even more slender in numbers than our chances of seeing any.

The ripe cranberries were jammed in heaps and handfuls, hiding under empty leaves, growing like jewels just over the fragrant moss bed. Some perfumed bush that was oddly familiar, but unidentifiable as to its source, kept inserting itself into the easy routine of tossing a handful of the high-potency fruit into my mouth for every four or five that went into the Mason jar.

"Why are there only cranberries growing here? Why not cloudberries, or salmon berries, or even blueberries?"

James appeared to think it was a good question, even as he had no ready answer. He was sixty-nine years old, an Elder, and he was still learning new things every day about the world around him with the amazement and innocence of a bright student for whom no question was too spurious or fanciful to be discussed aloud.

I had swallowed some dry bit of cranberry stem in the growing darkness, and James heard the coughing from his patch and immediately beckoned me to join him at a tree. A string of lumpy pearls hung from its bark—spruce tree gum. The same stuff that Wolverine gave up in exchange for his life, but seeing the white dripping here in the dark was more instructive than reading about it in a mythic account of Nehtruh (Wolverine). The crystallized sap looked like male ejaculate, pure and simple.

"Here! Stick this in your mouth and chew it!" James handed me a big sticky gob.

"All that?—Hm. Alright, alright."

I obligingly did as I was told. The spruce gum tasted strongly of menthol and stayed resolutely intact where it was on one side of my mouth while the cranberries continued to get chewed on the other side, not a bad combination, in fact. Perhaps there was profit to be made in designing a commercial product that combined the medicinal and culinary properties of the two indigenous plants, and it could be marketed under the brand "Old Crow's Wolverine-Strength Cranberry-Forest Gum," or some such, with 10 per cent of the profits going to a worthy northern cause.

We returned to the outdoor firepit. James occupied himself in the last minutes of the glowing twilight by clearing the loose brush and the dead weeds of late fall from around the cabin, and consigning it all to the shooting flames. Neither of us smoked or drank; we had both quit everything like that years ago, so the play of flames and smoke were all we had to bear witness to the memories of other campfires and other days spent out on the rivers and lakes of adventures past and illuminate the prospect of new adventures hopefully still to come.

After stoking up the iron woodstove in the cabin we went to sleep.

There was just the crackling of the spruce logs to break the utter silence of the northern night. The spruce gum had stubbornly remained where it was, sticking to my teeth, undiminished despite the rigorous chewing. I swallowed the tenacious lump at one go, vaguely wondering how Wolverine's spiritual medicine would affect my dreams once it had taken possession of my belly.

16 : Luck and Nothing

Hunting for caribou: "Saw six polar bears today, but no caribou." Sentry Island, Arviat, NU.

If I had missed that moose I'm going to make Charlie feel real bad, because I didn't listen. But I took a chance.

— STEPHEN FROST

IT IS NOW LATE FALL in the land of the Vuntut Gwich'in. The hills above the hamlet of Old Crow are dusted with sharp fragrant snow and framed with thin pillars of woodsmoke rising from cabins whose occupants are busy with preparations for winter: wood cutting, fish smoking, and making repairs to skidoos, snowshoes, and marten traps.

I am sitting on a deck, at peace with the sky after a late breakfast of fresh moose liver and onions, tea, bannock, and wild blueberry jam.

The ever-enterprising Allan Benjamin comes bouncing along on his ATV, loaded with salvaged lumber for an inside project he will do over the coming winter. He seems to have collected a mix of long boards and plywood sheets from the dump.

"You building a boat, Allan?"

"Don't know." He eyes his material speculatively. "It hasn't told me what it wants to be."

I don't know if he's joking; I understand that rivers and creeks and stones have their own personality and inner being, and they will speak if listened to, but a pile of lumber and nails? Reaching down, Allan shows off his new handmade snowshoes.

"Done the traditional way. Birch, moose hide, the works."

They are virtuoso snowshoes; Allan's fine workmanship is obvious from a dozen paces. I silently wonder if he will make another pair any time soon. A master of the crafted one-off, Allan cut only a single CD of his voluminous music repertoire, learned to play brand new instruments after he mastered the traditional "old time" fiddle, and invented a pair of language gloves, commercial work gloves stencilled with key words in Gwich'in, allowing him to study the finer points of his native language while performing outdoor chores. I must admit I identify with Allan's multitasking approach to daily life; he seems to be a polymath of the locally possible.

I pick up my overnight pack and head down to the muddy river shore. Elder Peter Kay has invited me to his hunt camp forty kilometres upstream, and we take off without ceremony, apart from a quick survey of the sky opening to the east. Despite the crisp broken sunshine and yellow leaves still hanging on in the Porcupine valley, it is unbelievably cold out on the water today.

The wind funnels through the tall wooded banks and creates a second invisible river above the watery first, starting straight at chest level and increasing in its motionless velocity with each twist and turn of our slow course east.

Movement on the shore.

There they are: the Porcupine caribou herd has finally arrived. A magnificent bull with three or four cows in attendance watch us with big rolling eyes before they go crashing off into the brush, their high bouncing rumps broadcasting a sequence of white flashes that makes one wonder whether the physical style of their flight sends a specific message to other deer. Is this flight style intentionally chosen to send that particular message out? Peter studies the deer herd intently but does not make a move for the wrapped .30-30 cradled beside him.

"We have to make it to camp before dark," Peter says, "No time for butchering them now and they'll be more down here, tomorrow."

Peter has already heard the main herd is on the way and that if they keep to their present course they will hit the river close to his camp. Some shots ahead. Peter cuts the motor as we turn around the bend. Two men, two caribou.

Esau Schafer and his young grandson have just shot two young bulls by the beach. They are dragging them up to the mossy granite bench that is conveniently set near the kill site. Maybe this encounter is not coincidental; it seems the hunters were watching from a rocky overlook that commands a view over the narrowest part of the river. We stop and talk further as we watch them put the two hides together as a kind of raw blanket for securing the chunks of steaming meat.

I decided to climb the rocky point, about five metres high, to have a look at the scene from the hunters' point of view. A late-season wasp, drawn by the smell of fresh blood, decides to investigate my head in the same way I am investigating the crown of the cliff. I do not feel like sharing my own crown with him, so I politely ask him to buzz off, just as Stephen Frost advised us to do with intruding bears—and the wasp careens off.

The caribou lookout offers a mossy, sun-dappled refuge from the wind. The roots and stumps of spruce and alder trees create a set of living room furniture in the wild style, complete with places to sit, hang my coat, and rest my head. Old brass gun shells to inspect as conversation pieces. It is all I can do not to nod off as I watch the scene from the Paleolithic era unfolding below.

It's the blood, of course. Bright red blood, lots of it. The scarlet flag marks the country of raw life, suppressed in our own society and kept hidden behind institutional walls: meat-processing plants, operating theatres, police tapes. The caribou kill site is a natural weir, a rocky funnel that directs the deer into a visibly narrow stretch of the river and limits their exposure out in the open water to the minimum. How many deer over the millennia have met their end at this spot? And still they keep coming.

There were two sorts of man-made caribou fences built with collective effort and maintained into historical times by the Vuntut Gwich'in, according to oral accounts by Sarah Abel, Moses Tizya, and others who recounted their history in the 1970s in *People of the Lakes: Stories of Our Van Tat Gwich'in Elders*, collected by the Vuntut Gwitchin First Nation and anthropologist Shirleen Smith.

The summer caribou fences were set up in the mountains under the direction of a hunt boss and used in August at the beginning of the hunt to collect caribou hides. During this season they reach the premium quality needed for clothing items, and for making "babouche" (corded hide) snares to catch more caribou, rabbits, etc.

The more temporary winter caribou fences were erected later in October and November, and these were set wherever the roaming hunters found a large number of overstaying caribou. When this critical task was done, they built their seasonal winter dwellings near the fences, using hides over domed timber huts that were partly dug down into the earth and filled with moss to keep out the wind. One informant says that such a moss hut could be built in a day and the real trick of their construction was getting the smoke hole at the top of the dome positioned properly in order to prevent the fumes from bothering the residents. One imagines that thick snow would have added its insulating qualities to the construction soon enough. Now the task became to visit the snares frequently and see what they caught before the wolves and wolverines did.

The oldest stories of the Vuntut Gwich'in tell us that traps and snares are two-sided devices. The Charlie family version of the Chit ta ho khei story cycle puts the hero in the position of a hunted and trapped animal. In that version, Tshii Choh, the relentless Giant Mosquito, chases the hero for days, getting hungrier and hungrier as his human quarry eludes him.

Finally, the monster decides to set a snare for Chit ta ho khei:

*So Chit ta ho khei grab his canoe and put it in the snare he throw [it] down
so Tshii Choh...got there was something caught so he started to make fire
to cook. He never even check his snare. After he make fire he make some
sharp stick to cook different parts of Chit ta ho Body. Pull with snare was
his canoe in it and he say turn to canoe by this time he is really starving
so he pinch himself all over on his leg [and] he cut off pieces of his leg and
started cook that, while Chit ta ho khei wait and watch him.*

The Vuntut Gwich'in snared and cooked caribou this way in the Yukon
areas of Black Fox Creek and King Edward Creek, using fences to herd the
deer into rawhide snares, stabbing them with spears, then cooking and
smoking the different parts, including the head, just as our reverse tale
relates. At the same time, the storyteller and his audience of hunters show
deep compassion for their principal prey, because stories like this one
insistently contemplate the caribou's silent terror from the perspective of
a human caribou.

The tale's hero hides and watches the monster eat himself in the
absence of his quarry, just as caribou did in delivering, or condoning, the
fate of starving local communities by failing to appear. And their people's
luck did run out from time to time, according to Vuntut Elders, who say
that whole communities have disappeared due to starvation. The omis-
sion in the story of reference to the caribou's name or its role in this tale
of wits suggests its primal sacred character. Primal myths do not use sim-
iles. Everything is already everything: Hero and Giant are setting the
hard rules for the world to follow. We see the same world-creating struggle between the Olympians and the Titans, as classical scholar Jane Ellen
Harrison points out; the Vuntut Gwich'in shamans described by Elder
Moses Tizya "killed their enemy partner" in order to mark their bodies
with scars indicating their victories.

Where the line was between real killings and spiritual ones is hard
to say, given that shamans in this culture "dream" their animals to know

where they are before killing them in actuality on the ground. Such concrete, object-driven dreaming is the basis of all sympathetic magic, used to manipulate reality via the inner realm of intimate, undifferentiated power on which all life depends and from which all life emanates. Yet the shaman is not always alone in his power-dreaming, is he? No, others are inside that oblique place, too, also seeking to influence the outcome of external events for their own benefit. It might be that an enemy partner always opposes a shaman, particularly if he is actively pursuing larger social or economic goals.

That was the gist of an extended account given by a contemporary Cree healer of his power battles with other shamans in northern Manitoba, as recounted in *Cry of the Eagle: Encounters with a Cree Healer*. The express Gwich'in rationale for the inevitability of the interpersonal conflict is that people are always ambivalent about the success of others and secretly wish to destroy them as possible threats to their own security. This was the Cree rationale, too. The Cree shaman, Russell Willier, describes in that study how he regularly encountered other unseen and malevolent (black) shamans working to oppose him at a distance, and so he was obliged to oppose them, in turn, or end up being destroyed himself.

The Gwich'in Elders' accounts acknowledge that shamans found the caribou by dreaming them but are otherwise reticent about any related, spirit-invoking activities. Apart from some references to the Duck Dance and a winter game played with a round white caribou hide with caribou hooves on it, which the players tried to catch, there are few references in these Elders' oral accounts to traditional Gwich'in seasonal ceremonials.

As elsewhere, church missionaries in the north actively opposed the shaman's role and authority and suppressed the open display of the old rites, and so it is likely elderly informants omitted mention of them for fear of censure or ridicule. It would be surprising if tales like that of Chit ta ho khei were *only* tales in the pre-missionary past; they seem to read more like a script for a series of public dance performances or even shadow plays, where Giant Mosquito chases an antler-adorned Chit ta ho khei around and over the campfire, the monster getting burned and cursing (even as he smells the roasting meat of his own flesh), and the hero skillfully eluding the proffered skewer and skillet, to triumph however briefly—for this cycle of various threatening monsters never actually ceases—over the thing-ness of nature.

Memory is the sense most often overlooked in the modern inventory of human perceptions because it has been so diminished by our growing reliance on external record keeping since the invention of script and then print. This effacement continues unabated in urban society: we have outsourced ourselves in hand-held devices, which now electronically oppose us with their glitches, structural obsolescence, and life-draining costs. No Gwich'in child seeing a weasel's black tail today will fail to recall the just-so story of the weasel's blackened tail, which inserts itself into the ongoing experiential reality of every listener, reminding him or her of the transformative power of timeless myth. In this way, Chit ta ho khei's willow wand continues to mark Gwich'in notions of nature and sex.

It may be pertinent to note that in the oldest hunting myth extant, the *Epic of Gilgamesh*, circa 2700 B C, the wild hunter Enkidu was, like the Gwich'in Hero with She-Otter, sexually tempted by a goddess or temple houri named Shamat, who lures him to her bed from his natural concourse with animals, and thence to the pleasures and griefs of civilization—the main grief being that civilization, unlike nature, *dies*.

Nature is the enemy partner, which must be separated from itself if men are to survive. Chit ta ho khei tricks nature itself by mimicking its cyclical processes, turning himself from prey "food" into useless "shit"— knowing nature will remain blind to its existential condition and that it can only do what it has done before in perpetuity.

Even if this particular reading is entirely wrong, it points to the extreme variability of readings provoked by traditional myths, which function as points of departure for further collective discussion, analysis, conjecture, and campfire entertainment. We know from the contemporary accounts in such sources as *The Jesuit Relations and Allied Documents: Travels and Explorations of the Jesuit Missionaries in New France 1610–1791* and the earlier Recollect accounts of Brother Sagard that other First Nations in

Canada at Contact performed midwinter rites whose purpose was to re-enact or historicize the phenomenal transformations of the seasonal cycle in public performances where participants wore wolf skins, growling and howling and biting themselves in a bloody frenzy, expressing the rapacity of an internalized beast that threatens to devour the social host without.

Accounts from the Contact era suggest that animal transformation was originally far more collective, and overtly aggressive, than expurgated modern accounts suggest (which tend to focus on lone shamanic activity). What we see of it in First Nations culture today may be both a reduced remnant form and tailored in the informants' accounts to the ideological biases of the dominant society. Anthropologist Bruce Trigger, writing in *The Huron: Farmers of the North*, about the Hurons (Wendat) before their decimation at the hands of the Iroquois in 1649, mentions historical institutions that all placed shamanic healing squarely into the realm of extreme social behaviour, where animal transformation, symbolic or otherwise, took place, as in this account of the Huron's *otakrendoiae* winter ritual:

In this dance the members of the society pretended to kill one another with charms such as bears' claws, wolves' teeth, stones and dog sinews. As the members fell under the spell of these charms, blood poured from their mouths and nostrils as they bit themselves...this society did not gain any recruits among the Attignawantan until 1636...This would not be the only ritual borrowed from the northern Algonkians.

That was then, but how shall we understand the following account, recounted recently, by a college-educated Aboriginal woman of high status, whom I had asked if animal transformations still occurred in her community?

People I know turn themselves into bees and hummingbirds, insects like grasshoppers, and, of course, hawks and eagles because of their perfect vision. The stories of animals who became humans, you know, are in our old stories, our myths. But today people become animals because of their powers.

She herself was transformed into a kingfisher; it was all part of a secretive rite with fasting, drumming, chanting, and it took place in a spiritually . energetic or sacred place. My informant did not specify if, by their powers, she meant *animal* powers, the individual *willpower* of the human seeker, or a *shared* power that somehow transcended and ecstatically linked the two in mutual self-possession, but she did acknowledge that, while mostly men sought out transformations, women were known to seek such self-alteration, too. That this complex practice continues to range across a wide swath of North America and has failed to disappear under the twin weights of religious suppression and secular skepticism points to an experiential anchor. The Gwich'in locate one of their traditional sacred sites at Bear Cave Mountain, *Chii Ch'a'an Ddhaa*, a site where I was given to understand certain shamanic healing rites take place each summer.

From these clues and small glimpses we see how a northern culture has dynamically developed and today continues to creatively develop among First Nations individuals who freely create and borrow useful solutions to the problem of living in a hazardous environment, an environment that itself keeps changing its own game, as animal populations come and go and the land deforms with climate change and new neighbours appear on the horizon. Nothing is static. And personality (or spirit, if you will) enters into the contest between order and change by taking on aspects of the Heroic. Heroes offer us the full possibility of life in all its human potentiality, embracing both nature and man's consciousness of himself, to come to the point of final departure: life for one means death for the other on the Great Hunt—there can be no other outcome.

The hunter is the chooser: historical reality is set in motion by the unrepeatability of his actions. There are no second chances when life or death is a daily act. The hunter makes history as he goes, surely one of the main reasons why the hunter is the perennially proud and tragic figure in world literature from its very first story. The hunter carries within him a lost civilization, and risks it at every turn, as we will see in our final account.

The Bluefish River is famous as the archeological site of early man's first arrival in North America from Asia. Stephen Frost, now the hale great-grandfather and esteemed patriarch of an attractive and widespread family, has spent seventy-eight winters in the surrounding Yukon forest, trapping marten, muskrat, lynx, and mink for most of them. He recounted this hunting story, dating from the late 1940s, over tea after a successful moose hunt with his grandson David.

Stephen Frost was a young boy of twelve, trapping marten with his first partner Charlie Abel, using dog teams on a trapline stretching over three hundred kilometres:

Out on the trap-line you have to be prepared to hunt before you run right out of food. We are out there till February, from right after freeze-up in October. With two toboggans! It would be hard to do now. Everybody did that. After Christmas out there we used to get cold weather, we used to get 65 below Fahrenheit. We'd just put a little more clothes on, and we'd still go out in it. Sleep in the tent.

So we ran out of dog food. It's hard to hunt when it's cold, you know. So we hunt moose four days. And lots of moose up there. But wherever we go to moose, moose run away, hear us long way away, from the noise. Christ you can't get up to moose, lots of birch and willows.

Ah Christ, we miss moose that third day. We were walking home after dark. A little flour's all we have, to cook for the dogs, bannock. Charlie, the wise old man, he got sack for emergency. So that's if we get stuck out there, we have to feed the dogs much as us, keep them going.

One more day to try: tomorrow. We went this way and hit this big valley, just around this side of Eagle Plains. There's a moose, 'way across. We could see its head, eating. So Charlie makes a decision. He told me, he's going to stay right there; and me, I'm going to get back on our track to get out of the noise. And to get the head of that god-darned creek, which is kind of steep creek, not far but I got to go right around. And try to pick up that big tree and that moose is right under it, pick up that tree from the other side and come up on top.

I did what he told me. But when I got where I supposed to be, that changed a little with the scenery. I remember I was scared, because where he told me to come over, wasn't the right place when I get there, and if I had missed that moose I'm going to make him feel real bad, because I didn't listen.

But I took a chance, I came a little to the right. I came over and god-darned, right down there that moose was standing there, close enough, one shot. Just dropped like that. In case like that, you don't only shoot only bulls, if you got chance you got to shoot a cow. This was a lone cow, no calves. So I just went to that moose and I took the knife, and the fat was like that, thick. That fat moose was like the best Christmas.

I went back to Charlie. I was tough that time, him, too. All day on snowshoes. When I got close to Charlie I tried not to smile and told him I got a bull moose, not too good. He saw that moose go down, "Ah, good, good, my boy." So I met him and we got there and he sees that cow moose, and man, it was just a lifesaver.

Lots of people did that. There's lots of stories, how we survived long ago.

What is striking is the narrator's recollected details of the landscape, sixty-five years later. Two things: a steep creek in the distance and the big tree. But then a shocker: the landscape changed on the boy. "That changed a little," and this, just in the short time it took the narrator to leave the company of his elder partner and make his way to where the moose was supposed to be. Young Stephen learns his life and the life of others depend on breaking with his received instruction and finding his own path through the winter forest.

Still, it is the intimate congress with wild animals that pervades northern consciousness and gives it its special quality of alertness, compassion, and a universal acceptance of our common destiny. Today, Gwich' in hunters still use a charm or spiritual animal token to invoke nature's protection from winter's annual threats: caribou hooves, which embody the idea of a final reserve of hope or grace by going the distance, are hung on an alder bush over the snow, close to the winter cabin.

Urban culture has lost more than the ability to understand animals: American photographer Ken Rockwell wrote an apt essay about the relationship of lens quality to subject focus. He distinguishes the richly detailed wilderness landscape work of Ansel Adams from the works of urban photographers, not on the basis of the elaborate efforts the Adams school made to lug their large-format box cameras to mountain peaks (as is so often attributed) but to the lack of fractal detail in the city, a world of smooth surfaces, simple graphics, primary colours, and seamless connections between signs and architecture—and, increasingly, the merging of people's faces and personalities with the trade logos of their branded apparel.

Rockwell says our urban environment is so visually impoverished that there is little to focus on, and urban photographers who keep upgrading perfectly good lenses are chasing moonbeams. Climb a hill and take a landscape shot in early morning before the mist and dust obliterate detail, and everything will be in focus, Rockwell recommends.

More significantly, however, the loss of fractal detail deprives urban residents of sensory connection and visceral cues. The city teaches us to read its signs but not the context. It hides the environment as a whole behind its billboards and the auditory din of emergency sirens and useless car alarms and the jumbo jets that take off at precisely 7:00 AM.

We have difficulty remembering things because we have been taught that memory is not important, dismissed as "rote learning" by contemporary academic theory, dismissed as the "unreliable eye witness" by contemporary jurisprudence, and dismissed as meaningless sentiment by glib retailers touting the new and improved. The First Nations' insistence on the supremacy of memory both as to its formal content and to the faculty itself strikes some urban residents as anachronistic if not stubbornly regressive. Yet this critical view is but a function of our wholesale immersion into the clinical history of a bureaucratic identity compiled by modern state practices. Who is to say which system shall prevail in the end, given that mass state data is always at risk of loss and distortion?

When formally introducing themselves, the Gwich'in will start by identifying where they were born, naming their parents and grandparents, and perhaps an illustrious ancestor, along with his or her community accomplishments. Except for mentioning a school they might have attended away, the typical Aboriginal informant will remain steadfastly out of their own account. Aristocrats live at the crosshairs of inherited status and individual action, and what defines them is their capacity for inhabiting the forefront of a sweeping narrative richly peopled with heroes, villains, wild animals, luck, and power. They need to remember who they are.

With mnemonic devices like escutcheons and crests, this is how European knights held themselves out to the medieval world. This is how First Nations hold themselves out in the modern world today as well. For it was in the courtier society and its military descendants that the hunting culture of Western history has been preserved, as social historians such as Jane Jacobs and Georges Demézil have confirmed.

There is something else. In the late 1970s, a research project by the Aboriginal Harvesting Research Committee, based on Inuit hunter informants, was conducted in northern Quebec, a study referred to here in an earlier chapter. On this occasion, the collected data was organized in a comprehensive report about animals taken by the hunters over the course of the year. It, too, provides us with a cultural map, in this case a map of Inuit food preferences and food availability in that mid-decade.

Once again, the preferred game food was caribou. A total of thirty-eight species was enumerated. Noteworthy are the animals not consumed: the wolf, the otter, the weasel, the mink, and the muskrat. This last, a vegetarian rodent, was and is still eaten regularly by the Gwich'in and other Dene, roasted whole on sticks, so its nonconsumption by the Inuit hunters marks a discretionary cultural preference on their part.

Conversely, predators like Arctic foxes, owls, fish-eating loons, and lynx were all eaten by the Inuit. Lynx are eaten by contemporary Gwich'in, too, who trap them for their valuable pelts and roast the "succulent" haunches in the field. According to Dene fisherman Burt Buckley, lynx provide local trappers with a white meat that tastes like the ptarmigan and rabbit it preys upon, so strictly structuralist conceptual categories like predator/ herbivore fail to account for all these mapped cultural preferences.

The Quebec researchers also noted how extrinsic factors determined the shape and accuracy of their database, citing such issues as political problems in one community; the tendency of successful hunters to skew the statistical results by over-reporting in comparison to the unsuccessful hunters who neglected to report their disappointing outcomes; the competition for cash-economy jobs in the fall by men who would otherwise be out hunting; and the extreme variability of weather patterns on the sea coast.

The ringed seal (*Pusa hispida*) forms 12.7 per cent of the total harvest in part because they are easily hunted at all times of the year. The numbers are staggering: fifty to 150 seals per hunter per year in the 1960s were the regional norm. In 1964, twelve Inuit hunters took 783 ringed seals in the Inuit community of Koartak, sixty-five seals per hunter, with a determined edible weight (bone in) of thirty-two pounds each for an average annual haul of 2,088 pounds per hunter just in seal meat.

Caribou, averaging five times more edible meat at 128 pounds, ranged from zero to twenty-five caribou per hunter taken annually; so the top tier, where the Inuit live in close proximity to the caribou's seasonal range, provides 3,200 pounds of meat to the successful hunter's kinship larder.

The researchers found the same contrasting community-wide catches for waterfowl. As their data disclosed, geese and ducks were less important as a food source going from the coast to inland, where the birds' lower concentrations were a given factor in determining the calculated optimization of local hunting efforts.

The report concluded that the 646 Inuit hunters in northern Quebec took 3,723,784 pounds of edible game weight in 1974, an average of 3.6 pounds of protein consumed per person in those communities, for a net intake of 2,000 calories per day. These hunters were occupied with satisfying objective nutritional standards, as such figures closely match the official nutritional needs of the healthy human diet.

Extrapolating from these figures, one can see that a theoretical band community of fifty individuals, with ten hunters aged nineteen to forty-nine (the optimal age of successful Aboriginal hunters, according to the Quebec data), might take 120 caribou per year, averaging twelve deer each. A seven-member wolf pack that kills a caribou every three or four days will kill the same number annually, about 120 deer per year.

What these statistics point to is the deep affective connections with these many species that the hunters maintain. It is safe to say that in some sense they not only communicate deeply, if mutely, with their principal prey like caribou but the hunters must also understand and fathom the habits and motivational lives of thirty-eight different prey species— in other words, speaking all their varied languages, to some degree. Is it too far to suggest that the wolves have also learned to speak the language of their prey? Or that the prey animals likewise know intimately the habits of their predators, and speak wolf and lynx and even human to some degree, as the myths recount about the old days?

At root, wolves and humans are the same; they have the same basic needs. Many First Nations groups recognize the common identity of a basic survival instinct with altruistic elements as between the wolf pack and human society. The Gwich'in acknowledged this identity by dividing their society into two exogamous clans: Wolf and Crow. Crow must marry Wolf to resolve the division that life imposes and culture ameliorates.

⋮ Just before leaving Old Crow, I went to the house of a local shaman and knocked on his door. No answer. It was only my second visit and I knew from all the old tales that I would have to go three times at least to prove my serious intent. I walked on with my bags to the little airport, enjoying the crisp forest breezes, the dogs that came to greet me, and the fat town ravens that watched me off with their shiny, overintelligent eyes. I got on the Hawker prop plane with half a dozen other people, all bundled for the approach of winter.

We rolled down the gravel runway and took off over the hamlet, banked, and headed toward the mountains as the spirals of blue woodsmoke and a few boats on the sparkling river soon disappeared into the immensity of the northern forest.

Afterword

IT'S WINTER ONCE AGAIN, a decade since I first travelled to the north-west. The local ravens circle the town's solitary high-rise tower in shrieky torrents and suddenly disappear from sight.

Snow lies fat on the bony ground. The scavengers must find food out there, but where? And how? Only a few hours of morose light at midday before the Subarctic gloom drops again. What sense do they use to find a meal in this murk?

At noon I gather up some kitchen scraps in a bag and trudge out to the frozen river. No birds around. I lay my offering on wind-scoured crust. How long will the egg bits and old cheese and leftover beans sit here?

Another look around. Empty sky, silent forest. Nothing moving.

I hike back up the riverbank and into the blue grove of trees.

A flash of black. A raven settles itself in a spruce between me and the loot.

He sits a moment and then launches himself. I think, naturally, he's heading for the grub—but, no, he circles back. It's me he wants to see up close. He hovers immediately overhead and peers down. Is he checking me over for a gun? A net?

I keep walking and glance back. The raven has careened down into the river to partake of the spread. Maybe he was just saying thanks? I hike back to town.

A few days pass. Lunchtime. I look out my apartment window at the unending spectacle of boreal winter. Flashes of black.

The ravens are circling the building again. The wing-flashes grow bigger, blacker. They are swooping my window. They've never done this before, I say to myself, a spoonful of bean soup halfway to my lips.

One of them unmistakably looks at me through the glass. *He knows me.* He knows where I live. He sees me eating my lunch in my concrete cave. What else does he know about me?

Does he know I brought food to the river last week?

Is he telling me he's hungry, to leave some bean soup for him?

Is he the same raven that flew over me in the forest?

Or have I become a character in an ongoing Raven Saga—*Humans Never Fly?*

ELEGY FOR THE GREAT HUNT

I saw three caribou below the hills in the morning, and I shot them.
I saw three caribou below the hills in the morning, and I shot them.
I saw three caribou below the hills in the morning.
I saw three caribou below the hills.
I saw three caribou.
Three caribou.
Three caribou.
Three...

Acknowledgements

I WOULD LIKE TO THANK the many far-flung people who contributed their time, wisdom, and experience to the success of this book. In Old Crow, YT: James Itsi, Esau Schafer, Peter Kay, Stephen Frost, Lawrence Dean Charlie, Allan Benjamin, Kennie Tetlichi, Megan Williams, and the Vuntut Gwitchin First Nation. In Whitehorse, YT: Jim Kemshead and Yukon Tourism. In the Mackenzie Delta, NT: Sharon Snowshoe, Alestine Andre, Ellen Firth, Noel Andre, and Johnny P. Charlie. In Inuvik, NT: Peter Clarkson, Robert Charlie, Evelyn DeBastien, Wanda McDonald, Mary Ann Ross, Diane and Mike Baxter, April and Martin Bourke, Greg Murphy, and Tara Gilmour. In Arviat, NU: Angie Eetak, Phillip Kigusiutnak, Peter Mikiyungiak, and Mary Mikiyungiak. In Rankin Inlet, NU: Tony Manernaluk. In Yellowknife, NT: Fred Koe.

Also, special thanks to Patrick Tomlinson, Paul Carlucci, Robert Murphy, Donald Weber, Steve Wilson, Ryan Carter, Jolene Armstrong, First Air, and the Canada Council for the Arts. Excerpts from the "Chit ta ho khei" manuscript have been reprinted with the permission of Lawrence Dean Charlie. *Mahsi Cho*!

Selected Reading List

Aboriginal Harvesting Research Committee. "Research to Establish Present Levels of
Harvesting by Aboriginal Peoples of Northern Quebec." 1988. pubs.aina.ucalgary.ca/
makivik/CI148.pdf.

Alaskool. Online Materials about Alaska Aboriginal History, Education, Languages, and
Cultures. http://alaskool.org/default.htm.

Andre, Alestine, and Alan Fehr. *Gwich'in Ethnobotany: Plants Used by the Gwich'in for Food,
Medicine, Shelter and Tools*. Tsiigehtchic, NT, and Yellowknife, NT: Gwich'in Social and
Cultural Institute and Aurora Research Institute, 2002.

Audubon. "Guide to North American Birds: Parasitic Jaeger." http://www.audubon.org/
field-guide/bird/parasitic-jaeger.

Boas, Franz. *Primitive Art*. New York: Dover Publications, 2010. First published 1927 by
H. Aschehoug & Company.

Boehm, Christopher. *Hierarchy in the Forest: The Evolution of Egalitarian Behavior*. Cambridge,
MA: Harvard University Press, 2001.

Bourdieu, Pierre. *Distinction: A Social Critique of the Judgement of Taste*. Translated by Richard
Nice. Cambridge, MA: Harvard University Press, 1984.

CBC News. "Gwich'in Social and Cultural Institute Launches Maps of Traditional Place
Names." *CBC News*, September 15, 2015. http://www.cbc.ca/news/canada/north/
gwichin-place-names-map-revealed-after-23-years-1.3229174.

———. "Tulita's Moosehide Boat Recreates Ancient Voyage," CBC News, August 27, 2013. http://www.cbc.ca/news/canada/north/tulita-s-moosehide-boat-recreates-ancient-voyage-1.1414126.

Colpitts, George. "Conservation, Science and Canada's Fur Farming Industry, 1913–1945." Histoire Sociale/Social History 30, no. 59 (1997): 77–107. http://hssh.journals.yorku.ca/index.php/hssh/article/view/4729/3923.

Cranston, James Herbert. Étienne Brûlé: Immortal Scoundrel. Toronto, ON: The Ryerson Press, 1949.

Dumézil, Georges. Mitra-Varuna. Translated by Derek Coltman. New York: Zone Books, 1988.

Dunbar, Robin. "The Social Brain Hypothesis." Evolutionary Anthropology: Issues, News, and Reviews 6, no. 5 (1998): 562–72.

Ellul, Jacques. Propaganda: The Formation of Men's Attitudes. Translated by Konrad Kellen and Jean Lerner. New York: Vintage Books, 1973.

El-Shemy, Hany A., Ahmed M. Aboul-Enein, Khalid Mostafa Aboul-Enein, and Kounosuke Fujita. "Willow Leaves' Extracts Contain Anti-Tumor Agents Effective against Three Cell Types." PLOS ONE 2.1 (2007): e178. doi:10.1371/journal.pone.0000178.

"Factors Influencing the Contents of Provitamin A and Vitamin C in Plants." Nutrition Reviews 2, no. 9 (September 1944): 271–274. doi:10.1111/j.1753-4887.1944.tb08307.x.

Frolick, Vernon. Descent into Madness: The Diary of a Killer. Surrey, BC: Hancock House, 2004.

Geertz, Clifford. The Interpretation of Cultures: Selected Essays. New York: Basic Books, 1973.

Gwichin Social and Cultural Institute. Gwichin Territorial Park (Campbell Lake) Oral History Project Final Report. Tsiigehtchic, NT: Gwichin Social and Cultural Institute, 1994.

Harrison, Jane Ellen. Prolegomena to the Study of Greek Religion...A Wonder Book. London: Hodder and Stoughton, 1922.

Heine, Michael, Alestine Andre, Ingrid Kritsch, and Alma Cardinal. Gwichya Gwich'in Googwandak: The History and Stories of the Gwichya Gwich'in, as Told by the Elders of Tsiigehtshik. Tsiigehtchic, NT, and Yellowknife, NT: Gwich'in Social and Cultural Institute, 2001; 2007.

Hume, David. A Treatise of Human Nature. New York: Dover Publications, 2003.

Innis, Harold A. The Fur Trade in Canada: An Introduction to Canadian Economic History. Toronto, ON: University of Toronto Press, 1999. First published 1930 by Yale University Press.

Jacobs, Jane. Dark Age Ahead. Toronto, ON: Random House, 2004.

———. Systems of Survival. New York: Random House, 1992

Krakauer, Jon. Into the Wild. New York: Villard Books, 1996.

Kuntz, Delphine, and Sandrine Costamagno. "Relationships between Reindeer and Man in Southwestern France during the Magdalenian." Quaternary International 238 (2011): 12–24. http://www.academia.edu/3627844/Relationships_between_reindeer_and_man_in_southwestern_France_during_the_Magdalenian.

Lévi-Strauss, Claude. *The Savage Mind*. Chicago, IL: University of Chicago Press, 1966.

Lin, Juan, James P. Gibbs, and Lawrence B. Smart, "Population Genetic Structure of Native versus Naturalized Sympatric Shrub Willows (*Salix*; Salicaceae)." *American Journal of Botany* 96, no. 4 (April 2009): 771–785. doi:10.3732/ajb.0800321.

Lippmann, Walter. *Public Opinion*. New York: Harcourt, Brace and Co., 1922.

Mackenzie, Alexander. *Voyages from Montreal through the Continent of North America to the Frozen and Pacific Oceans in 1789 and 1793 with an Account of the Rise and State of the Fur Trade*, vol. I. New York: A.S. Barnes and Company, 1903. http://www.gutenberg.org/ebooks/35658?msg=welcome_stranger.

Mlodinow, Leonard. *Subliminal: How Your Unconscious Mind Rules Your Behaviour*. New York: Vintage, 2012.

Moffat, Charles. "Anthropological Art." *Prehistoric & Ancient Art*, December 2007. http://www.arthistoryarchive.com/arthistory/prehistoricart/.

Müller, Friedrich Max, trans. *Immanuel Kant's Critique of Pure Reason. In Commemoration of the Centenary of Its First Publication*, 2nd rev. ed. New York: Macmillan, 1922.

Nittono, Hiroshi, Michiko Fukushima, Akihiro Yano, and Hiroki Moriya. "The Power of *Kawaii*: Viewing Cute Images Promotes a Careful Behavior and Narrows Attentional Focus." PLOS ONE 7, no. 9 (2012): e46362. doi:10.1371/journal.pone.0046362.

Rockwell, Ken. "Lens Sharpness." http://www.kenrockwell.com/tech/lens-sharpness.htm.

Sagard, Gabriel, and George M. Wrong. *Sagard's Long Journey to the Country of the Hurons*. Toronto, ON: Champlain Society, 1939.

San Diego Zoo Global. "Short-Faced Bear, *Arctodus*." July 2009. http://library.sandiegozoo.org/factsheets/_extinct/shortfaced_bear/bear_shortfaced.htm.

Schulz, Kathryn. *Being Wrong: Adventures in the Margin of Error*. New York: Ecco, 2010.

Shipman, Pat. "Dog Domestication May Have Helped Humans Thrive While Neanderthals Declined." *American Scientist* 100, no. 3 (May–June 2012): 198.

Stromberg, Joseph. "This 33,000-Year-Old Skull Belonged to One of the World's First Dogs." *Smithsonian*, March 6, 2013. http://www.smithsonianmag.com/science-nature/this-33000-year-old-skull-belonged-to-one-of-the-worlds-first-dogs-763615/?no-ist.

Surovell, Todd A., and Nicole M. Waguespack. "How Many Elephant Kills Are 14? Clovis Mammoth and Mastodon Kills in Context." *Quaternary International* 191, no. 1 (2008): 82–97. doi:10.1016/j.quaint.2007.12.001. http://www.uwyo.edu/surovell/pdfs/qi%202008.pdf.

Thwaites, Reuben Gold. *The Jesuit Relations and Allied Documents: Travels and Explorations of the Jesuit Missionaries in New France 1610–1791*. http://puffin.creighton.edu/jesuit/relations/.

Trigger, Bruce. *The Huron: Farmers of the North*. New York: Holt, Rinehart and Winston, 1969; revised edition 1990.

Turner, Victor W. *The Ritual Process: Structure and Anti-Structure*. Piscataway, NJ: Transaction Publishers, 2008.

Veblen, Thorstein. *The Theory of the Leisure Class*. New York: Dover Publications, 1994. First published 1899 by Macmillan.

Vuntut Gwitchin First Nation and Shirleen Smith. *People of the Lakes: Stories of Our Van Tat Gwich'in Elders/Googwandak Nakhwach'ànjòo Van Tat Gwich'in*. Edmonton, AB: University of Alberta Press, 2009.

Warner, Kathryn. "'The Feast of the Swan, 22 May 1306." *Edward II* (blog), May 22, 2006. http://edwardthesecond.blogspot.ca/2006/05/feast-of-swan-22-may-1306.html.

Wingert, June M. "At What Frequencies Do Grizzly Bears and Black Bears Hear?" *MadSci Network*, October 3, 2000. http://www.madsci.org/posts/archives/2000-10/970614897.Zo.r.html.

Yao, Bo, Milica Vasiljevic, Mario Weick, Margaret E. Sereno, Patrick J. O'Donnell, and Sara C. Sereno. "Semantic Size of Abstract Concepts: It Gets Emotional When You Can't See It." *PLOS ONE* 8, no. 9 (2013): e75000. doi:10.1371/journal.pone.0075000.

Young, David, Grant Ingram, and Lise Swartz. *Cry of the Eagle: Encounters with a Cree Healer*. Toronto, ON: University of Toronto Press, 1990.

Index

Dene, 90, 115–16, 124, 142, 162–63

desclimax, 125–26

dogs

    ability to read human emotions, 36–37

    bear dogs, 42–44

    breeding, 39–41

    danger to, 33, 41–42

    human dimension of, 241–42

    intelligence, 34–35

    of P. Kigusiutnak, 177

    role in human evolution, 46–48

    as sled racers, 36–41, 98

    and spring ice, 95–96

    varieties of northern, 45

dreams, 257–58

drive fences, 25, 256, 257

Duck Dance, 114, 258

eagles, xviii, 170, 239, 247

Earl (fly fisher friend), 199

earth force, 147, 164

Eetak, Angie, 183–91, 204–05

Elders

    and difficult times, 15

    respect for, 23, 108, 134

    stories from, 168, 256–58

    wisdom of, 9, 206–07, 249

Europeans

    and clocks, 147–48

    clothing, 118–19

    first contact with Indigenous people,
        3–4

    Indigenous adaptation to, 30, 70–73,
        162–64

    romantic notions of Indigenous people,
        6–7

    stunted senses of, 79–80. *See also* urban
        society

fires, 5–6, 60, 157

fireweed, 163–64

First Nations. *See* Indigenous peoples

Firth, Ellen, 8, 12–16, 17, **20**

floe-jumping, 96–97

flood-dwelling societies, 92–94

floods/flooding, xix, 52, 90–94, 125, 127, 238

food preferences, 28, 54, 265–67

food taboos, 4–5

forest

    camping, 164–65

    checking and laying rabbit snares in,
        8–17

    described, 51–52

    earth force, 147, 164

    effect of on Gwich'in, 81–82

    Indigenous view of reality in, 65–66

    silence of, 9–10

    survival, 208–09

    tracking, 65–66

    trails through, 52–53, 137

    wilderness, 56, 57–58

fox, 220

freezers, 44

Frost, David, 230, 262

Frost, Harold, 160–61

Frost, Stephen

    on fire lookouts, 60

    as fossil collector, 231

    on game, 29–30

    on his early life, 26

    as hunter, 230

    moose hunting story, 262–63

    range of foods available to, 159–60, 161,
        162